THE RISE OF SHARING

The LTCB International Library Trust

The LTCB (Long-Term Credit Bank of Japan) International Library Trust, established in July 2000, is the successor to the LTCB International Library Foundation. It carries on the mission that the foundation's founders articulated as follows:

> The world is moving steadily toward a borderless economy and deepening international interdependence. Amid economic globalization, Japan is developing ever-closer ties with nations worldwide through trade, through investment, and through manufacturing and other localized business operations.
>
> Japan's global activity is drawing attention to its political, economic, and social systems and to the concepts and values that underlie those systems. But the supply of translations of Japanese books about those and other Japan-related subjects has not kept pace with demand.
>
> The shortage of foreign-language translations of Japanese books about Japanese subjects is attributable largely to the high cost of translating and publishing. To address that issue, the LTCB International Library Foundation funds the translation and the distribution of selected Japanese works about Japan's politics, economy, society, and culture.

International House of Japan, Inc., manages the publishing activities of the LTCB International Library Trust, and Sumitomo Mitsui Trust Bank, Ltd., manages the trust's financial assets.

LTCB International Library Selection No. 35

THE RISE OF SHARING

FOURTH-STAGE CONSUMER SOCIETY IN JAPAN

MIURA ATSUSHI

translated by DANA LEWIS

 LTCB International Library Trust/International House of Japan

Transliteration of Foreign Words

The Hepburn system of romanization is used for Japanese terms, including the names of persons and places. Except in familiar place names, long vowels are indicated by macrons. An apostrophe is used to distinguish syllable-final *n* from *n* at the beginning of a syllable. The spelling of non-Japanese words that have been incorporated into Japanese reflects the way these words are pronounced by Japanese speakers.

The local custom of placing the family name first has been followed for the names of Japanese, Chinese, and Korean persons.

This book originally appeared in Japanese as *Daiyon no shōhi: Tsunagari o umidasu shakai e* (Tokyo: Asahi Shimbun Publications, 2012). International House of Japan retains the English-language translation rights under contract with Miura Atsushi.

First English edition published June 2014 by International House of Japan
11-16, Roppongi 5-chome, Minato-ku, Tokyo 106-0032, Japan
Tel: +81-3-3470-9271   Fax: +81-3-3470-9368
E-mail: ihj@i-house.or.jp
URL: http://www.i-house.or.jp/

Printed in Japan
ISBN 978-4-924971-38-7

Contents

PART ONE

THE FOUR STAGES OF CONSUMER SOCIETY

Chapter One

An Overview of Consumer Society in Japan

PART TWO

THE TRANSITION FROM
SECOND-STAGE TO THIRD-STAGE CONSUMER SOCIETY

Chapter Two

Differences Between Second- and Third-stage
Consumer Society

Chapter Three

Individualization and Sophistication of Demand

Chapter Four

Evolving Consumer Psychology

Chapter Five

Splintering of the Masses and Harbingers of a Divided Society

Chapter Six

An Age of Amorphous Desire

Chapter Seven

Consumer Society at Saturation Point

PART THREE

THE TRANSITION FROM THIRD-STAGE TO FOURTH-STAGE CONSUMER SOCIETY

Chapter Eight

Fourth-stage Consumer Society: An Age of Sharing

Chapter Nine

The Sharing Lifestyle

Chapter Ten

Simplicity, Localism, and the Japanese Way

Chapter Eleven

The Ultimate Consumer Society

PART FOUR
THE FUTURE OF CONSUMER SOCIETY

Chapter Twelve
The Search for New Ways of Living

Chapter Thirteen
Creating the Sharing Society

APPENDICES

APPENDIX I: CASE STUDY

APPENDIX II: INTERVIEWS

INTERVIEW WITH YAMAZAKI RYŌ

INTERVIEW WITH ASADA WATARU

Figures and Tables

TABLES

Preface to the English Edition

I t is a true honor to have one of my books published in English. Ten of my titles have come out in China, Taiwan, and South Korea, but this is the first to be made available to English-speaking readers. Almost all contemporary Japanese books in English translation are literary works by writers like Murakami Haruki and Yoshimoto Banana, and I have long felt it would be valuable if more Japanese books of a sociological bent were available widely overseas to help foreign readers understand conditions in contemporary Japanese society. I am delighted that one of my own books was chosen as one of those texts.

To tell you a little about my background, after graduating from college in 1982 I spent eight years at Parco, one of the symbols of Japanese consumer culture in the 1980s, editing the marketing magazine *Across*. I think many people working in marketing, product development, advertising, and similar fields in the 1980s had occasion to read *Across*.

From there I joined the Mitsubishi Research Institute (MRI), where I spent the next nine years. Part of my work at MRI involved marketing but I also did research related to management consulting, social security, and labor policy. Since leaving MRI I have worked as a researcher on consumer society and as a marketing analyst at my own think tank, Culturestudies. Along the way, I have written numerous books on consumption, the family, cities, youth, and more. As I write this, just over three decades have passed since I left the university.

Across was a marketing magazine, but it was a marketing magazine that also engaged in sociological and social psychological analysis. It did not simply investigate consumer preferences, but was known for its qualitative analysis and forecasting on changing consumer values. At the same time—and because Parco was in essence a real estate company—we did not limit ourselves solely to consumption but also wrote extensively on urban studies, community, regional planning, and the history and structure of Tokyo. For a marketing magazine, we had an extremely broad reach.

Since the primary object of my own analysis is consumer behavior, my books have often been categorized as marketing texts. I believe marketers can find much of value in them, but in reality it has never been my intention to write specifically about marketing itself. In fact, my readership reaches far beyond those in marketing to include practitioners in city planning, architecture, housing studies, juvenile and youth issues, and family studies.

One reason I have wound up writing books with such a collage of content is that in university I studied that jumbled stew of a discipline, sociology. But another reason is that *Across* was exactly that kind of broad-based magazine.

My research themes since leaving Parco have included Japanese consumer society, the nation's *dankai* baby-boom generation, and suburbia. For years I have thought I would like to pull together my research results in all these fields.

I published my first book on the baby boomers, *Ōinaru meisō: Dankai sedai samayoi no rekishi to genzai* (The Great Run-around: The Wandering History and Present Day of the Baby-boom Generation),[1] in 1989 while I was still at Parco. This was well received, and you could say that my 2005 *Dankai sedai o sōkatsu suru* (Summing up the Baby-boom Generation),[2] reissued in 2007 in the Bunshun Bunko paperback series as *Dankai sedai no sengoshi* (A Postwar History of the Baby-boom Generation),[3] and my 2007 *Dankai kakusa* (*Dankai* Divided: The Stratification of the Baby Boomers)[4] largely summarize my subsequent research on the subject.

On suburbia, I published *"Kazoku" to "kōfuku" no sengoshi* (Family and Happiness: A Postwar History of Suburbanization in Japan)[5] back in 1999, then revisited the subject in 2011 with *Kōgai wa kore kara dō naru?* (What Will Become of the Suburbs Now?),[6] followed the next year by *Tokyo wa kōgai kara kiete iku!* (The Vanishing Suburbs: The Coming Decline of Metropolitan Tokyo).[7]

Which brings me at last to *Fourth-Stage Consumer Society*. I have written this work about consumption, the main theme of *Across* magazine, based on thirty years of personal experience. It is my own attempt to lay out a theory of consumption. The process of writing it has reminded me anew of just how broad that subject is, and how it cannot possibly be contained within a single volume. I found I could not avoid referring time and again to youth consumption, but was unable to cite as many hit products and trends as I had originally hoped. The Internet, *anime*, and *manga* are not among my strong points, and I wound up barely mentioning them at all. I spent considerable time on housing, but was unable to write anything on the relationship between gender and consumption. Our consumer society converts even love between a man and a woman and marriage into consumer behavior, but I did not discuss that either. No doubt I should have included more basic analysis of key consumption statistics like the Ministry of Internal Affairs and Communications' "Family Income and Expenditure Survey." I also wanted to write on the linkage between consumption and politics, but in the end I simply could not get to it.

There were no ulterior motives behind these various omissions. I simply found myself with a book-length manuscript after addressing just the main themes of consumer society. Since consumerism renders virtually every aspect of our lives into objects of consumption, it is all but impossible to write a thoroughly comprehensive overview of consumer society itself. If I have the opportunity in the future, I would like to assay a theory of consumer society three times the length of this one, but for the time being I must stop right here.

For that reason, this volume addresses only certain aspects of consumer society. At the same time, however, I am confident that the aspects it does address are fundamental. In essence, this book attempts to answer the related questions: "Where did consumer society come from, and where is it headed next?" Or, to express it another way, it asks—rather like the paintings of Gauguin after he escaped to his South Sea Islands—"Where did we human beings come from, and where are we headed?" Further still, and especially so since this book overlays my own life story atop the history of consumerism in Japan, it harbors within it the very personal question, "Where did I come from, and where am I headed?" I feel that even more strongly now that I have finally reached the end.

In writing this book I went back and looked at the old scrapbook of newspaper clippings I kept between 1975 and 1976 when I was still in high school. When I opened it I was amazed by the clippings I had saved: an essay by the playwright Yamazaki Masakazu who appears repeatedly in this book, an article about Mochizuki Teruhiko who was researching Dōjunkai apartments in Daikanyama, an article about the Kadokawa Shoten advertising slogan, "*Josei yo, terebi o keshinasai* (Women, turn off your televisions!)" directed by Ishioka Eiko who went on to reign over an entire era with her advertisements for Parco. There were items on the publication of the *Whole Earth Catalog* in the United States, the spread of DIY and the growing popularity of making things by hand, the furniture of the Shakers sect that aspires to simplicity and frugality, participation in management by West German laborers, the nuclear power issue, the food crisis, the preservation of old brick buildings in Japan, the labor market for women, and lifetime education. I had pasted in newspaper cuttings on a veritable kaleidoscope of themes.

Judging from my old scrapbook, it seems my interests have not really changed that much over time. Or perhaps I should say I am astonished to find that the starting point for my interests of today goes back thirty-eight, even thirty-nine years. That was the dawn of third-stage consumerism. The Oil Crisis had brought Japan's high growth era to a sudden halt, and people were seeking new models for society. The Vietnam War had ended, all the war news was gone from newspapers, and very likely those one-sided articles extolling progress and growth had begun to dwindle as well. In their place there would have been a rising demand for new themes and new values, be it the reevaluation of Dōjunkai apartments from the early Shōwa period or new ways for women to live out their lives.

As for myself, I went on to university and in time joined Parco, the company that was known for the advertisements of Ishioka Eiko (who herself passed away in 2012, the year the Japanese edition of this book came out). I went on to find Mochizuki Teruhiko's name in the pages of *Across*, and to write my own theory of consumer society quoting the works of Yamazaki Masakazu. It is as if everything started from that high school scrapbook of thirty-eight years ago.

⚭

Readers of this book may find my usage of some English phrases and terminology that appear here unusual. This is because many of the words and terms that have entered Japan from other countries have, over the course of becoming part of the Japanese language, acquired different nuances than what they had in their original tongue. This is particularly true in fields like marketing and advertising, and for words like "needs," "wants," "do," "be" and others that you will encounter here. However, as this is ultimately a book about Japan, I hope that you will accept these different nuances as a reflection of the historical reality of how certain words came to be used in certain industries in certain eras in Japan.

I also suspect that many readers will find themselves wondering if Japan is the only country where consumer society can be divided into these four stages, or if the model applies to other countries as well. This is a question I am often asked by Japanese readers, too.

Fundamentally, I believe that Japan is the only country where the rise of consumer society can be divided into these four distinct stages. In the first place, only the Western industrialized states, Japan, and South Korea have attained mass-production, mass-consumption second-stage of consumer society as I define it here. It is only recently that China and other developing nations have reached or begun to approach this level. It may well be that these latter countries will jump straight into a second-stage consumer society without having traversed a first.

In this light, Germany's experience seems to be comparatively close to Japan's. Urbanization advanced rapidly in Germany in the early twentieth century, with office buildings, movie houses, and theaters springing up in German cities. In that respect, it did resemble

Japan's trajectory from first-stage consumer society on into its postwar second-stage consumer society. I cannot say with confidence, however, whether or not Germany has experienced a similar third-stage consumer society. I suspect that the processes shaping Japan's third-stage consumer society were not as salient there.

England, France, and other countries have also had an influence on Japan, but it was the United States in particular that became the model for Japan's postwar consumer society, and it is my belief that it experienced the first and second stages of consumer society described here some thirty years earlier than did Japan. The Model-T Ford was in mass production and a mass-consumption society already beginning to take shape in the United States by 1908.

Likewise, the United States in the 1950s strikes me as similar in many ways to Japan's third-stage consumer society. High school students rode around in their own cars, and homes overflowed with merchandise that could hardly be called necessities.

Again, in the Vietnam-era antiwar movement and the counter-culture explosion of the late 1960s and early 1970s we can find trends in American society that presaged Japan's later fourth-stage consumer society. The value placed on a simple life, on ecology, on Zen, on the do-it-yourself ethic all resembles what we are seeing in contemporary Japan today. More to the point, and especially as far as Japan's youth culture is concerned, I believe that era in the United States was one of the wellsprings of today's fourth-stage consumer society in Japan.

That being said, every country has its own unique historical currents, and as those currents themselves are not necessarily single-tracked but split and diverge, not every consumer society will pass through four distinct stages as Japan's has. Nor, even should they by chance follow a similar progression, is there any telling if that will unfold in roughly thirty-year stages as I argue it has in Japan.

It also goes without saying that, even regarding Japan, my argument that the development of consumer society can be divided into four distinct stages is only one hypothesis. Yet having said that, it is also true that this hypothesis has proven persuasive to a great many people in Japan, and especially so to the younger generations. I think there can be no doubt that Japan's consumer society is entering a new stage.

This has been particularly true after the devastating earthquake of March 11, 2011. Ever since the disaster, increasing numbers of Japanese who saw the video images of houses and automobiles being swept away by the tsunami have begun to feel in a very personal way the futility of material possessions. It is said that the number of people who would now say that it is other human beings, not material possessions, that are most important in life is on the rise. That is certainly true among my own acquaintances.

While it may not be as well known overseas as the March 11 disaster, there was another catastrophic earthquake in Japan, in 1995, that inflicted severe damage on the central districts of the city of Kobe. There are many people in Japan today for whom this calamity was the trigger that turned their attention from their previous work in architecture and designing and creating products to community design and revitalization. These changing values are particularly evident among the younger generations born in the 1970s and after. They are the people who are shaping Japan's fourth-stage consumer society today, and who will be entering their sixties when this stage of consumer society comes to an end. At that time, Japan will be the grayest society in the world. If there will indeed be a fifth stage of consumer society in Japan, the foundations for that new society's social systems will have to be laid during today's fourth-stage.

In closing I would like to offer my deepest thanks to everyone who has given me permission to include interviews and conversations that I have had with them over the years in this book. Let me thank in particular Asada Wataru, Yamazaki Ryō, Nishimura Hiroshi, Naruse Yuri, Koizumi Hideki, Inokuma Jun, Gotō Chikako, and of course, Tsujii Takashi. It saddens me deeply that Tsujii-san passed away in 2013. It had been his intention to write a book on the economics of consumption as a grand compendium of his thoughts and experience as a business leader and an intellectual. It is a sad loss for us all that we will never be able to read his book.

I would also like to thank everyone who contributed so greatly to the publication of the Japanese edition of *Fourth-Stage Consumer Society*. To my staff, Sakajiri Junko and Shimizu Fumiko, I am sorry

I made you work so hard on the timeline. In the course of writing the manuscript I benefitted greatly from the wise advice of my old friend Ishii Nobusuke. And in the editing of this book I am in the greatest debt to my editor, Yamada Tomoko.

On the occasion of the publication of this English edition, I would also like to offer my sincere thanks to Dana Lewis, Janet Ashby, and Takechi Manabu and to Saji Yasuo of the International House of Japan who have all worked with such dedication on this translation and on bibliographic information far superior to the Japanese original.

Miura Atsushi
Spring 2014

Preface to the Japanese Edition

Looking Beyond
Material Possessions for Happiness

This year and this month, April 2012, mark thirty full years since I became a working member of society. For all that time, virtually without pause, I have been studying consumer society. The intent of this book is to first quickly review the history of consumerism in Japan, and then to discuss the latest evolutions in its consumer society, all grounded in my own personal experience.

I was born in 1958. That was the year that Tokyo Tower was completed and that the everyman's Subaru 360 minicar, the ubiquitous Honda Super Cub motorcycle, and Nisshin Chicken Ramen instant noodles all went to market for the first time. In a sense, I entered the world at the very dawn of Japan's postwar high-growth era.

The Oil Crisis of 1973 struck during my third year of middle school, which also happened to be the year my teenage growth spurt came to an end. It was as if my own body were in lockstep with Japan's economic growth.

Then, during the 1980s—the decade known in Japan as the age of the "advanced consumption society" and that ended in Japan's economic bubble—I joined Parco, a trendy apparel chain in the Seibu Saison Group that can fairly be called the symbol of Japan's 1980s consumer culture, and as a young employee began working on Japan's seminal marketing monthly, *Across*.

So, in a way, you could say that my own personal history has been virtually inseparable from the history of Japan's postwar consumer society, and that there may indeed be—based on my career and perspective—some point to me writing about the history and future of consumer society and consumerism in this country. Of course, I may retain some lingering bias from my years with Parco and the Saison Group, but as at the time they were the two leading corporate entities of Japan's new age of consumerism, I think one can make the case that my biases may actually throw the unique characteristics of those days into even sharper relief.

⚘

It is surprisingly difficult to write about consumption. That is because there is so little literature on the subject that addresses with any authority how a particular product was conceived, or what kind of people living in what kind of period of social change purchased it in sufficient quantity to make it a success.

In actual practice, a product only goes to market after a thorough analysis of countless factors: the background of the times; the target population and their tastes; changes in the nature of the parent-child relationship, in the ties between husband and wife; shifting family structures; changing income levels; shifts in the values that people seek in their lives. Yet that sort of analysis is rarely published in a format available to the public, while even if an analyst does know the full backstory of one or another company's products, he or she may know nothing about the products of other companies or other industries.

Likewise, consumers buy products every day, yet they are also constantly evolving themselves in the changing times. Their values and their tastes morph without their even noticing it. Some of the factors driving these changes may be age-sensitive, but others may be social. Are they single or married? What is their relationship with their parents? With their spouses? What is their income? On and on, countless factors play out within each individual consumer, and it is the composite of all these factors that ultimately manifests in one very specific behavior: do they or do they not buy the product?

Similarly, all people consume. Yet consumption is only one aspect of any one person's behavior. Therefore, when analyzing consumer behavior it is necessary to know everything you can about the consumers in question. To know everything about these consumers you have to know about the society and the city or community that surrounds them, which means you also have to know the history of that society or city and the transformations they have gone through. And on and on. It has at least been my intention, as I have studied consumerism and consumer society over the years, to do so from as broad and comprehensive a perspective as possible.

There is no single text that will tell you all you need to know about consumer society. There is no text that lets you understand, simply by reading it, all you need to know about the changing trends in consumption from the past to the present, and the transformations in consumer society over time.

That being the case, it can actually be quickest and easiest to just ask an experienced practitioner who has lived and worked in the heart of it all. I think I can be considered one of those practitioners. My experience is not the experience of creating one particular product. Instead, I write from my experience editing a marketing magazine, executing many a marketing survey for many a company, and analyzing the relationships between consumption and society from a multifaceted perspective for the last thirty years.

᱐

In closing, what do I mean when I declare that Japanese consumerism has entered its fourth stage? I discuss this in much more detail in the book, of course, but back when I first joined Parco Japan was just entering its third-stage consumer society. I personally believe that Parco in particular and the Saison Group to which it belonged were a driving force in shaping that new consumerism.

It is for precisely this reason, I believe, that I can see so clearly the passing of Japan's third-stage consumerism. If I were to summarize that passing in a single phrase, it is the end of the era of "trying to buy happiness by buying things."

It is my belief that the beginning of this particular end came in the waning days of the 1990s. With its passing a new era began, an era when Japanese would begin to ask themselves for the first time if they could find happiness in something other than material possessions.

As for myself, I quit my job and went independent in 1999, the very end of that decade. With the clarity of hindsight, you could almost say I went independent just to argue the case for fourth-stage consumerism in Japan.

Miura Atsushi
March 2012

PART ONE

THE FOUR STAGES OF
CONSUMER SOCIETY

A society where all people with the desire and capacity to work can use their skills to the fullest, a society where, through that, every person has the opportunity to earn a high income not in the least inferior to their counterparts in the nations of the West, a society that no longer generates the poor or the unfortunate, a society that can apply toward the enhancement of the welfare of its people and the construction of a cultured national life the bountiful economic power achieved by allowing those very people to freely develop their own great creativity. We stand today at a point where, depending only upon our own hard work, the building of such a society will no longer be a dream.

Shimomura Osamu, *Nihon keizai seichōron*
(A Theory of Japanese Economic Growth)

Chapter One

An Overview of Consumer Society in Japan

onsumerism has entered its fourth stage in Japan. That is the main theme of this book.

People have consumed in every era. In ancient Rome, in Renaissance Italy, in thirteenth-century Hangzhou in China, in Edo and Osaka during the Edo period (1603–1867), people were active consumers. It is safe to say that all of these societies were consumer societies.

However, the consumer societies that are the subject of this book are limited to those postdating the Industrial Revolution. In other words, these are not consumer societies that simply consumed the output of primary industries. Rather, they are consumer societies that arose in the modern era, once modern industry—its productivity boosted by technological innovation—began to need vast numbers of consumers to consume all the products that it made.

In addition, this book confines itself to consumer society in Japan, as the specific stages in the development of consumer society will differ from country to country.

First-stage Consumer Society (1912–42)

Consumer society in the modern sense can be said to have appeared in Japan in the early twentieth century. Having emerged victorious from the Sino-Japanese and Russo-Japanese wars, the country was bubbling with the boom-time economy of the First World War. At the same time,

3

however, sky-high inflation was eroding workers' real incomes, and Japan experienced rice riots and other unrest as the wealth gap widened between the rich and the poor. The 1920 collapse of the silk and cotton yarn market triggered a financial panic. Big Capital's hand was strengthened, and there was a surge in the ranks of the nouveau riche.

Nevertheless, thanks to the growing populations of Japan's big cities, consumption began to expand rapidly in urban areas, giving birth to a true mass consumer society in Japan's largest cities by the early days of the Shōwa period (the reign of the Shōwa Emperor, December 1926 to January 1989).

This, then, was the first stage of consumer society in Japan. In this book, let us define it as lasting for the three decades from 1912 to 1941, from the first year of the Taishō period (the reign of the Taishō Emperor, July 1912 to December 1926) until Japan's 1941 entry into World War II.

It is safe to say that Japan's first-stage consumer society unfolded exclusively in Tokyo, Osaka, and a few other major cities. Indeed, while in 1920 only some 3.7 million, or 6.6 percent, of Japan's total population of 56 million lived in metropolitan Tokyo, just ten years later in 1930 Tokyo had a population of 5.4 million, or 8.4 percent of a total national population of 64.5 million. By 1940 the city's share would exceed a tenth of the national population at 7.4 million, or 10.2 percent of a total population of 71.9 million (fig. 1-1).

Osaka Prefecture, home to Japan's second largest urban concentration, was also growing, with its population surging from 2.6 million in 1920 to 3.5 million in 1930, and on to 4.7 million by 1940. Clearly Japan's first-stage consumer society found its footing in tandem with the rapid consolidation of the nation's population into urban areas.

Young people swathed in the latest fashions began to throng the streets of big-city shopping districts. These were the *mobo* and the *moga*, the so-called "modern boys" and "modern girls" of the new urban Japan. To be *modan* (modern) was to be progressive, to be *modan* was to be cultured, and to be both progressive and cultured was a good thing in every aspect of food, clothes and shelter. There was a boom in *yōshoku*, or Western food, so much so that curry rice, pork cutlets, and croquettes were called the "Three Great *Yōshoku* of Taishō."

4

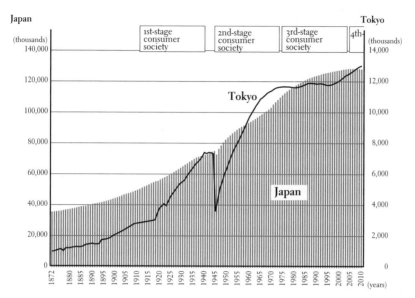

FIGURE 1-1 Population Trends: Japan and Tokyo Metropolitan Prefecture

Source: Primarily based on Japan Statistical Association, *Statistical Handbook of Japan 2012*, edited by Statistical Research and Training Institute (Statistical Bureau, Ministry of International Affairs and Communications).

In the United States the 1920s are sometimes called the golden days of radio. So, too, in Japan. Radio broadcasting began in Tokyo, Osaka and Nagoya in 1925. It was the start of the mass media age; from now on the media would create the masses.

The Taishō period also brought the beginnings of mass production. In 1913 confectioner Morinaga Seika began selling the milk caramel candy that generations of Japanese children have grown up eating since, while Ginza Senbikiya announced the first of the elegant "fruit parlors" that customers still pack today. It was also in 1913 that Tokyo Denki (the first incarnation of today's Toshiba Corporation) succeeded in the mass production of a tungsten light bulb, marketed as the "Matsuda Lamp." That same year Singer Mishin, the Japanese subsidiary of today's Singer Corporation, began selling sewing machines for the home as Western clothing spread across Japan.

This era also saw the flowering of Japan's modern entertainment industry. In Osaka, the Takarazuka Chorus Group (later the Takarazuka Revue, with its cast of female starlets performing all the roles) was founded in 1913. The Takarazuka Grand Theater opened its doors on the outskirts of the city in 1924. In 1920, Osaka's Hankyu railway company built a five-story building in front of its Umeda Station rail terminus with a branch of Shirokiya, one of the country's oldest and then largest retailers, on the second floor. It was the forerunner of the grand train terminal department stores that have since become such a feature of Japan's urban landscape. Nine years later, in 1929, this first building would be reborn as the Hankyu Department Store, which still dominates Umeda today in a gleaming new skyscraper.

By the mid-1920s the pattern had already been set in Osaka for a new style of consumerism in Japan: live in the suburbs, commute downtown on the electrical railway to work, and on your days off take the train again to recreational facilities even further out of town.

This lifestyle quickly spread to Tokyo. In 1928 Shirokiya opened a train terminal department store in front of Gotanda Station. Other grand department stores soon sprang up in Shibuya, Shinjuku, and other terminals where the suburban commuter trains fed into the city center. Shinjuku's Mitsukoshi Department Store opened in 1929, followed by the Shinjuku Isetan Department Store in 1933. Matsuya Asakusa opened its doors in 1931, and the Tokyu railway company opened its Shibuya department store in 1934.

The year 1919 had already brought the release of Japan's long-selling fermented soft drink Calpis. In 1921 Morinaga Seika *dorai miruku* (powdered milk) went on sale, and in 1922 Ezaki Shōten (today's Glico Group) began selling Glico candy. Weekly news and entertainment magazines *Asahi Weekly* and *Sunday Mainichi* went to print in 1922, followed the next year by the monthly opinion journal *Bungei Shunjū* and the *Asahi Gurafu* (Asahi Graphic; initially published daily, later weekly). It was the birth of the great mass media rival to radio: the popular magazine.

In 1923 the landmark Marunouchi Building was completed in the Marunouchi business district between Tokyo Station and the Imperial Palace, Frank Lloyd Wright's new Imperial Hotel building was topped off in downtown Hibiya, and the subdivision of Den'en Chōfu, soon to become the suburban garden home of Japan's wealthy, got underway. The previous year, in 1922, the Peace Memorial Tokyo Exposition had been held in Tokyo's Ueno Park; fourteen red-tile-roofed Western-style small housing units called *bunka jūtaku*, or "culture homes," were on display. Suburban housing developments started being branded as *bunkamura* ("culture towns"). Office buildings filled city centers, and the development of suburban housing plots began in earnest.

Cosmetics maker Shiseido launched its chain store system, Kotobukiya (today's Suntory Ltd.) began distilling Japan's first domestic whiskey, the progenitor of household staple S&B Curry—*Kujaku jirushi* Curry (Peacock Indian Curry)—went on sale, Cemedine glue hit the market, and Kikuchi Seisakusho (today's Tiger Corporation) started selling its tiger-mark vacuum bottles, all in 1923.

That year, on September 1, the Great Kantō Earthquake struck the Tokyo region. The old wooden *shitamachi* traditional neighborhoods of Tokyo and much around them were destroyed. Yet ironically, the vast destruction and subsequent reconstruction only accelerated the transformation of Tokyo into a modern city.

The start of the Shōwa period (1926–89) brought even more change. The expansion of the Mitsukoshi Department Store in Tokyo's central Nihonbashi was completed in 1934. The subway station in front of it, Mitsukoshi-Mae Station, had already opened its gates two years earlier in 1932. That was also the year that Tokyo's administrative structure of thirty-five wards—precursor of today's twenty-three-ward system— was put in place. Construction began on earthquake-resistant reinforced concrete apartment buildings, of which those built by the government-backed Dōjunkai, created to accelerate Tokyo's reemergence from the earthquake as a modern city, were representative examples.

In this way, we can say that Japan's first-stage consumer society existed primarily for city dwellers, and particularly for the urban middle class, which at the time accounted for no more than 10 or 20 percent of the population. Yet, limited though it may have been, this nonetheless was the time when the prototype for our life today—in short, for Japan's modern, Westernized lifestyle—was first put into place.

Second-stage Consumer Society (1945–74)

After surviving the global panic of 1929, the war years (1937–45), and the desperate poverty of the early postwar years, Japan succeeded in rebuilding itself and ushering in an era of virtually unprecedented high growth. In 1955, the country's two leading conservative political parties, the Jiyūtō (Liberal Party) and the Nihon Minshutō (Japan Democratic Party), merged in a grand conservative political alliance, creating the Jiyū Minshutō (Liberal Democratic Party) that has held a nearly continuous grip on power ever since, thereby laying the framework for the country's postwar democratic system.

That same year the semi-public Japan Productivity Center and the Japan Housing Corporation (today's Urban Renaissance Agency) were established. Together with the creation of the Japan Highway Public Corporation in 1956, these and similar measures launched Japan on the road to an American-style mass-production, mass-consumption society symbolized by such popular catchphrases of the time as "My Car" and "My Home." By then Japanese aspirations for the "American way of life" had already been whetted by marketing like the lavish America Fair exposition held in 1950 at the Nishinomiya ballpark outside of Osaka.

Prime Minister Ikeda Hayato's Income-doubling Plan was announced in 1960, the Tokyo Olympics were held in 1964, and in 1968 Japan's GDP became the second largest in the world after the United States, marking Japan's arrival as a global economic powerhouse. The new catchphrase of the day was "Shōwa Genroku," after the wealthy and flamboyant Genroku era in late seventeenth-century Japan. The Expo '70 Osaka World Fair was a triumphant success, followed by the equally successful 1972 Sapporo Winter Olympics.

Let us then define Japan's second-stage consumer society as one that covers the period running from Japan's defeat in World War II up until the abrupt end of high growth with the Oil Crisis of 1973, known in Japan as the "Oil Shock"— the three decades running from 1945 to the country's first postwar descent into negative growth in 1974.

As with Japan's first-stage consumerism, the nation's second-stage consumer society was distinguished by the ever-accelerating concentration of

The opening ceremonies of the Tokyo Olympics, held under a perfect blue sky. Public broadcaster NHK reported in its live coverage that it was as if all the blue sky from across Japan had been collected in a single spot. It was one of the best days that Tokyo, and Japan, would ever have. (Photograph: Asahi Newspaper Company)

population in urban centers (fig. 1-1). This time, however, the new consumerism was not limited to Tokyo and other big cities, but reached out across the whole country. Needless to say, it was this nationwide diffusion of mass-produced products, best symbolized by home appliances, that constituted the dominant characteristic of Japan's second-stage consumer society.

As mentioned earlier, you could already see the first pale blossoming of mass production during Japan's first-stage consumer society. Most consumer products, however, were still being made by hand in small family enterprises. They were hard to mass-produce, and perforce tended to be expensive. The simple reality of first-stage consumer society was that huge numbers of working-class people were still laboring to make products and provide services to a tiny minority of middle- and upper-class consumers.

Put differently, the pool of people who could actually indulge in consumerism was limited to the big-city middle and upper classes, while the vast majority of Japanese still struggled in poverty. In short, Japan's first-stage consumer society was a society burdened with all of the contradictions of consumption inequality. It would take the arrival of second-stage consumer society to resolve those contradictions, and to give an ever-greater number of people around the country the opportunity to enjoy the fruits of consumption.

In Japan's second-stage consumer society, the full-scale modernization of industry finally enabled mass-produced goods to penetrate every corner of national life. The journalist Ōya Sōichi dubbed 1953—the year that Sanyo Electric Company began selling Japan's first electric washing machine—"Denka Gannen" (Year One of Electric Living).

During the fourth decade of the Shōwa period (1955–64) the "Three Sacred Treasures" spread across the country like wildfire. These holy "treasures"—as they were called after the three sacred *sanshu no jingi* regalia of Japan's Imperial Household—were the washing machine, the refrigerator, and the television. Fast on their heels came yet another acronym—the "3 Cs" (cars, coolers [air conditioners], and color televisions) of the fifth decade of Shōwa (1965–74)—as Japan put the finishing touches on its simulacrum of the American way of life (fig. 1-2).

(a) Second-stage Consumer Society: Diffusion Rate of the "Three Sacred Treasures"

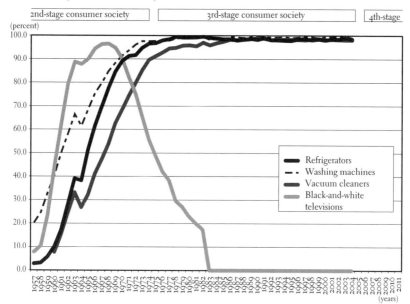

(b) Third-stage Consumer Society: Diffusion Rate of the "3 Cs"

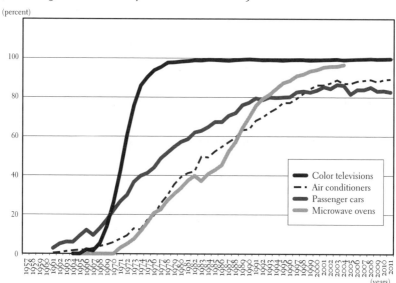

FIGURE 1-2 Diffusion Rates for Key Consumer Durables

Source: Based on Cabinet Office, "Shōhi dōkō chōsa" (Survey of Consumption Trends).

It was in 1966 that the Toyota Corolla first went on sale. As with the Denka Gannen of washing machines before it, that year has been celebrated ever since as "Jidōsha Gannen" (Year One of the Automobile), and marked a sudden acceleration in the diffusion of automobiles across the country. The Corolla itself went on to become a true "monster product," topping the chart of best-selling automobiles in the Japanese domestic market for thirty-three consecutive years from 1969 until 2001. As of 2012 it had sold more than 39 million units at home and abroad.

In 1955 the Ministry of International Trade and Industry (MITI, precursor of today's MEITI, the Ministry of Economy, Trade and Industry) announced its "People's Car Concept." According to the website of the Japan Automobile Manufacturers Association (JAMA), MITI's concept called for producing passenger cars that could carry two to four passengers at maximum speeds in excess of 100 km/h (62 mph) and to do it no later than the autumn of 1958. In the end, the MITI "People's Car" failed to materialize, but the very idea of it left Japanese automakers hungry to develop cars that could at least approach the ministry's ambitious specifications. The Japanese people, for their part, took the proposal as proof that their government wanted them to have cars. Many famous automobiles of that era—the Subaru 360 (1958), the Mitsubishi 500 (1957), the Mazda R360 coupe (1960), and more—are said to have been developed in direct response to MITI's "People's Car."

Yet that was just the beginning. In 1964 Mazda released its Familia Sedan, closely followed in 1966 by the Corolla and by the Nissan (then Datsun) Sunny. The family car had taken its place in the pantheon of essential consumer products.

Jump ahead five decades. In February 2012, the same Fuji Heavy Industries that gave the world the Subaru 360 a half-century before announced that it was pulling out of small car production for good. One cannot help but feel the end of an era.

As a side note, if you track annual domestic per unit sales for the Toyota Corolla and annual sales volume for instant ramen noodles on a graph, you find that they trace almost identical curves (fig. 1-3). Perhaps this was characteristic of mass-market products in Japan's second-stage consumer society.

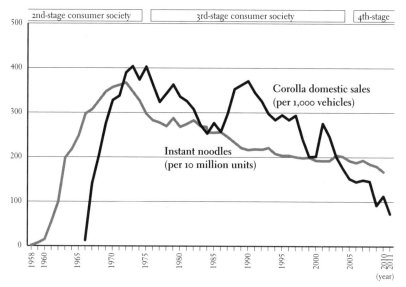

FIGURE 1-3 Sales Volume: Toyota Corolla vs. Instant Noodles

Sources: Toyota Motor Corporation and Japan Instant Foods Industry Association (Nihon Sokuseki Shokuhin Kōgyōkai).

A Toyota Corolla.

A Subaru 360 (1958).

The key demographic characteristic was a shift in the primary unit of consumption from the extended family to the new nuclear family, composed of husband, wife, and two children. There were only 7.5 million nuclear families in Japan in 1955, but by 1975 they had doubled to 15 million. This rapid change was due primarily to a flood of young people born into extended families in small-town and countryside Japan pouring into Tokyo and other big cities for work or education, and staying on to marry and have children.

A cautionary note is in order. While it may not have been as pronounced as it was in Japan's first-stage consumer society, it is undeniable that Japan's second-stage consumer society also emerged first and foremost in large urban areas. Automobile ownership began first in the cities, then spread to the countryside. The Westernized lifestyle epitomized by ranks of new reinforced concrete apartment blocks took hold in Japan's big cities

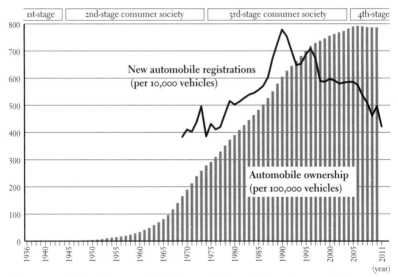

FIGURE 1-4 Total Automobile Ownership and New Automobile Registration

Sources: Ministry of Land, Infrastructure, Transport, and Tourism (MLIT), "Jidōsha hoyū sharyō-sū" (Automobile Ownership by Vehicle Numbers); Japanese Automobile Dealers Association (JADA); Japan Light Motor Vehicle and Motorcycle Association.

by the fourth decade of the period (1955–64), but did not permeate the rest of the country for many more years to come.

Even given this regional differential, however, it is still safe to say that—at least in the sense that people in small-town and rural Japan were longing for the big-city life even if they could not yet have it for themselves—Japan's second-stage consumer society was the era when consumption patterns finally became national in scope.

I might add that in 1945 there were a mere 144,000 private automobiles in all of Japan. By 1960 that number had jumped to 3.4 million, and by 1975 had soared to 29.1 million. That by itself was impressive enough. Yet just fifteen years later private car ownership would be more than double that, reaching 60.5 million in 1990 (fig. 1-4). This last big jump was due to a surge in car ownership outside of Japan's big cities.

Third-stage Consumer Society (1975–2004)

The years that followed the 1973 Oil Crisis are often called the low-growth era. Growth rates that had been averaging an annual 9.1 percent for eighteen years straight from 1956 through 1973 fell abruptly into negative growth in 1974, and for the next seventeen years from 1974 through 1990 they would average only 4.2 percent per annum. Even during the so-called "bubble" economy of the late 1980s the annual growth rate was only in the 6 percent range (fig. 1-5). In 1993 land prices went into freefall with the puncturing of the real estate bubble, and the growth rate again slid into negative territory. Growth revived briefly after that, but not enough: 1997 and 1998 brought the failure of landmark Japanese financial institutions like the Hokkaido Takushoku Bank, Yamaichi Securities, and the Long-Term Credit Bank of Japan. Growth went negative yet again in 1998, partly under the impact of a hike in the national consumption tax. Taken together, these years marked the beginning of the end of Japan's third-stage consumer society.

I will discuss the distinguishing characteristics of this period in much greater detail later. To summarize quickly here, however, it was during this time that the principal unit of consumption in Japan began to shift again—this time from the family unit to the individual. This

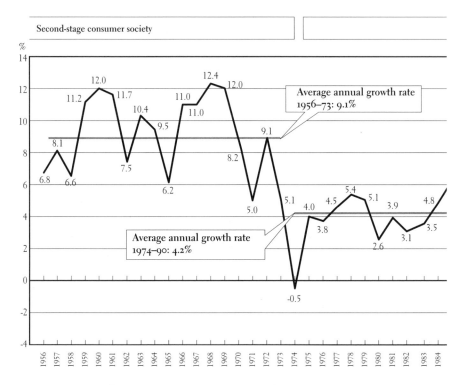

FIGURE 1-5 Trends in Japan's Economic Growth Rate (%)

Note: Fiscal year base. Data based on 1993 System of National Accounts (SNA), calculated
using the chain-linked method. Averages are simple averages by fiscal year. Figures prior
to fiscal 1980 from *Heisei 12-nenban Kokumin keizai keisan nempyō* (FY2000 System of
National Accounts Annual Report; 1968 SNA base). Figures for 1981–94 from *Annual
Report* (FY2009 annual revision). Figures thereafter from the 2011 third quarter second
preliminary estimate (released December 9, 2011).

trend has sometimes been called in Japan the switch from family budgets to personal budgets. It was during these years, for example that
koshoku, or "single meal" food items just big enough for one person
to eat by himself or herself, began appearing in the grocery section of
Japanese department stores in response to a rising tide of customers who
were eating alone at home.

At the same time, there was also a boom in products like the Sony
Walkman portable tape player (later CD player) that in effect individualized stereo sound systems—"*keihakutanshō*" (lighter, thinner, smaller,

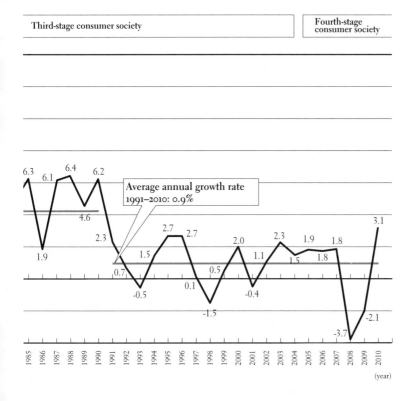

| Third-stage consumer society | Fourth-stage consumer society |

Source: Honkawa Data Tribune website.

shorter; sometimes translated today as "downsized") was suddenly the hot new secret to creating hit products.

Right when I began work at Parco, *Nikkei Business* magazine ran a cover story on *keihakutanshō* that would be the first of many such articles to appear in Japan. It was titled: "Industrial Structure: The Lighter, Thinner, Shorter, Smaller Shockwave."[1] I think I can safely say *keihakutanshō* was the first marketing slogan I learned in my life.

According to the *Nikkei Business* article, in the previous year, 1981, *keihakutanshō* products had completely dominated the *Nikkei*

Marketing Journal newspaper's much-watched December ranking of hit products in Japan. The big winners included personal computers, subcompact cars, mini-component stereo systems for the home, and portable headphone stereos. Consumer tastes, *Nikkei Business* declared, had changed for good. The new Japanese consumer thought traditional *"jūkōchōdai"* products ("heavy, thick, long, big," the antithesis of *keihakutanshō*) were *yabo*, or old-fashioned. *Keihakutanshō* products were chic, and *naui* (very "now").

I will also explore this in more detail in the next chapter. But let me just note for now that behind the rise of *keihakutanshō* were a series of fundamental transformations in Japanese society itself: a shift in the ratio of unmarried singles; an increase in the number of so-called "parasite single" young people indulging in conspicuous consumption while living off their parents at home; and a growing number of *tanshin* (solo assignment) households: company employees forced to leave their families behind and live by themselves when reassigned to offices in other cities.

Clearly this was a society where consumption, once familial, was turning individual. It was, in short, a third-stage consumer society.

Fourth-stage Consumer Society (2005–34)

When did Japan's third-stage consumer society end and its fourth-stage consumer society begin? The turning point was not defeat in war, nor an oil crisis, nor any other single event clear for all to see. In hindsight, however, it is obvious that the financial crash of 1997 was a critical turning point. After all, many of the mighty corporations that had been synonymous with Japan, Inc., in its heyday had gone bankrupt. At the time many commentators and journalists described this catastrophe as a kind of defeat in battle, equivalent to Japan's defeat in World War II. So in that sense, we could perhaps point to 1997 as the real turning point.

The next year, 1998, marked the start of a surge in suicides that has continued to the present day, with more that 30,000 Japanese now taking their lives each year. This would be another good reason to view the late 1990s as the time that the eras changed. Sociologist Yamada Masahiro has argued the case for a "1998 Problem," based on the sharp increases in suicides, violent crime, and the number of children refusing to go to school that all began manifesting around that year.[2] Reviewing the public opinion polls of the time—which I will discuss in more detail in Part Three—many show a striking change in the consciousness of the Japanese people beginning in 1998.

In addition to these transformations, we might also cite as our turning point the peaking of Japan's working-age population, the cohort of Japanese aged fifteen to sixty-four. The working population peaked in 1995, and has been shrinking ever since (fig. 1-6). Similarly, Japan's population as a whole began a steady decline in 2007, making this a conceivable turning point as well. Since a decline in the working

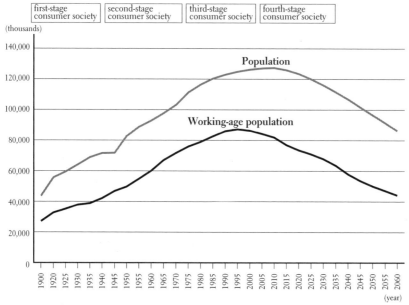

FIGURE 1-6 **Japan's Total Population and Working-age Population: History and Projected Future**

Sources: Based on Ministry of Internal Affairs and Communications, "Kokusei chōsa" (National Census); National Institute of Population and Social Security Research (IPSS), "Nihon no shōrai suikei jinkō" (Estimate of Japan's Future Population) (January, 2012 estimate).

population is synonymous with a decline in the income-earning population, this shift in and of itself signaled a coming decline in Japan's economic strength and purchasing power. And of course a shrinking population also shrinks a society's total expenditures on consumption. It remorselessly forces a total reconfiguration of consumer society.

Yet another change telegraphing the shift to a fourth-stage consumer society has been the sharp increase in the number of temporary workers in Japan. We will also examine this in more detail in Part Three but, in brief, the free market policies pursued by the administration of Prime Minister Jun'ichirō Koizumi from 2001 to 2006, while spurring an economic recovery driven by big business, also led to what has been called Japan's jobless recovery, drastically increasing the numbers of temporary workers in the economy.

Sociologically speaking, the shift from full-time to temporary workers meant an increase in the number of "individualized" Japanese living outside the postwar Gemeinschaft community of the corporation. Even as it changed the basic unit of consumption, the individualization that was such a defining characteristic of third-stage consumer society in Japan has also increased the risk of social isolation. In that sense, we could say that the new employment volatility in Japan's later third-stage consumer society ultimately served to accelerate the birth of the coming fourth-stage consumer society, a new model of consumerism that conversely seeks to rebuild connections among people.

With this last point in mind, there are some who would say that the 1995 earthquake that devastated the port city of Kobe marks the real turning point in the shift from a third- to a fourth-stage consumer society in Japan. This human tragedy at once exposed—as the Tohoku earthquake of March 11, 2011, would do again some sixteen years later—the spiritual emptiness of Japan's consumption-centric society, and gave Japanese a first-hand reminder of the importance of the bonds between people, be it within the family, within neighborhood society, or even reaching beyond to volunteers and NPO staffers. We can thus say that this terrible catastrophe, too, was a major impetus for Japan's evolution into a fourth-stage consumer society.

Taking into account all of the above, we can confidently peg Japan's transformation from a third- to a fourth-stage consumer society as having taken place between the years 1995 and 2007. However, it is not the intent of this book to fuss over strict chronological divisions. Let us instead define the eras in broader strokes: for Japan's third-stage consumer society, the thirty years from 1975 to 2004; and for today's new fourth-stage consumer society, the thirty years from 2005 to 2034.

And thus, the great question. Will Japan's fourth-stage consumer society be a dark and hopeless time as the nation's population shrinks and its economic power wanes?

No. Not at all.

Quite the contrary, it is exactly because Japan's problems have grown so intractable that we are finally beginning to see a new dynamic emerge in response.

In Parts Two and Three we will examine in much more detail both Japan's transition from a second-stage consumer society to a third-stage consumer society, and today's ongoing shift from yesterday's third-stage consumer society to today's fourth. As the transition from a first-stage to a second-stage consumer society was primarily quantitative, and also departs from the core concerns of this book, we will not spend more time on it than we have already. My primary concern in this volume is first to document what Japan's transformation from a second-stage to third-stage consumer society was all about, and then to ponder how it was that those forces came to manifest themselves in yet a further evolution: from a third- to a fourth-stage consumer society.

On a cautionary note, let me observe that just because eras change — for example, from yesterday's third-stage consumer society to the fourth of today — it does not follow that the traits of those past stages all vanish with the arrival of the new. Even in today's fourth-stage consumer society, many characteristics of Japan's third-stage, and indeed its first- and second-stage consumer societies, still live on. In a sense, you could say that the fourth-stage consumer society we are living in today is one in which all of the characteristics and traits of Japan's consumer societies, from the first stage to the present, exist side by side (fig. 1-7).

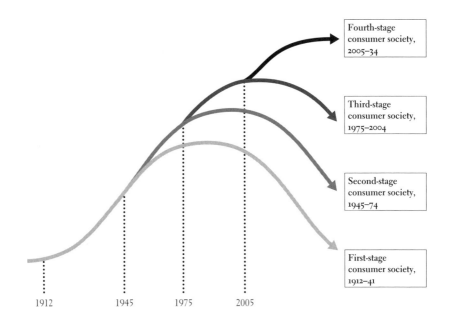

Fourth-stage
consumer society,
2005–34

Third-stage
consumer society,
1975–2004

Second-stage
consumer society,
1945–74

First-stage
consumer society,
1912–41

1912   1945   1975   2005

FIGURE 1-7 The Present as Composite: Four Overlapping Stages
            of Consumer Society

TABLE 1-1 Characteristics of Consumerism in the Four Stages of Consumer Society

	First-stage 1912–41	Second-stage 1945–74	Third-stage 1975–2004	Fourth-stage 2005–34
Social Backdrop	From victory in the Russo-Japanese War of 1904–05 through the Sino-Japanese War of 1937–45. The birth of an urban middle class in Tokyo, Osaka and other big cities.	From defeat in World War II through reconstruction and high growth to the Oil Crisis (1973). Mass production, mass consumption. The era of the "100-million-strong middle class."	From the Oil Crisis through low growth, the Bubble years, financial collapse and the Koizumi reforms. Widening income gap.	Global fiscal crisis (2008), two catastrophic earthquakes, recession and declining incomes from employment instability. Contraction of the consumer economy as population shrinks.
Population	Growing population	Growing population	Slowly growing population	Shrinking population
Total fertility rate	5	5 → 2	2 → 1.3–1.4	1.3–1.4
Ratio of seniors	5%	5–6%	6–20%	20–30%
People's value systems	National— Consumption is personal, but the nation comes first.	Family— Consumption is personal, but family and society come first.	Individual— Consumption is personal, and the individual comes first.	Social— Sharing is good, and society comes first.
Consumer aspirations	Westernization, big-city living.	Mass consumption, bigger is better, big-city living, America.	Individualization, diversification, differentiation, name brands, big-city living, Europe.	Non-brand, simple, casual, Japan, regional.
Consumer themes	Cultural, modern.	One per household, My Car, My Home, Three Sacred Treasures, 3 Cs.	Quality over quantity, multiple per household, one per person, multiple per person.	Connection, one per multiple people, shared housing, casual.
Primary consumer	Yamanote middle-class households, *mobo* and *moga*.	Nuclear family, full-time housewives.	Working-age singles and "parasite singles."	All-generation singles, the individual.

Katei Gahō *monthly, September 1962 (Miura collection).*

1950s National ad (from the Toyota Museum exhibition, "The Coming of the 'My Car' Era") (Miura collection).

Sunday Mainichi *weekly, November 20, 1966 (Miura collection).*

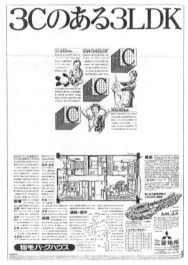

Asahi Shimbun *newspaper, 1974 (Miura collection).*

(Upper left) *We can glimpse the longing for the American way of life in this ad for Sunwave Corporation's latest sink.*

(Upper right) *For its ads heralding a modern new life with the "Three Sacred Treasures," Matsushita Electric (maker of National home appliances; today's Panasonic Corporation), hired the popular Japanese movie actress Wakao Ayako as "Miss National." In her 1960 movie* Chinkasai, *Wakao even played herself playing "Miss National," just one indication of the exceptional effort Matsushita put into the campaign.*

(Lower left) *"My Car," one of the "3 Cs," was yet another dream of Japan's new middle class.*

(Lower right) *The "3 C"-equipped 3 LDK (apartment with three rooms plus a combined living room, dining rooms and kitchen) is an ad for a new Mitsubishi Estate Company, Ltd. manshon ("mansion") apartment building in the suburbs. At the time, manshon apartments were considered luxury housing.*

PART TWO

THE TRANSITION FROM SECOND-STAGE TO THIRD-STAGE CONSUMER SOCIETY

We will see that the kind of demand that industrial society devalued, that it dismissed as a waste of resources, ineffective for industrial society's future advancement, will be exactly the kind of demand that most flourishes in the future. If affluence in an industrial society is to be defined as providing an overabundance of material possessions, then the coming "Sensibility Society" will take the luxurious sharing of "expression" and the creation of "objects of expression" as its own proof of affluence. Replacing the first-stage affluence of the past will be the second-stage affluence of the Sensibility Society that humanity will have searched out for itself at last.

Fujioka Wakao, *Sayonara taishū*
(Farewell to the Masses)

Chapter Two

Differences Between Second- and Third-stage Consumer Society

The Five Transformations

There were five key transformations in Japan's shift from second-stage consumer society to third-stage consumer society:

1. From the family to the individual (from one per family to one per person)
2. From goods to services
3. From volume to quality (from mass-produced products to luxury and brand products)
4. From rationality and convenience to sensibility and "being yourself"
5. From full-time housewife to working woman

Ever since the Meiji period (the reign of the Meiji Emperor, 1868-1912, and the time of Japan's re-opening to the West), the Japanese people had shared an overarching narrative of modernization and *fukoku kyōhei* ("Enrich the nation; strengthen the military"). Defeat in World War II snatched away that nationalistic identity, but in its place arose a new narrative of economic superpower, high growth, and a rising middle class. The prewar *Gemeinschaft* communities of the "village" and the "military" were reorganized into the new production community called the corporation, and the employees of industry went on to form their own individual consumption communities called the family. These production and consumption communities complemented one another, and soon became the locomotive driving society forward. The Japanese people stood astride the two wheels, keeping them both spinning and in the process discovering a new identity for themselves through their identification with both.

Postwar consumption was tied inextricably to the new narrative of "high growth." From the "Three Sacred Treasures" to "My Home," "My Car," and "white collar," new images of the good life were spun out one after another, driving people to consume. As symbolized by catchphrases of the time—"*Shōhi wa bitoku*" (Consumption is a virtue) or "*Ōkii koto wa ii koto da*" (Bigger is better), for example—consuming

When the Nissan Sunny took on its rival Toyota Corolla with the advertising slogan, "It makes your neighbor's car look small" (right), Toyota retaliated with "We haven't just made it bigger. It's the luxurious, luxurious Corolla 1200" (top).

The tit-for-tat was a perfect expression of second-stage consumer society values.
(Top) Taiyō, *August 1970; (right)* Taiyō, *March 1970. (Miura Collection).*

more and more was tightly tied to the formation of people's identities as citizens, as company employees, and even as families.[1]

Bigger Is Better

Second-stage consumer society adopted mass production and mass consumption as its greatest organizing principles. At the time, production meant by definition the mass production of a limited variety of goods. Since most of the products people had in their lives were necessities, they bought them without much regard for uniqueness or design. So long as they had the same things in their homes as their neighbors did, that was good enough for them.

When consumers did replace something, it was standard to buy a bigger version of what they had before. If their first car was a Subaru 360 minicar, then their next would be a Toyota Publica, then a Corolla, a Corona, a Crown, and finally a Mercedes Benz. Their televisions, too, would start with a 14-inch set, and then climb the ladder to 20-inchers and 30-inchers, getting bigger each time they bought a replacement.

This was the classic style of consumption in second-stage consumer society in Japan. Of course, it was the high-growth period, a time when base wages were going up by 20 percent a year and annual raises by even more. It was natural to buy up the ladder to bigger and bigger models. Family excursions to the movie theater to watch the latest films together plunged (fig. 2-1). Instead, they were enjoying television in the privacy of their own homes. It was, in short, the triumph of the principle of private, as opposed to public, property.

People who were inculcated back then with the value of "bigger is better" still doggedly pursue that lifestyle, even in today's fourth-stage consumer society. This is particularly true of Japan's baby-boomers, the so-called *dankai-sedai*, or *dankai* (mass) generation. After all, they were born and raised in a second-stage consumer society. They were imprinted with a value system that believed happiness equaled buying bigger and better things, and keeping them for yourself.

The prime characteristic of Japan's second-stage consumer society was that, as mentioned earlier, consumption was centered on the family. This was the period when the nuclear family came into ascendancy

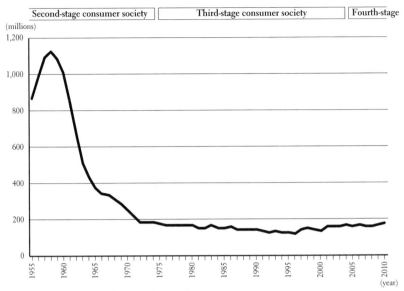

| Second-stage consumer society | Third-stage consumer society | Fourth-stage |

FIGURE 2-1 Movie Theater Attendance

Source: Motion Picture Producers Association of Japan website.

in Japan (fig. 2-2). If parents kept buying replacement products as their children grew, then naturally they would replace their cars and even their homes with ever-bigger models, and that purchasing pattern in turn would keep the economy booming. That was the mechanism of Japan's economic growth, and the *dankai* generation, Japan's largest age cohort, was at its heart.[2]

The Homogeneous Consumer

Since companies were selling to such a large cohort, their products became increasingly homogeneous as they searched for the highest possible common denominator. Furthermore—and very differently from today—the vast majority of *dankai*-generation women were already married and had their first child by age twenty-five. Most men had wives and two children by the time they were thirty. Since large generational cohorts tend to behave in much the same way at much the same age, from a corporate perspective you could not have begged for more efficient

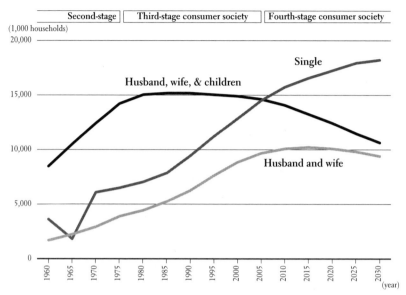

FIGURE 2-2 Trends and Projected Trends in Family Type

Sources: Ministry of Internal Affairs and Communications, "National Census"; National Institute of Population and Social Security Research, "Population Projection for Japan." [http://www.ipss.go.jp/index-e.asp]

consumers. Thanks to the *dankai* generation consuming en masse in such vast numbers, Japanese companies had no trouble growing.

At the same time, however, I personally feel that their marketing power failed to keep pace with their growth. It was just so simple to sell their products that they never learned more elaborate marketing techniques.

If any members of the *dankai* generation are reading this book, no doubt you are protesting at this point that you are not the cookie-cutter consumers I make you out to be and that in fact you are all different, each and every one. Yet since all the baby boomers I speak to insist to the man or woman that they are not uniform and are in fact highly individualistic, I cannot help but wind up thinking, well yes, they really are all the same.

All joking aside, most of the baby boomers reading this book are by self-selection likely to come from the elite of their generation as far as marketing savvy is concerned. The best of the *dankai* generation really did despise uniformity and asserted their own individuality in the face

A line of virtually identical "my cars" belonging to the residents of Tama New Town, looking like they're on a conveyer belt. It's an emblematic image of Japan's second-stage consumer society. (Photo credit: Asahi Newspaper Company, 1971)

of the pressure to conform. But the general public as a whole was not like that. If you asked them to discuss their individuality they would have been at a loss. And they were the *dankai* majority.

In point of fact, around 1980 the then Japan Housing Corporation introduced a new kind of apartment at its vast Tama New Town housing development in western Tokyo. Unlike the old cookie-cutter units, apartment hunters were able to select their own unique floor plans. JHC assumed the *dankai* generation would love the new residences, but in practice they failed to win over the baby boomers. It seems Japan's *dankai* generation preferred "normal" housing.

The vast majority of baby boomers were (and still are) truly "normal." And that is how it came to be that not just industrial products like home appliances and automobiles, but even the houses, the *manshon* and other residences all across Japan came to be standardized, industrialized, and built to the same specifications, be they in *danchi* complexes, *manshon* towers, or sprawling "new town" developments.

In 1951, early in Japan's second-stage consumer society, there had been only 210,000 housing starts. By 1972, just before the Oil Shock, housing starts had soared nearly nine times over to a historic peak of 1,860,000 units a year. The pace slowed thereafter, but picked up again during the economic bubble of the late 1980s, hitting a second peak of 1,730,000 units in 1987.

In recent years it has been a far different story. Housing starts were poking along at 820,000 units in 2010, less than half the level of the heyday of Japan's third-stage consumer society (fig. 2-3).

Contradictions of Second-stage Consumer Society and the "Individuality" of the Dankai Generation

As I discussed in the previous chapter, filling one's home to bursting with goods and possessions was the ultimate goal of consumption in Japan's second- and third-stage consumer societies. It was its joy and its happiness. With the world oil crisis of 1973, however, Japan's second-stage consumer society came to an abrupt end and consumer society entered its third stage.

As the nation entered this third-stage consumer society people began to feel a growing disconnect with the uniform consumerism that had felt so natural in second-stage consumer society. More and more they

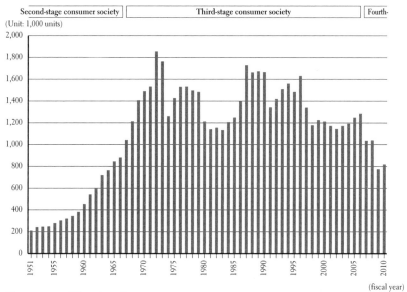

FIGURE 2-3 Housing Starts

Source: Ministry of Land, Infrastructure, Transport and Tourism, "Construction Starts Statistics."

began asking themselves if they shouldn't be consuming in more individualistic ways.

Even in Japan's *dankai* generation there were always cutting-edge types who had felt that way all along. But now a new, younger generation of Japanese began to find the faceless consumerism of their baby-boom predecessors to be downright pathetic.

You can see the change in the advertising. By the first half of the 1970s, Japanese were abuzz about new campaigns like the "Ken and Mary" car commercials for the Nissan Skyline featuring a *dankai* generation guy and his girlfriend, or the Marui department store's "*Aijō hatsuratsu*" (Bouncy Love) campaign with *dankai*-generation newlyweds. The Suntory campaign "*Kinyōbi ni wain o*" (A little wine on Friday night; photo p. 315) painted a picture of a husband and wife enjoying a little time in their own private world away from the children.

Each one of these campaigns showed people enjoying rich private lives separate from their formal roles in society and the workplace. It was a message that was also being taken up and reinforced in hit pop songs like *"Sekai wa futari no tame ni"* (The world is just for us), which won Sagara Naomi the Japan Record Award Best New Artist Award in 1967, or Inoue Yōsui's 1973 smash hit, *"Kasa ga nai"* (I can't find my umbrella). Inoue's whimsical lyrics said it all:

> Young suicides are on the rise in the cities
> But the real problem is today's rain.
> I can't find my umbrella
> And I have to get going
> So I can be with you.

Consumption patterns were shifting, too. Until now consumption had kept the wheels of Japan's "family community" and "corporate community" spinning in sync. Now it was becoming visibly more individualistic. Traditional domestic tasks were increasingly being outsourced to service providers, and even dining itself was starting to shift from the home to restaurants, another service industry. Apparel was changing, too. As it became easier than ever to just go out and buy something new, it was increasingly rare to find anyone who still mended, much less made, clothes at home.

In addition—and initially to supplement their husbands' salaries which had hit a wall in the post-Oil Shock recession—Japan's housewives left the home in droves to take on part-time work. From the perspective of struggling corporate Japan, there was ample merit to having women join the workforce. Without the economic leeway to hire more regular employees or even give raises to the staffers they already had, they could plug the labor gap with wives.

Now working outside the home, Japan's housewives increasingly turned to instant and pre-prepared foods instead of homemade cooking, and to eating out, thereby accelerating the trend toward dining alone. Ironically, the places they found to work were often in the same food processing and restaurant industries they were patronizing. If they cooked at home they were paid nothing, but if they cooked for a living they could collect a salary. It was the kind of slightly cockeyed phenomenon that would begin popping up across Japan's third-stage consumer society.

Of course, by taking on part-time work outside the home housewives were not just supplementing the family budget; they were also earning money they could use on themselves. In this sense, too, consumption that had heretofore been centered on the family unit began shifting gradually to the individual.

Individualization involves people developing their own strong, personal "preferences." That phrase seen so commonly in Japanese marketing today—*kodawari shōhi* (preference consumption)—probably could not have existed in a second-stage consumer society. It only appeared as consumerism in Japan entered its third stage.

In 1975, in the dawning days of third-stage consumerism, the *Nikkei*, Japan's leading business newspaper, published a book titled, quite appropriately, *Shōhisha wa kawatta* (The Consumer Has Changed). It identified a significant shift in public attitudes.

According to the book, respondents to the Leisure Development Center's 1971 "Research Survey on the Lifestyle Composition of the Japanese People in an Age of Leisure"* were asked to pick from among thirty possible responses to the question: "How strongly would you like to do the following in your life?" Possible choices ranged from "Have ample possessions" to "Live a simple life" and even "Be true to myself." When taking the survey, the authors reported, respondents "immediately aspired to a 'healthy, materially and spiritually rich life.'" Their likeliest second choice was "To give expression to my own nature." Noted the testers: "It is an expression of the desire to value their own individuality and to strive to express it, to create a lifestyle that suits their own likes and dislikes without being yanked to and fro by fashion and the mass media. In short, 'to be authentic in the midst of affluence.' If we were to boil it down to its essence, that is the lifestyle aspiration revealed by our study . . . 'Being true to yourself in your daily life.' We should recognize this lifestyle as something entirely new."

In this way, Japan's third-stage consumer society began as the start of a new era, a moment in time when people could finally begin to

* Today's "Survey on Leisure Activities," now run by the Japan Productivity Center.

infuse the material wealth generated by second-stage consumerism with their own authentic individuality.

From Politics to Consumption: The Rise of the Shin-jinrui Generation

The trend toward greater individualism that had already begun to assert itself in the first half of the 1970s would clearly gain strength through the second half of the decade and on into the 1980s. But on top of it would come a change of generation

The so-called *shin-jinrui* Generation (sometimes translated into English as the "New People," or even the "New Humans") was very different from the *dankai* generation that preceded it. Where the *dankai* generation had been politically active, the *shin-jinrui* were said to be virulently apolitical.[3] That tendency had already been present even among Japanese like myself who were born in the late 1950s and were just a few years older than the *shin-jinrui*. Already in the late 1970s people had been astounded to learn that support for the conservative Liberal Democratic Party (LDP) was on the rise among the students at the University of Tokyo, one of the bastions of left-wing student radicalism during the 1960s and early '70s.[4]

Of course, it would be wrong to suggest that the *shin-jinrui* turned against politics spontaneously. The fall of the University of Tokyo's student-occupied Yasuda Auditorium to riot police in 1969 had already signaled the beginning of the end for Japan's student movement. That was followed in 1970 by the hijacking of a Japan Airlines jetliner to North Korea by the extremist Red Army Faction. The following months and years brought violent internal purges within the student movement. It culminated in the bloody hostage rescue and arrest of armed Red Army Faction radicals holed up in the Asama Mountain Lodge in the swanky resort town of Karuizawa, all broadcast live on Japanese television.

It goes without saying that such violence was already eroding sympathy for the student movement in society at large. Then came the 1974 bombing of the headquarters of Mitsubishi Heavy Industries by the ultra-radical East Asia Anti-Japan Armed Front in Tokyo's central business district, with eight dead and hundreds injured.

Up until then, some in the media had been attacking Mitsubishi for profiting from the Vietnam War. The bombing redefined the firm as a victim. Radical students attacking each other was one thing, but the killing of innocent civilians was another, dealing the movement a decisive blow as sympathy for the Left evaporated overnight. (In retrospect, it was also the moment when Japan's formerly skeptical media began to actively promote nuclear power, another Mitsubishi business.)

This abrupt shift in political sentiment helped mold the politically averse nature of the *shin-jinrui*. In place of politics, the attention of the young swung to consumption. Or perhaps a more penetrating analysis would be to say that an establishment unhappy with the excessive politicization of Japan's youth seized on the opportunity to redirect a new generation's interest from politics to consumerism.

Combined with the *shin-jinrui's* rejection of politics and social change, the arrival of third-stage consumer society in Japan also hastened the demise of intellectuals. Japan's postwar intelligentsia had found its *raison d'être* in debate within the Cold War-era polarities of capitalism versus socialism, conservative versus liberal. Young people chose to either learn from these opinion leaders, or to challenge them. If you could take away youth's interest in politics and society, however, you could also render the intellectuals superfluous.

In the meantime, the East Bloc began to collapse of its own accord. With the fall of the Berlin Wall in 1989, the postwar Cold War structure itself was winding to a close.

Those taking on the mantle of the intellectual in Japan's third-stage consumer society were proponents of the so-called "New Academism," and were either openly positive toward or at very least not universally critical of consumer capitalism. The *shin-jinrui* generation embraced the New Academism, so much so that the obtuse 1983 book *Kōzō to chikara: Kigōron o koete* (Structure and Power—Beyond Semiotics) by the young scholar Asada Akira became a bestseller despite being a work of philosophy, selling 150,000 copies and catapulting its author into stardom.

The *shin-jinrui* generation was born and raised in the latter half of Japan's second-stage consumer society, but the term itself was first coined by *Across* in our June 1983 edition. At the time, we identified the archetypal *shin-jinrui* as a young person born in 1968. One of our motivations for the article was the string of Japanese athletic records set during the run-up to the Los Angeles Olympics by young people born on or around that year and still not even out of middle school.

Even in the world of *shōgi*, a Japanese strategy game often compared to chess, fourteen-year-old Hayashiba Naoko had just claimed the coveted women's Ōshō title. Parco pounced on her for its advertising, so big was the uproar.

All that aside, the phrase *shin-jinrui* quickly caught on in articles like "Flag Bearers of the *Shin-jinrui*" profile series in the opinion-leading *Asahi Journal*. Along the way the public image of the *shin-jinrui* solidified around the generation born between 1957 and 1968.

That definition is not far off the mark. As mentioned earlier, both the Japan Housing Corporation and the Japan Highway Public Corporation were founded in 1957, the year that launched Japan's high-growth era. And 1968 was the year Japan's GDP became the second largest in the world, second only to the United States.

Nonetheless, I personally have come to feel based on my own generational marketing research that the most accurate definition of the *shin-jinrui* is the generation born between 1963 and 1969. For one thing, Japan's high-growth spurt ran from 1955 to 1973. The generation born in the very middle of that era—1963 to 1969—should be the one most indelibly imprinted with the values of the high-growth age. From a year before the Tokyo Olympics in 1964 to a year before the Osaka Expo World's Fair in 1970—that was the golden age of postwar Japan.

Many of the *shin-jinrui* generation were also born in Tokyo. Their parents, the 1930s generation, had poured into the city in search of work, and it was there that they married and had their children. Consequently, while Japan's national birthrate peaked between 1947 and 1949, the years the *dankai* generation came into the world, the birthrate in Tokyo itself peaked much later, from 1965 to 1974. With the exception of 1966, a *hinoe-uma* (Year of the Fire Horse) that comes once every sixty years in the traditional Japanese zodiac, considered an ill-starred time to have children, more than 200,000 children were born in Tokyo in each year of that decade (fig. 2-4).

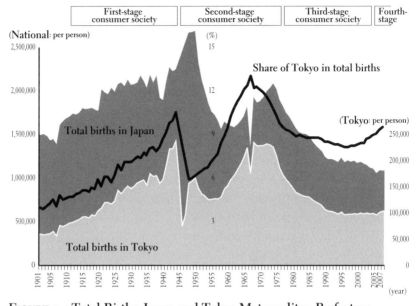

| First-stage consumer society | Second-stage consumer society | Third-stage consumer society | Fourth-stage |

FIGURE 2-4 Total Births: Japan and Tokyo Metropolitan Prefecture

Source: "Statistics on Population Dynamics," prepared by Miura Atsushi; Ministry of Health, Labor, and Welfare.

We might also note that in 1941 and 1942 during the early Pacific War years the birth rate in Tokyo topped 200,000 a year. Since women born during those years would have begun having children around 1964, we can safely assume that many of the *shin-jinrui* generation were native Tokyoites going back at least to their parent's generation. The ratio of Tokyoites to Japan's total *shin-jinrui* population would have peaked between 1962 and 1972.

Taking all these factors together, I prefer to define the *shin-jinrui* generation as the generation of Japanese born in the 1960s, and in particular, between the years 1963 and 1969.

What impact would it have on your life to have been born in those years? In terms of employment, you would have entered the work force between 1986 and 1992 for four-year college graduates, and 1984 to 1990 for two-year college graduates. Since this period embraces the beginning of Japan's 1980s economic bubble to just before the ice age post-bubble, you would have been able to find work under extremely advantageous conditions. In that sense as well, I think we can call the 1960s generation, and particularly the 1963–69 generation, the most "bubbly," the most "*shin-jinrui*-esque," of them all.

Born to Consume

The *shin-jinrui* generation, born in the heart of Japan's high-growth period, and so many of them born in Tokyo itself, were naturally voracious consumers. From childhood they found it normal to go to chic Ginza stores with their parents. Upon reaching high school they easily gravitated to the youth fashion center of Shibuya to play. They would have been in high school at least sometime between 1979 and 1987, meaning that by the time I joined Parco they were in the full flush of their teenage years. From there, they would go on to carry Japan's third-stage consumer society on their shoulders.

The *dankai* generation—born and raised in the second-stage consumer society—reached adulthood between 1967 and 1969. They were there when Japan's GDP became the second largest in the world.

The *shin-jinrui* generation that would lead Japan's third-stage consumer society reached adulthood between 1983 and 1989. This was an era stretching from the eve of Japan's bubble economy to the very peak of the bubble itself.

The *dankai* generation and the *shin-jinrui* generation thus had very different traits, but they did share a powerful inclination toward materialism. If materialism sounds too harsh, let me rephrase. They shared a belief that buying things would buy them happiness. That belief would finally begin to weaken in the next, fourth stage of consumer society.

When the *shin-jinrui* were children, Japan was already an economic powerhouse. By the time they became aware of the world around them, their homes were outfitted with a full panoply of electric appliances. It must be a rare member of their generation who can remember, like their predecessors in the *dankai* generation easily could, the day the first television was delivered to his or her home. When the *shin-jinrui* were growing up, it was already a given that there would be a television in every residence. This would have been especially true in Tokyo, the trend-setter for consumption in Japan.

However, if every household now had a television and the market had reached the saturation point, that spelt trouble for the country's consumer electronics firms. The strategy the makers adopted in response was to push the principle, not of one television per household, but of one per family member, one per room. Of course you should want to have a television not only in the living room, but also in your bedroom, and in the children's rooms. Let's make telephones with extra handsets. Let's have two automobiles, one for Dad to drive to the golf course, and one for Mom to go shopping. Stereo systems? Separate them out. One for listening to classical music in the living room, a mini-component stereo for your son to play his rock 'n' roll, and a radio cassette player for your daughter to listen to singer-songwriter Yuming's [Matsutōya Yumi] latest hits. And of course, every room should have its own air conditioner. In this way, the appetites of Japan's consumers were whetted to buy two or even three of everything for their homes.

The one product best symbolizing this shift from family to individual is the Sony Walkman. First released in 1979, with the even sleeker, more compact WM-2 appearing in stores in 1982, the Walkman was so popular that by 1988 Sony would ship 186 million of its cassette-tape Walkmans alone. And the people walking around town with their Walkmans on their hips were none other than the *shin-jinrui*, as they made their journey from high school kid to college student.

Chapter Three

Individualization and Sophistication of Demand

"Parasite Singles"

T he 1980s brought a wave of social change to Japan. It was in this decade that the Japanese began marrying later in life, with more and more men and women staying single into their late twenties (fig. 3-1). And of these new singles, more and more chose to live at home with their parents instead of going out on their own. It was this latter group, the stay-at-home, unmarried twenty-somethings, that were dubbed the "parasite singles."

Behind this shift in lifestyles was another demographic shift: a decline in the number of Japanese graduating from high school in the hinterland and moving to Tokyo to attend university or find work, and a rise in the number of young people who had been born in Tokyo and could commute to campus or the job from their parents' homes. This change boosted the number of young people who did not have to pay for such basic living expenses as food and housing, leaving them free to use all of their disposable income solely on themselves. Inevitably this accelerated the trend toward one-person, one-product demand.

According to statistics from the Ministry of Internal Affairs and Communications Statistics Bureau, in 1980 the percentage of

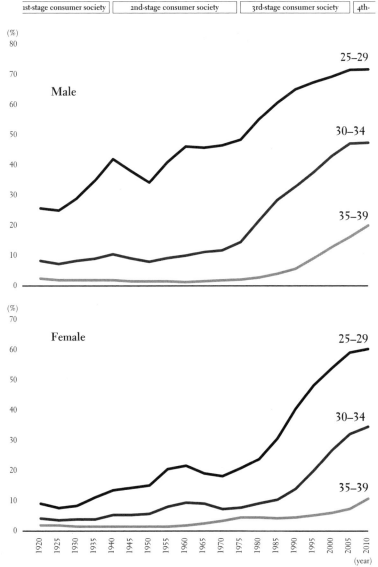

FIGURE 3-1 Trends in Japanese Unmarried Adult Population by Age

Note: Composition of total population exempting those whose marital status was unknown.
  2010 figures from sample tabulation advance report.
Source: National Census (prior to 2005 from *Nihon no chōkiteki tōkei keiretsu* (Historical
  Statistics of Japan).

unmarried males aged twenty to thirty-four who were still living at home with their parents—the very definition of a "parasite single"—was 32.9 percent. For females it was 26.1 percent. In 1990, just ten years later, it had jumped to 44.6 percent for males and 38.8 percent for females (fig. 3-2).

The share of so-called parasite singles continued to grow into the late 2000s, but you can see from these figures that the biggest increase came during the 1980s. This was because, as I noted earlier, the cohort of Japanese who would have been somewhere between twenty and thirty-four during that decade included the 1960s generation whose parents were already living in Tokyo when they were born. Viewed in absolute numbers, the population of twenty- to thirty-four-year-old parasite single men rose from 4,580,000 to 6,380,000 between 1980 and 1997, while the number of parasite single women increased from 3,590,000 to 5,630,00 (fig. 3-3).

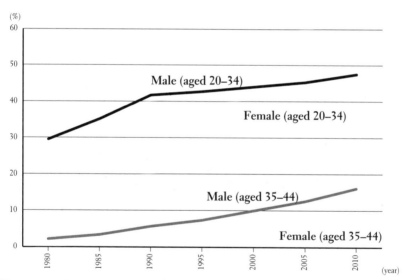

FIGURE 3-2 Percentage of "Parasite Singles" among Total Unmarried Adults

Note: "Parasite singles" refers to young unmarried adults who are still living with their parents.
Source: Ministry of Internal Affairs and Communications Statistical Research and Training Institute website.

(a) Aged 20–34

(Unit: 10,000)

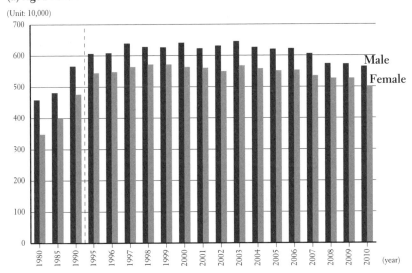

(b) Aged 35–44

(Unit: 10,000)

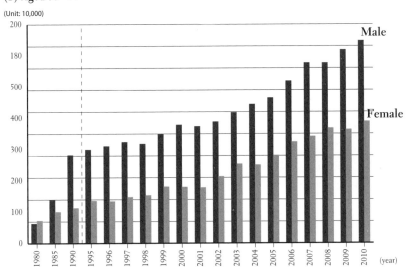

FIGURE 3-3 Trends in Number of Unmarried Children Living at Home by Gender

Source: Ministry of Internal Affairs and Communications Statistical Research and Training Institute website.

You can see the signs of this shift in the women's magazine market in Japan. *More* magazine, targeted specifically at twenty-five-year-olds, was launched in 1977, followed in 1980 by a Japanese-language edition of *Cosmopolitan* and *Torabāyu* (named after the French word for "work," "*travail*," and featuring job listings for women). It was further evidence of how common it had become for Japanese women to put off marriage and continue working, even changing jobs to do so, well into their mid- and late-twenties.

Needless to say, these singletons, liberated from rent and other living expenses, had a voracious appetite for consumption. And most of their money went into fashion.

As I mentioned in the preface, I joined Parco in 1982, right when the "New People" *shin-jinrui* kids were in high school or university. One of the very first articles I was assigned to write for *Across* was on sales results at Shibuya Parco Part 2, our ultra-hip fashion tower. It turned out that Part 2's sales of so-called "DC brands"[1]—the top-of-the-line Japanese designer brands like Rei Kawakubo's Comme des Garçons, Issey Miyake, and Yohji Yamamoto's Y'z and high-end fashion lines from larger Japanese clothing manufacturers—were soaring. In fact, they were up nearly 30 percent from a year before.

Fashion sales accelerated even faster in 1983. Once mid-market retailers like Marui started handling DC brands, the designers' sales soared, with some companies posting increases of more than 300 percent year-on-year. The numbers were truly jaw dropping, as the DC brands achieved bubble-era growth before the Japanese economic bubble had even begun.

It's an ironic aside that the Shibuya Parco Part 2 building has been standing empty on Kōen-dōri for several years after closing in 2007. Rumor has it that it has left Parco's hands and will be completely rebuilt. I cannot help but remember those famous opening words from the *Tale of the Heike*:

> The sound of Gion Shōja bells echoes the impermanence of all things; the color of the sāla flowers reveals the truth that the prosperous must decline.[2]

From Household to Personal Goods

The increase in the number of unmarried young people in their twenties and of single-person households also served to accelerate another 1980s transformation: the shift from home appliances (*kaden* 家電) to "personal appliances" (*koden* 個電), the first sign of a broader shift in the market from household to personal goods.

Nowadays it's common for one person to own several wristwatches, but it was a different story thirty years ago. Another article I was assigned to work on shortly after joining Parco happened to be a consumer survey on wristwatches. Leading Japanese watchmaker Seiko had just launched an advertising campaign asking consumers the question, "Why don't you change your watch along with your clothes?"[*] (This catchphrase had actually been around since 1979, but was now elevated to a nation-wide campaign.) The idea here was that everyone should own multiple watches: a watch for work, a watch for dating, a watch for sports. At the time people were still so wedded to the idea of one item per person that it was actually necessary to suggest this new way of thinking.

Again—and this is something else younger readers may have trouble believing—in the early 1960s the apartment of a young, independent single in Japan would have been virtually devoid of household appliances. Indeed, only a minority of singles were even living in their own apartments—the conventional wisdom at the time was that you lived at the shop or factory where you worked. If you didn't have that kind of live-in job, then you probably were living with other young people in a boardinghouse with meals, or in a company dorm. It was not until the late 1960s that the number of young people living by themselves in their own places really began to climb. And it was not until the 1970s that you began to see young, solo singles outfitting their apartments with televisions and other appliances.

Looking at 1969 statistics on consumer durable ownership among live-alone singles under age thirty compiled by the then Economic Planning Agency (now part of the Cabinet Office), even refrigerators

* *Naze, tokei mo kigaenai no.*

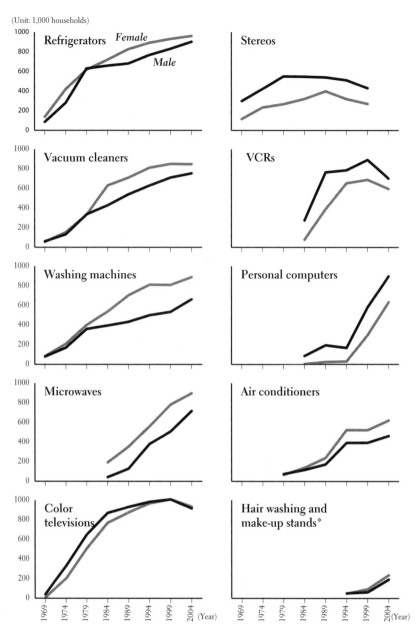

(Unit: 1,000 households)

FIGURE 3-4 Consumer Durable Ownership among Individuals under the Age of Thirty Living Alone

Source: Economic Planning Agency (now part of the Cabinet Office)
* Many Japanese apartments do not come with pre-installed mirror-sink sets in the bathroom area.

were still a rarity: just 86 out of every thousand singleton households in Japan (fig. 3-4). By 1979, the number had soared to 630 per thousand, and was up again to 902 per thousand singleton households by 2004. Vacuum cleaners and washing machines displayed the same rapid diffusion rate, until by the late 1970s it had become the norm for a young Japanese living alone to own the full set of electric home appliances.

Not surprisingly, it was when Japan became a third-stage consumer society—and consumption shifted from the family unit to the individual—that ownership rates for consumer durables surged among live-alone singles.

As an aside, Japanese singles today are more likely to have microwaves in their homes than they are to own rice cookers. It's standard now to just buy precooked rice packs and side dishes at the local convenience store and microwave them for dinner, instead of going to the trouble of fixing your own rice.

From Consumption to "Creative Consuming"

Japan's third-stage consumer society put a special emphasis on fashion sense and diversification as a way of responding to the increasing individualization of the consumer. The premise was that since all people wanted to be themselves and no two people were the same, the design and functions of their products should also be more diverse. If you were targeting young women consumers in particular, then your products had to be extremely fashionable, without at the same time boxing these new, more individualistic Japanese women into traditional notions of femininity.

In Parco's case, our 1975 advertising slogans included "Don't look at nudes. BE nude,"[*] and "It takes more than a [pretty] face to be a model"[†](pboto p. 315). Over at Seibu Department Stores, the 1980 campaign was "Yourself, Rediscovered."[‡] Ads like these heralded the dawn of "The Age of the Self," the age of individuality.

---

[*] *Hadaka o miru na. Hadaka ni nare.*
[†] *Moderu datte kao dake ja dame nan da.*
[‡] *Jibun, shinhakken.*

Advertisements expressing a new thirst for individualism freed of firm and family prolif-
erated from 1975 on. This ad for the Seibu Department Store in Tokyo's Ikebukuro reads:
"Yourself, rediscovered" (Jibun shinhakken; Advertising Museum Tokyo collection).

At *Across* magazine, we posited the concept of *sōhisha* 創費者, a pun on *shōhisha* 消費者, the Japanese word for "consumer." In Parco parlance, a *sōhisha* was literally a "creative spender." This term didn't gain much currency beyond the pages of our magazine, but since *Across* had so many paid subscribers at Dentsu, Hakuhodo and other Japanese advertising agencies, the idea itself seems to have spread.

It was none other than then Parco senior managing director, and later chairman, Masuda Tsūji who invented *"sōhisha"* as well as the earlier famous Parco advertising slogan "The Fourth Yamanote," taking the affluence of the traditional wealthy core of Tokyo and spreading it out across the suburbs.[7] This is what I remember Masuda telling us staffers at *Across* one memorable day way back then:

What is consumption (*shōhi* 消費) anyway? Look at the Chinese characters we use to write it. *Kesu* 消, "erase." *Tsuiyasu* 費, "use up." But

51

our consumers aren't actually erasing or using up anything, right? Buying fashion at Parco, buying interior goods at Parco, that's not the same as buying radishes at the supermarket. They're not just "consuming," right? They're "creating 創." They're consuming to create their own lifestyles. That's why I say this isn't *shōhi* (消費, consumption). It's *sōhi* (創費, creative spending/consumption).

Now of course I don't remember Masuda's exact words after all these years, but this captures the essence of what he had to say. People were beginning to create their own individual lifestyles, their own ways of living. The place that could help them to do that was Parco.

The mass society consumers that one studies in university sociology classes are as scattered as the sand, pulled this way and that way by powerful corporations. It cannot be denied that a housewife may watch a TV show, see an ad for detergent or food, and then, when she goes to the supermarket that evening and finds the actual product on the shelf, think to herself, "Oh, I just saw that on TV!" and buy it.

This chain of events is a classic example of "rational" consumer behavior in the sense that it is the direct result of calculated marketing. If consumers never behaved "rationally" in this way, then there would be no point to making commercials. And, while it would be an overstatement to say that consumers are at the mercy of the corporations, it is true that for the most part consumers are passive recipients of the messages that the corporations pump out.

It is not all that uncommon for someone who studied sociology in college to join an advertising agency and wind up working on the marketing side. However, sociology as an academic discipline is highly critical of the way the establishment manipulates the emotions of the masses. Since manipulating consumers is at the heart of advertising, it's small wonder that people in the industry with sociology backgrounds sometimes feel ashamed of what they do.

At Parco, however, we saw things differently. We did not perceive the consumer as passive or weak, but rather as active, strong, and creative. Since fashion consumers in particular are purchasing items that are not essential, not time sensitive, not daily necessities, they really study up on the merchandise. Unlike buying radishes, or detergent, or ramen noodles, when it comes to fashion, you want to buy things that really suit you and make you look fabulous; you want to be on top of the latest trends. Parco consumers were coming to our stores and picking their clothes with all of those factors in mind—they didn't just pop in and buy whatever we wanted them to buy. If anything, our customers were in a stronger position than Parco itself. Parco didn't create a trend and then consumers hopped on board. It was the consumers who started the trends through their interactions with one another, and it was our job to spot those trends and respond as quickly as possible.

You may challenge me on whether the consumer is really as powerful as I suggest, but in the fashion industry, at least, the most popular models out there today are the "reader models," normal shoppers who are actually out on the street wearing their own fashions. The "reader models" you might see in today's fashion magazines are not wearing styles imposed on them by the fashion industry. Instead, the fashion industry is being shaped by these women and others like them who are checking each other out and thinking, "Oh, her clothes are really nice," or, "I love the way she's put herself together," admiring and adopting each other's looks. These aren't passive consumers who simply gulp down whatever is fed them by the fashion industry. They are consumers who beam their own image back at the fashion houses. They are exactly the creative *sōhisha* of whom Masuda spoke.

The advertising copy Parco used when opening its Shibuya store was particularly apt: "The people you're passing are all so beautiful. Shibuya Park Drive."* In other words, the consumer on the street is the real star.

This way of thinking was classic third-stage consumerism. Yet at the same time it hinted at the coming of the next, fourth-stage consumer society. In the sense that people were trying to find products that matched their own personal lifestyles and life choices, it was still a third-stage consumer society. But in the sense that the consumer, the person living in society, had taken control of the process, it was fourth-stage consumerism in action.

* *Surechigau hito ga utsukushii. Shibuya Kōen-dōri.*

If consumption in third-stage consumer society is not just about consuming and expending, but is actually a creative act, then you require an audience to view your "creations." You need neither the gaze nor the praise of others if you're buying radishes. But buying and wearing fashion requires more than your own self-satisfaction—it requires the admiring, the approving, the envious eyes of others. Consumers pick their fashions not just for themselves, but for the positive evaluation of others.

In April 1983, *Across* published an article[4] that broadly divided consumer goods into three categories: (1) daily life essentials (basic food, clothes, and shelter); (2) social life essentials (radios, televisions, automobiles); and (3) goods for differentiation and self-expression (fashion, brand goods, furs). However, the article then went on to propose a fourth category: goods for personal growth and fulfillment (hobbies, reading, the arts). When you purchased these products, the article argued, you were engaged in *sōhi*, consumption as creation.

As it happens, the four categories in the article also correspond to the four stages of consumer society discussed in this book.

We can say, then, that *sōhi* intersects to some degree with the concept of *kyōhi*—or "shared consumption"—that distinguishes Japan's fourth-stage consumer society. It already contains within it some aspects of the definition of *kyōhi*: consumption as a joint undertaking carried out by independent, self-aware individuals. I will speak more of this in Part Three.

Just as an aside, when I first found myself working for a marketing magazine I felt very uncomfortable with the term *sabetsuka*, often translated as "discrimination" or "differentiation." In general (and especially so for those of us who studied sociology and social policy in school), *sabetsuka* in the older sense of sexual or racial discrimination is bad. But in the marketing world—and I'm not exaggerating—you say "*sabetsuka* this, *sabetsuka* that" every day, all day long. And in the beginning I did indeed feel a lot of resistance to this loaded term.

Of course, there is a clear difference between *sabetsuka* as used in a societal sense ("discrimination") and *sabetsuka* as used in the marketing sense ("differentiation"). Yet I would be hard put even now to argue that they're unrelated. People differ from one another. They flaunt those differences. They think they're superior to each other based on those differences. That is the value system embodied by *sabetsuka*.

From Supermarket to Convenience Store

In business terms, the above individualization of the consumer led to a surge in convenience store sales.

Japan's supermarkets had their heyday in the country's second-stage consumer society, posting their strongest sales growth back when the family was still the primary unit of consumption (fig. 3-5). There was actually an historic moment in 1972 when the giant supermarket chain Daiei overtook the venerable Mitsukoshi department stores in sales. As noted earlier, department stores are a first-stage consumer society business model. Their sales peaked during the economic bubble, and they have been falling steadily for the more than twenty years since. Third-stage consumerism's strong preference for brand products helped stabilize

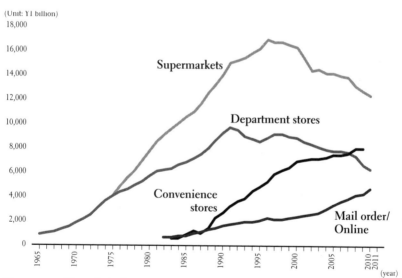

FIGURE 3-5 Trends in Department Store, Supermarket, Convenience Store, and Mail Order/Online Sales

Sources: Japan Department Store Association, Japan Chain Store Association, Japan Franchise Association, and Japan Direct Marketing Association.

department stores for a time, but it seems that their very existence may now be at risk with the arrival of a fourth-stage consumer society.

Japan's first convenience store is generally agreed to have been a 7-Eleven that opened its doors in Tokyo's Toyosu district in 1974. Now there are some fifty thousand convenience stores across the country. Their combined sales exceed 8 trillion yen annually, leaving department stores in the dust. Even the second-stage consumerism supermarkets are seeing their sales stumble under the convenience store onslaught.

Meanwhile, the spread of the Internet combined with a changing pace of life as more and more women join the workforce has set the stage for increased online, catalog, telephone, and mail order sales.

From Physical Goods to Service: The Rise of the Food Service Industry

The individualization of demand in Japan also forced a shift in the structure of consumption from physical goods to service.

To take a simple example, when one of today's new individualized consumers wants something to eat, he or she is far more likely to eat out than to cook up something at home. In short, it is not the consumption of goods that is increasing, but the consumption of service.

The sector that has benefited most directly from this trend is the food service industry, with its family restaurant chains, fast food outlets, and other eateries. It was 1971 when McDonald's opened its first Japan branch, picking for its location one of the most prestigious addresses in Japan: the first floor of the Ginza Mitsukoshi Department Store. Skylark, Kentucky Fried Chicken and several other family restaurant and fast-food chains all debuted in 1970.

In 1975, the food service industry's market size was ¥8,580 billion. Just ten years later in 1985 it was ¥19,277 billion. Sales of instant "cup noodles," which also went on sale about the time that the first McDonalds's and Skylarks appeared, have posted a very similar growth curve (fig. 3-6).

Supporting this rapid expansion of family restaurants and other food service industry business were the so-called "new families" of the baby boom generation. In that sense, the very term "family restaurant"

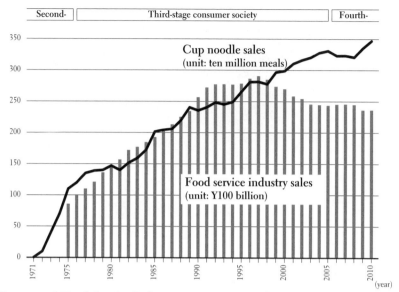

FIGURE 3-6 Food Service Industry vs. Instant Noodles

Sources: Foundation of Food Safety and Security, Japan Instant Foods Industry Association.

identified these new restaurants as a business model tailored to second-stage consumer society.

McDonald's first targets in Japan were the young people strolling along the Ginza on Pedestrian Paradise days when traffic is banned from Japan's most famous street. For many years after, its image in Japan was as a chain focused primarily on young urban singles, even though the company had originally expanded across the United States as a family-oriented chain outside the city center. Yet as the young folk in the 1970s went on to marry and have children of their own in the 1980s, they still continued to eat at McDonald's, only this time they were patronizing suburban branches with their kids in tow. In that sense, McDonald's was actually a second-stage consumer society business, just like Japan's indigenous family restaurant chains.

However, as Japan entered the 1980s family restaurant chains started to increasingly be a place for young singles living alone to eat. In fact, when I myself entered college in 1977 and moved into my own

A picture from a newspaper article on the popularity of family restaurants from the days when the sector was growing 30 percent year-on-year. The photograph was taken in Koganei City, where the author lived at the time. (Asahi Shimbun, April 28, 1977)

place in Koganei City in the western exurbs of Tokyo, there was already a Skylark restaurant near my apartment. Eating a hamburger there with a fried egg perched atop it was a wee bit of luxury for a poor college student living on fried rice and Chinese pot stickers.

During my junior year at Hitotsubashi University I moved to Kunitachi City, which is even further out, and, sure enough, there was a Skylark restaurant right near my apartment there as well, as there would be again when I relocated even further west to Kokubunji. I particularly remember stopping by that Kokubunji Skylark on many a late night for dinner. Perhaps it was around then that demand from night-owl singles like myself took its place alongside the chain's core demand from daytime moms with kids and weekend family diners?

No doubt the young people patronizing family restaurants today don't think of them as places for families but as all-purpose hangouts, be it for coffee and tea with their friends or even a relaxed drink or two. When they were children their parents took them to these restaurants for dinner. When they reached high school they went there with their friends after school. Then later, they were back again on dates. As adults today, they may still drop by to have a beer. In that way, it's become natural to go to the local family restaurant at every stage of your life. This suggests that the family restaurant business model itself has evolved from a second-stage consumer society staple to a business model for third-stage consumerism.

Starting in 1992, however, sales growth began leveling off across Japan's entire food service industry. The economic bubble had burst, and the "lost decades" of economic malaise lay ahead. Industry sales finally peaked in 1997 at 29,000,700 million yen, and they have been in continuous decline ever since. The market for Japan's food service industry began shrinking together with the dawn of the fourth-stage consumer society.

The single biggest factor behind this contraction was the long post-bubble economic recession, leading consumers to eat out less and eat in more. However, there was a powerful second factor at work as well: the rise of ready-to-eat food, or *nakashoku*.[5] Groceries, department stores, and convenience stores anywhere in Japan today are stocked with a cornucopia of food items and even complete meals that can be eaten as is or quickly warmed up in a microwave.

When you buy such pre-prepared food you may not, technically speaking, be eating out. Yet neither are you cooking at home. You can simply pick up some takeout or deli items to have at the office or when you get back to the house. Or while you're walking around town. Or even sitting on the grass.[6]

In 1997 the share of *nakashoku* in Japan's total food consumption was just 4.7 percent. By 2009 it had nearly doubled to 8.1 percent (fig. 3-7). These figures do not include instant noodles, which are listed under a different category, so we can assume that the actual number of times a week that people are cooking their own food in their own home has actually fallen farther than even these numbers suggest. Instant noodle sales continue to grow even today.

What, then, is behind the decline in eating out and the surging popularity of ready-to-eat and instant food? The biggest factor is simply

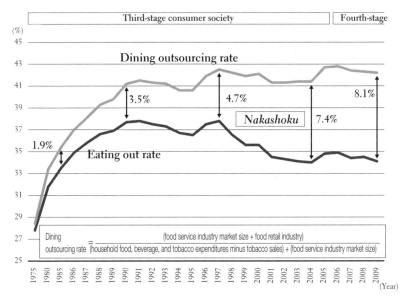

FIGURE 3-7 Trends in Eating Out and the Outsourcing of Dining

Source: Foundation of Food Safety and Security.

consumers' desire for less expensive and/or simpler ways to eat. At the same time, however, I do not consider it too much of a stretch to suggest that it is also a product of people wanting to have more direct connection with their families and their friends rather than spend their time cooking or sitting in restaurants. In that sense, the *nakashoku* boom harbors within it some distinctly fourth-stage consumerism traits.

Or perhaps I could put it this way instead. The food service industry is categorized as a service industry. Yet the reality today is that many family restaurants simply truck in frozen meals from a central kitchen, zap them in the back kitchen microwave, and serve them to the customer with just a modicum of additional preparation. This hardly deserves to be called "service."

Back in the 1970s family restaurants provided much more attentive service, so you could make the case that at least originally they belonged in the service industry. Now, however, in the wake of the fierce price competition following the bursting of Japan's bubble, staffs have been slashed and self-service, all-you-can-drink "drink bars" and similar innovations have been rolled out across the industry. It seems that "service" is no longer on the menu.

If, as I will argue later, fourth-stage consumer society places a premium on quality service, then today's family restaurants will have a hard time adapting to the coming age. They may well revert to the old mass-production, second-stage consumer society business model of their origins.

Brand Consciousness

Another key aspect of the migration from second-stage to third-stage consumerism in Japan was a new focus on quality. "From quantity to quality"[*] was a phrase worked virtually to death in the Japanese marketing industry of the 1990s.

By that time, virtually the entire baby boom (*dankai*) generation was in its child-rearing years, and the cohort that had taken its place in the privileged singles market was the same *shin-jinrui* (New People) generation that we met before.

The defining characteristic of *shin-jinrui* consumption was brand consciousness. Theirs was a society in which even college coeds were turned out in the world's top luxury brands. Imported luxury car sales surged (fig. 3-8). The "from quantity to quality" ethos meshed perfectly with the *shin-jinrui* hunger for brand name products, and from there went on to permeate every corner of Japanese society.

A novel that perfectly captures the brand orientation of Japan's third-stage consumer society is *Nantonaku, kurisutaru* (Somehow, Crystal, 1980), by Japanese novelist and later liberal politician Tanaka Yasuo. This best-selling novel received the prestigious Bungei Prize for emerging writers in 1980, exactly when the *shin-jinrui* kids were in high school and college. Tanaka's fictional characters were obsessed with brands and after his book came out the real-world young people

[*] *Ryō kara shitsu e.*

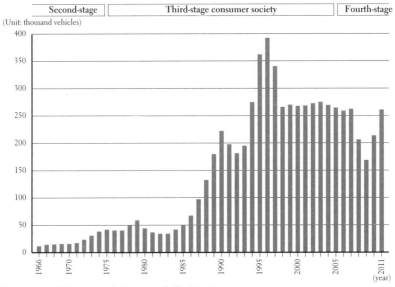

FIGURE 3-8 Imported Automobile Registration

Note: 1966 figures for March-December only.
Source: Japan Automobile Importers Association.

who shared this obsession were mocked by adults as the *Crystal-zoku* (Crystal Tribe).

As it happened, I was just a year behind Tanaka at our shared alma mater, Hitotsubashi University. A person like Tanaka really stood out at a school like Hitotsubashi, that back then was known for its test-taking grinds who had survived Japan's rigorous national university entrance exams to get in. Tanaka was already wearing brand-name clothes as a student, even around campus (not that I had a clue then as to what brands they were). He was also notorious for heading out night after night for the jam-packed discotheques of Tokyo's flashy Roppongi district.

Thinking back on my university days today, I can safely say that the students from Tokyo and Yokohama—especially the coeds—were far more stylish than the rest of us, and also wore more brands. Yet even compared to them Tanaka stood out. I suspect you would have found more students like him at private universities around Tokyo like Keio University, Aoyama Gakuin, and Rikkyō University.

Yet once I graduated and joined Parco I suddenly found myself—and what else should I have expected?—surrounded by colleagues who might all have been Tanaka Yasuo doppelgangers. Everyone was a member of the Crystal Tribe.

Now, I myself was an old-school public university student. True, I had applied to work at trendy Parco, but my dream was to join the publishing wing and create art books. I had zero interest in fashion or brands, and I was totally unprepared for how many Crystal Tribe staffers there were. I remember my shock at seeing some of my fellow employees actually come to work in sweatshirts—albeit sweatshirts from the then-hot Boat House brand.

People who choose a discipline like sociology—or at very least, we sociology students back in the day—tend to dismiss fashion as some foolish behavior of the masses, so I went through severe culture shock when I joined a workplace populated with fashionistas. Nor was it just our office. The Shibuya sidewalks of ultra-hip Kōen-dōri (Park Drive) outside our front door thronged with college girls dressed just like the models in popular fashion magazine *JJ*. I remember feeling like I had tumbled into the maw of mass society incarnate.

Looking back on it now, however, I should have known that I could never really learn about society by lazing around reading books on a college campus in leafy, suburban Kunitachi. A community like that is hardly the best environment for studying a discipline that seeks to analyze cutting-edge social trends. And that was doubly true for me as I lived a life even further divorced from the "floating world" of Tokyo than most, immersing myself in Max Weber's sociology of religion in the original German. I can see now that I spent my entire college life without once experiencing the realities of mass society.

As it happened, upon joining Parco I was assigned not to the art book publishing of my dreams but to the editorial department of a marketing magazine. I was fated to spend my days analyzing the newest trends in consumption. I tried to tell myself that if I could just view consumption as the religion of our day, then I might still get some good out of my expertise in the sociology of religion. And indeed, looking back at those times today, I really do think 1980s Shibuya was a town ruled by a new religion: the Church of Consumption.

The Dawn of "Catalog Culture"

At the time, it was popular to dismiss Japan's new brand-conscious consumer culture as a "catalog culture." Indeed, not a few critics scathingly declared Tanaka's *Nantonaku, kurisutaru*—with its walking dress-up doll heroine falling in love in the hot spots of Tokyo—a "catalog novel."

But where did this catalog culture come from? Catalogs had been around in Japan for a very long time. But it was not until the 1970s that today's ubiquitous for-pay catalog magazines first made their debut.

The trigger was a book from the United States: the 1968 *Whole Earth Catalog*. Created by writer and editor Stewart Brand, *Whole Earth Catalog* was a counterculture catalog that promoted the "do-it-yourself" message that people should be able to create the things they need in their lives with their own hands. Brand used a very specific set of criteria to choose the items he introduced in the catalog, including relevant to independent education, high quality or low cost, not already common knowledge, and easily available by mail.

At heart, his work was the antithesis of post-1950s American society dominated by mass production and mass consumption, a society where people had devolved into consumers who did nothing with their lives but shop and buy.

The *Whole Earth Catalog* went through many editions, but it was not until the 1970s that it became better known in Japan and the first imitations appeared in Japanese bookstores. The first to hit the stands was the "Zentoshi katarogu" (Whole City Catalog) special section of the November 1975 edition of *Takarajima* magazine, published by JICC Shuppankyoku (today's Takarajima Co). It was followed in April 1976 by the *Zentoshi katarogu* (Whole City Catalog), the first edition of the company's new line of *Bessatsu Takarajima* magazine anthologies, which itself has gone on to become an influential trendsetter.

Another example was the *Made in U.S.A. Catalog* (see illustration at right), published as a special edition of *Shūkan Yomiuri* (Weekly Yomiuri) magazine in June 1975. This "catalog" included on-the-ground

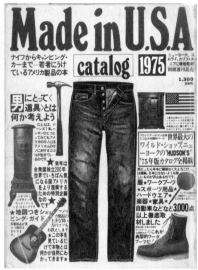

(Author's collection).

The Whole Earth Catalog *and "catalog culture" comes to Japan.*

reporting from New York, Colorado, and California and was described grandly as "Naifu kara kyanpingu-kā made—wakamono ni ukete iru Amerika seihin no hon" (From knives to camping cars: The book of American products popular among young people). It may seem hard to believe today, but back then the United States was still the wellspring of youth fashion in Japan.

There is an interesting backstory to the *Made in U.S.A. Catalog*. This special issue actually originated with Kinameri Yoshihisa, a legendary editor at the lifestyle publishing powerhouse Magazine House (then Heibon Shuppan), who eventually went on to become editor-in-chief of popular men's magazines *Popeye* and *Brutus* and president of Magazine House itself. Kinameri saw a copy of the original *Whole Earth Catalog* and proposed to his then boss that they produce a Japanese version. His boss slapped the idea down, declaring, "People get catalogs for free!" And Kinameri took his proposal to Yomiuri instead.

So in short, the *Made in U.S.A. Catalog* was virtually a Japanese version of *Whole Earth Catalog*. Matsuyama Takeshi, who would also later be an editior at *Brutus*, joined Kinameri's team as well. Which makes it even more ironic that, after all the original internal opposition to Kinameri's proposal at Magazine House, the company turned around the next year and launched *Popeye* magazine, the flagship of catalog magazine culture in Japan.

The *Whole Earth Catalog* influence extended to Japanese women's magazines, starting with *Saison de non-no*, published in 1974 as a special edition of leading fashion journal *non-no*. Regretfully, I still have never seen an actual copy of the inaugural issue, but the 1976 eleventh edition—which I did secure for my collection—uses "catalog" in the title of almost every article between its covers. For instance, there's "Daitokushū: Yutaka na kurashi no katarogu" (Giant Special Section: A Catalog for an Abundant Life), and "Ima o ikiru onna no ko no yottsu no raifu katarogu" (Four Life Catalogs for Women Living in the Moment), "Fasshon katarogu" (Fashion Catalog), and more. So we may not be amiss in anointing *Saison de non-no* the ancestor of women's catalog magazines as they exist in Japan today. In that same vein, 1975 saw the publication of both *An-an zōkan: Katarogushū* (An-An Expanded Edition: The Catalog

Collection) and the *Shūkan Sankei tokubetsu zōkan Do Catalog* (Weekly Sankei Special Expanded Edition Do Catalog).

In this way, a new catalog media, springing originally from the counterculture pages of the *Whole Earth Catalog*, evolved in Japan into a powerful force for the promotion of materialistic consumption. And this wave of catalog magazines, led by popular titles like *Popeye* and *Brutus,* became in turn the template for today's even more brand conscious and consumption-centric *butsuyoku-zasshi* ("gear lust" magazines) and *burando-zasshi* (brand magazines) targeting Japanese youth. Truly it was a change of eras: from politics to consumption.

Before moving on, I should note parenthetically that the do-it-yourself philosophy promoted by the original *Whole Earth Catalog* did in fact go on to take tangible form in Japan as well. We can see it in today's proliferation of giant Tokyū Hands DIY emporiums and other smaller DIY shops in Japanese cities. The layout of the sales floors at a Tokyū Hands may strike one as more "catalog-like" than that of smaller DIY shops, but we have to give Hands credit for melding the *Whole Earth Catalog* ethos with Japan's catalog consumption culture.[7]

"Luxury" Instant Food and "Luxury-car" Dating

The fashion industry was not alone in turning to branding and climbing the luxury ladder to satisfy consumers' new hunger for "differentiation." Even instant ramen, the archetypal mass-market product of second-stage Japanese consumerism, was fair game. In 1981, Myōjō Foods released its Chūka Zanmai line of "luxury" instant ramen with fancy packaging and higher-quality ingredients. The product aspired to being a luxury item, even though it was just instant noodles. And, in fact, Chūka Zanmai is still selling briskly today.

Nestlé Japan, a leading purveyor of instant coffee, also played the luxury card. It launched a series of TV commercials featuring a "Crown Prince Rudolph, heir to the Belgian throne," to promote its new "luxury" instant coffee, Nescafé President. The campaign caused quite a stir, even though skeptics questioned whether aristocrats really drank instant coffee at home.

The full-color ad on the back cover of the inaugural issue of women's fashion magazine non-no *was not for clothes but for the just-released Toyota Celica. The ad copy clearly positioned it as a "date car": "Koi wa Serika de"* (Love is better in a Celica). *In those days it would have been highly unlikely that the* non-no *reader herself would be driving, so the ad was no doubt calculated to leave her longing for a boyfriend who did drive one. The Celica also offered a broad selection of exteriors and interiors for the time. Hence one of the ad's other sales points: "Anata ni pittari na Serika o chūmon"* (Order the perfect Celica for you). *(Author's Collection).*

Adopting luxury product differentiation strategies for something like instant foods is actually quite common for mid-range products in a saturated market. Japan's home appliance industry could move its customers up the ladder from one unit per household to several per household and on to one-per-person and even several-per-person. But there is only so much food a person can eat. The food industry needed "luxurification" to raise its unit prices.

In the case of automobiles, Japan's carmakers were working hard to both increase the number of vehicles per household and to move its customers up the luxury ladder, all at the same time. The classic example was the sporty "specialty car" primarily targeting the young, single male, exemplified by new models like the 1981 Toyota Soarer, the 1975 re-released Nissan Silvia, and above all the Toyota Celica.

What were the specialty cars? Let me quote from the website of the Japan Automobile Manufacturers Association (JAMA):

> The car that created the "specialty car" category was the Ford Mustang . . . . The first-generation Mustang released in 1964 was lauded as Ford's biggest hit in the U.S. market since the Model T. It stole people's hearts with its sporty exterior design and excellent performance, a price tag within reach of young people, and a kaleidoscope of options dubbed the "full choice system." The success of the Mustang had a profound impact on automakers around the world. In Japan, a whole range of specialty cars were released from the 1970s on through the 1990s.

The first Japanese car to truly succeed in the Mustang's sporty niche, says JAMA, was the 1970 Toyota Celica. It even came with a customizable "full choice system" of its own. But it was hardly alone. The Isuzu 117 coupe (1968–81), the Mazda Cosmo Sports (1967–72), the Nissan Skyline hardtop (1970–73 models), and the Mitsubishi Galant GTO (1970–76) all came to market at just about this time.

The Japanese government introduced rigorous auto emission standards following the 1973 Oil Shock, but that did not stop the specialty cars. Explains the JAMA article: "The demand for specialty cars showed no sign of slowing down." The Nissan Silvia (1975–79, 1979–83), the Honda Prelude (1978–82, 1982–87), and other models all joined the race.

Furthermore, JAMA notes, "During the 1980s there was a boom among Japanese young people for the *haiso-kā*" [a contraction of "high-society car," a term widely used at the time for Japanese-built luxury cars]. The car that triggered the *haiso-kā* craze was the Toyota

Cresta but, says JAMA, "the pinnacle of the *haiso-kā* was the first generation two-door Toyota Soarer hardtop."

According to JAMA, *haiso-kā* were "objects of desire for the young . . . . To establish its image as a 'date car,' Toyota assumed even in the development stage that it would advertise the Soarer not with the standard scenes of sports driving on winding roads but with a Soarer cruising down a seaside highway on a date."

It comes as a bit of a shock today to learn that Honda's second-generation Prelude came with a passenger seat that could be lowered by remote control from the driver's side. Come to think of it, even Masuda Tsūji—by then the president of Parco—bought a Soarer for his own private car. You can really get a sense of those very different times.

In a sidenote, speeding has actually been declining as a cause of traffic fatalities involving young drivers age 16–24, dropping from 1,600 deaths in 1990 to 628 in 1999, and just 120 in 2009. Perhaps that's because today's young Japanese—unlike their predecessors who hurtled around the country in high-powered sports and specialty sedans—now putt along in tiny subcompacts like the Nissan Cube.

Chapter Four

Evolving Consumer Psychology

Sophisticated Consumption

T he theology of Japan's Church of Consumption differs between second- and third-stage consumer society.

The dogma of second-stage consumer society is "the bigger the better" and "*Oitsuke, oikose*" (Catch up and surpass). In practice, that always meant a quantitative expansion.

In contrast, the dogma of Japan's third-stage consumer society involved a better, more refined lifestyle, a beauty that could manifest itself even in the "high-society" car, and the bringing of luxury to all aspects of life, even instant noodles. In short, it was all about the quality of life. Lying behind this radical reformation was the growing number of consumers who had themselves converted from the pursuit of material abundance to the pursuit of spiritual richness.

The shift appears clearly in the Cabinet Office's annual National Survey on Lifestyle Preferences. In the section of the survey devoted to how one would like to live in the future, respondents are asked to choose between (1) "For the time being I would like to emphasize improving my material life" and (2) "Since I have attained a certain degree of material abundance, from now on I would like to emphasize a spiritually rich and relaxed lifestyle."

Back in the early 1970s, during the last phase of Japan's second-stage consumer society, a majority of survey respondents still indicated they were seeking material wealth (fig. 4-1). But by the late 1970s—the beginning of

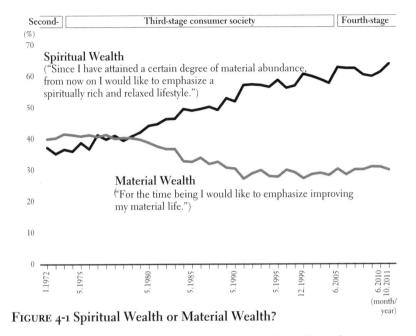

FIGURE 4-1 Spiritual Wealth or Material Wealth?

Source: Cabinet Office, "National Survey on Lifestyle Preferences" (*Kokumin-seikatsu ni kansuru yoron chōsa*).

Japan's third-stage consumer society—the aspiration for a richer spiritual life was already coming into ascendance. And post–1998—as we begin to see the first signs of fourth-stage consumerism in Japan—more than 60 percent of those polled said that they desired greater spiritual wealth (although it should be noted that the desire for material wealth appears to have made a modest comeback since the 2008 worldwide financial crisis and subsequent recession; the number of Japanese seeking a richer material life may rise again as income inequality widens).

The Healthy Living Boom

When we contemplate this striking reorientation from the material to the spiritual, it is no surprise that the move from quantity to quality was not limited to brand consciousness alone, but appeared in many other ways as well.

An archetypal example is Japan's "healthy living" boom. This new aspiration for a healthier lifestyle first emerged in food and diet during the mid-1970s. It appeared initially as a desire for food that did not simply fill your empty stomach, did not simply fill you with calories and make you bigger, but that actually contributed to a healthy body.

Likewise, the current popularity of jogging and other sports in Japan also dates back to the mid-'70s, suggesting that this concern about healthy living is part of a long-term trend that has already lasted nearly four decades.

That said, however, as we enter the latter half of Japan's third-stage consumer society we can detect a subtle shift, with a growing emphasis on the pursuit of not so much physical health as mental and spiritual well-being. This is the trend now widely referred to in Japan as "healing" (*hiiringu*).

In English, the etymological roots of "health" and "healing" are the same. But in Japanese the term hiiringu—as opposed to *kenkō*, the traditional word for health—has come to be used exclusively to mean resolving mental and spiritual stress and controlling *kokoro*, the spirit and heart. It is a movement that first appeared in the United States in the 1990s, and has now swept over Japan as well. Needless to say, the "healing" boom is yet another manifestation of the new emphasis on physical and spiritual health.

As to where the healthy living trend will go from here, I personally believe that health in Japan's fourth-stage consumer society will be holistic. In English, "holistic" shares etymological roots with "health" and "healing," and means "the totality, the whole." It reflects a belief that one is unhealthy when there is something missing from the wholeness that should be the natural state of all human beings, and that if you can only restore that wholeness to its natural state then you will also restore your health. Yoga, as omnipresent in Japan today as it is in the West, is considered a quintessential technique for restoring wholeness to your life.

However, should you ask a believer what constitutes wholeness, you will be assured that it is not just about the body nor just about the heart. You cannot achieve wellness, it seems, unless you reevaluate all aspects of your life and the way you live it. In that sense, I expect that

Japan's fourth-stage consumer society will go far beyond simple physical health or even spiritual healing to demand a holistic reassessment of one's entire way of being.

Moving Beyond the Material: The Yūrakuchō Seibu Experience

As we have seen, the individualization of consumption in Japan's third-stage consumer society triggered a shift from products to services, with convenience stores overtaking department stores, and the rise of New People *shin-jinrui* consumers driving fashion consciousness to new heights. Consequently, Japan's retail industry began to look for new business models. Parco's fashion buildings were one answer, supermarket chain Nichii (later absorbed into Aeon) opened Vivre, and Tokyū built the 109 Building in the center of Shibuya. In 1978 the first Tokyū Hands opened in Shibuya, followed in 1987 by lifestyle products megastore LoFt, as consumers embraced the idea of giant specialty stores.

The Japanese word for department store is *hyakkaten*, or literally, a "hundred-product store." Now, the new theory went, all you really needed was a *jikkaten*, or "ten-item store," providing a more carefully targeted range of quality items. The search was on for new ways to persuade Japanese consumers—their homes already overflowing with products—to purchase even more.

It was in this context that the department store industry came up with a new concept of its own. This new model department store would not simply sell goods: it would sell services. It would sell information. Instead of dealing in *mono* (things), it would deal in *koto*, the intangible, the happening, the "experience." The crystalization of this new model was Yūrakuchō Seibu, a towering shopping complex that would dominate the gateway to the Ginza for sixteen years until closing its doors in 2010.

Yūrakuchō Seibu opened for business in 1984 under the moniker Life Information Building (Seikatsu Jōhōkan). On its first floor it had its own Yūrakuchō Seibu television station, and on its specialty food floor it offered a delivery service for the chic cake and delicacies store Lenôtre of Paris. In its lingerie department it didn't just sell lingerie, it repaired lingerie. It had fashion advisors for customers to consult on what looks were best for them. It organized a Ralph Lauren fan club called the Polo Club. In its furniture department you could use computers to generate color coordination and floor-layout simulations for your home. It even had a counter that helped customers self-publish their own books.

In this way, Yūrakuchō Seibu truly was the new model department store, declaring front and center that it was not just there to sell products but to sell services, to sell information, to sell *koto*. And yet in practice the grand experiment did not necessarily turn out as hoped. Especially once Japan's economy entered the overheated bubble years, Yūrakuchō Seibu reoriented itself into just another high-end department store selling top luxury brands, and its original aspirations fell by the wayside.

Yet while this experiment in moving from *mono* to *koto* ultimately did prove a flower that bloomed too soon, it should still be remembered as an effort worthy of the Saison Group and its innovative leader, Tsutsumi Seiji. In fact, many of the services that were first tested at Yūrakuchō Seibu have since become common practice not only in department stores but in many other businesses as well. We may take the services first offered by Yūrakuchō Seibu for granted today, but thirty years ago it truly was a daring venture.

Having said that, however, the *koto* that Yūrakuchō Seibu made so much of also ultimately turned out to be just another way to sell a product, in this case a product called "service." In that sense, it was still not a model that could generate the person-to-person connections that will be so essential in fourth-stage consumer society.

The "From Driven to Beautiful" and "Discover Japan" Ad Campaigns

I am now going to step back a little in time. Obviously, the transition from a second-stage to a third-stage consumer society in Japan was not just triggered by the 1973 Oil Crisis. As we can see in seminal ad campaigns like the 1970 "*Mōretsu kara byūtifuru e*" (From Driven to Beautiful) campaign[1] for office equipment maker Fuji-Xerox and the "Discover Japan" campaign launched that same year by Japan National Railways, the public precursor of today's privatized JR rail companies, expressions were already popping up in Japanese advertising that in retrospect can almost be read as the starting point not just for Japan's third-stage consumer society but even for its fourth.

These two memorable campaigns—"From Driven to Beautiful" and "Discover Japan" (photo p. 313)—were both created by the same man: Fujioka Wakao, then with Japan's top advertising agency Dentsu. In 1988, Fujioka took a look back on his campaigns:

> This year, 1988, is the year that new values will sprout in Japan. For so many years we have fought with a single arrow in our quiver. Everything has been about the economic axis. We haven't been able to comprehend anything that we could not measure in terms of its economic value. Yet while that era has lasted so very, very long, recently we really are beginning to see the signs of something different . . . We are beginning to see the signs of a willingness to foster within each and every one of us and in society at large a simple, unadorned appreciation that, even if we might have to sacrifice a little economic value here or a little economic efficiency there, that which is beautiful is still beautiful all of itself, and that is good enough. . . .
>
> If that is true, people ask, then is that what we meant by "From Driven to Beautiful"? Yes, that is exactly what we meant. Those words we shouted out seventeen years ago have now, finally, begun to carry the weight of reality. We needed all of those seventeen long years for it to happen. What has awoken this new awareness is a realization, a gut sense rooted in people's real-world lives, that one cannot become rich from economic prosperity alone.[2]

Should Japanese, especially younger Japanese, read Fujioka's words today, they would probably feel like they had hopped a time machine back to an older age. "That which is beautiful is still beautiful all of itself, and that is good enough"? "One cannot become rich from economic prosperity alone"? Most Japanese nowadays consider those givens.

When these campaigns came out back in 1970 it was just a year before the start of Japan's second baby boom. The generation that turned forty in 2011 was born in an era when "From Driven to Beautiful" was a powerfully fresh message. But they have grown to adulthood in parallel with changes in Japanese society that have turned that from a radical notion into the new normal.

Nonetheless, when the first "From Driven to Beautiful" television ad appeared, with its young flower-child youth wordlessly carrying a hand-written "beautiful" sign through crowds of hurrying office workers on the blurry streets of a big city, it was revolutionary.

Fujioka's second campaign, Discover Japan, is discussed at length in my 2010 *Aikoku shōhi: Hoshii no wa Nihon bunka to Nihon e no hokori* (Consumption as Nationalism: What We Want is Japanese Culture and Pride in Japan). Let me point out here, however, that strictly speaking the campaign copy was not actually "Discover Japan," but rather "Discover Japan: Utsukushii Nippon to Watakushi" (Discover Japan: Beautiful Japan and I).

Running for seven continuous years from 1970 to 1977, Discover Japan was, in Fujioka's own words, "the longest campaign without a tumble in the history of advertising." In 1988 he shared these thoughts about the campaign's message:

> If you want to visualize the ugliest form a civilization that has developed totally indiscriminately could possibly take, it is enough to simply recall today's environmental pollution . . . However, rather than approaching pollution as a problem of civilization, we need to teach everyone to position pollution as a problem of heart.
>
> Beyond a doubt, what has actually become indiscriminate is not our civilization per se, but our own hearts . . . When the willow trees along the Ginza withered, when the fish died in the Sumida River, what did we actually feel? Can it really be true that as we sang the praises of economic growth, driven by our own materialistic desires, we felt not a single twinge of regret at their passing?[3]

℀

Traditionally, travel has in some sense been little more than the marketing of destinations, a kind of glorified postcard. That kind of travel can never transcend simple tourism, and provides no more information than you might get from watching TV. The true joys of travel must be joys you create for yourself. True travel in Japan should be a kind of journey where you discover Japan for yourself and through that process of discovery rediscover yourself.

That is the sense in which we called the campaign "Discover Japan." A dusty road in a nameless countryside. Perhaps it was once a road steeped in history. Perhaps countless dramas and romances played out along its length. Standing there, maybe you catch the smell of sweat, or hear the harvest songs. When you stand at a place like that on your own two feet, that is when you are traveling. That is when you truly "Discover Japan."[4]

In this way, for what may have been the first time in the history of advertising, problems of the spirit were taken up in an ad campaign in the form of a reevaluation of the materialism inherent in second-stage consumer society. Fujioka himself later went independent, and at the time of this writing is embarked on a journey across Japan to visit what few unspoiled landscapes still remain. For Fujioka, the "From Driven to Beautiful" and "Discover Japan" ad campaigns were not just work—they were his own view of life.

"I Can't Depict a Happy World . . ."

I know I am writing a lot about myself in these pages, but the "From Driven to Beautiful" campaign brings back a number of other television commercials and popular catchphrases from that time.

The popular slang term "*yukkurizumu*" (take it slow-ism), a call to push back against the driven *mōretsu* lifestyle by setting a more relaxed pace for yourself, was on everyone's lips. It was also this era that brought us the traffic safety slogan, "*Semai Nippon, son'na ni isoide doko e iku?*" (Where are you going in such a hurry in crowded little Japan?) in response to surging traffic accidents.

One thing I particularly remember was an episode of *Sazae-san*,[5] Sazae's father Namihei is sitting in the guest room of his house with a group of his colleagues when he declares, "*Nihonjin mo, motto yukkuri shinakereba narimasen na*" (We Japanese have to slow down and take it easy). His colleagues all agree, crying out, "*Sō desu, sō desu. Yukkuri*

Undō o shimashō!" (You're right! You're right! Let's launch a Take-it-easy Movement!). The punch line comes when they spring to their feet and dash out of the room, crying, "*Sore de wa, sassoku yarimashō!*" (Let's get on it immediately!).

That was how it was back then. The times demanded speed, and everyone was in a hurry. That had been the unbroken thread running through Japanese attitudes toward life since the prewar days and war-time militarism. No, it went even farther back. Back to the era of the Meiji Revolution in the late nineteenth century that ushered Japan out of isolation into the modern world. That was the kind of age we were immersed in when people first began talking about "beautiful" and "Take it slow."

One of the things that left the deepest impression on me in those days were the lyrics to a Mobile Oil advertising song:

Kiraku ni ikō yo
Oretachi wa
Asette mitatte
Onaji koto

(Let's just let it all hang out, all of us. Even if you rush, it all comes out the same).

This commercial with its archetypal images of freedom-seeking 1970s young people was especially memorable, and the art director behind it was Sugiyama Toshi.

Sugiyama was a genius of Japanese advertising, having worked on campaigns for cosmetics maker Shiseido, soft drink company Calpis, Toyota, and others since the 1960s. Of course as a teenager I had never heard his name, but I certainly knew his work. I had been watching it constantly on TV since elementary school.

However, one day at the end of 1973 a shocking article with Sugiyama's photograph popped out at me from the pages of the *Asahi Shimbun* newspaper. The famous art director had taken his own life. The article said he had left behind a suicide note, and quoted the following passage:

Ritchi de nai no ni ritchi na sekai nado wakarimasen.
Happii de nai no ni happii na sekai nado egakemasen.
"Yume" ga nai no ni "yume" o uru koto nado wa . . . totemo.
Uso o tsuite mo bareru mono desu.

(I can't understand "rich" when I'm not rich.
I can't depict a happy world when I'm not happy.
When I have no dreams, selling dreams is . . . out of the question.
Tell a lie, and someday you will be exposed.)

The death of a creative genius in the wake of the Oil Crisis. Truly it telegraphed the end of an era.

Yet speaking only for myself, I cannot really say I ever felt any "richness" or "happiness" or "dreams" in Sugiyama's TV spots. They were simply great commercials with a fine sensibility, beautiful ads full of humor. I guess my middle-school self was too young to understand the inner torments of a creator.

One day after entering university I spotted a book in a bookstore near my apartment titled *CM ni chan'neru o awaseta hi* (The Day I Switched My Channel to a Commercial). It turned out to be an anthology of Sugiyama Toshi's work. I thought, "My god, they've published a book about that Sugiyama Toshi!" I practically danced with joy and bought it on the spot.

The collection turned out to have been published by Parco, and one of the editors was the great art director Ishioka Eiko. Ishioka, who passed away too young in January 2012, had worked under Sugiyama during his Shiseido years and later was one of the art directors behind the golden age of Parco advertising. It goes without saying that she went on to become an Oscar-winning director and designer on the world stage.

As fate would have it, I myself would go from dreaming of a Parco that had published a book on Sugiyama and where Ishioka Eiko was creating the advertising to joining that company and editing a marketing magazine telling of consumer dreams and the joys of fashion. And even now I cannot help but wonder what commercials Sugiyama might have made if he had lived on into Japan's third-stage consumer society.

The Tower of the Sun and Contradictions of Economic Growth

As if encapsulated in Sugiyama's death, a wave of doubt about economic growth swept the world in the early 1970s. In 1972 the Club of Rome think tank, founded by Aurelio Peccei, president of Italy's Olivetti S.p.A., and British scientist and policy advisor Alexander King, published *The Limits to Growth*. This ground-breaking report was an alarm bell, warning that if population growth, environmental pollution, and other trends were to continue unchecked, growth on Planet Earth would reach its limit within the next hundred years.

In Japan, pollution, environmental destruction, soaring traffic deaths, and many other consequences of the deep contradictions in the country's all too rapid postwar growth were emerging as serious social problems. Sickening smells wafted up from the rivers, and the surrounding seas were fouled with sludge. Traffic fatalities soared (fig. 4-2).

In response, the government implemented the Environmental Pollution Prevention Act in 1967, and in 1970 an Environmental Pollution Prevention Headquarters was established within the Cabinet Office. The Environment Agency was created the next year. The ecology movement was in full swing, and there were calls for a "bikecology" movement to get people onto bicycles to protect the environment.

Then in 1973 the British economist E. F. Schumacher caused a sensation with his book *Small Is Beautiful*. The author was a former economic advisor to the British Coal Authority, and in his book he predicted a coming energy crisis, which almost instantly became a reality with the first Oil Crisis later that year. In the same book Schumacher questioned the core assumptions of modern economics with its emphasis on mass consumption as an indicator of happiness, and of "scientism," the era's unbridled belief in the benefits of science. He went on to propose achieving full employment under an economy free of government interference.

And of course, the theme of the 1970 World Exposition when it had opened in Osaka three years earlier was "Progress and Harmony of Mankind." Implicit in the Expo theme was a critique of the many contradictions of progress. Japanese avant-garde artist and sculptor Okamoto Tarō punched a hole right through the roof of the Festival Plaza designed by world-renowned Japanese architect Tange Kenzō to erect

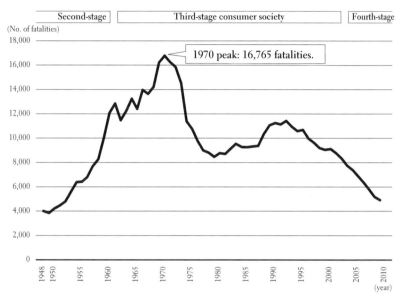

FIGURE 4-2 Trends in Traffic Fatalities

Source: National Police Agency Traffic Bureau, *Heisei 22-nenchū no kōtsūjikoshisa ni tsuite* (Report on Traffic Accident Fatalities 2010).

his Tower of the Sun (photo at right), turning to pottery from Japan's prehistoric Jōmon period for design hints. Inside the tower he erected a Tree of Life tracing the world's progress from primitive cells to the human race, drawing a sharp contrast with modern civilization.

Okamoto himself says it best. Let me quote him at length:

> I proclaimed that I was going to create something nonsensical, something absurd. That was because I think that the Japanese, while a hard-working people and pure at heart, are a bit short on cheerful idiocy. I thought it would be good if 1970 marked the beginning of a new image for the Japanese. No matter how much we grow our economy, no matter how skillfully we jockey and maneuver, wouldn't it be boring if that was all we were? I wanted us to have a rounded, rich, wide-ranging, appealing humanity.... Human beings are all filled with the universe, shining with innocence just the way they are. The Tower of the Sun, standing there so innocently with its arms outstretched, is supposed to

82

The Tower of the Sun was imbued with a critique of modern civilization (Photo: Kyodo News)

be a symbol of that. With a buck-naked heart, it merges with the sun and all creation, escaping from our fidgety everyday selves. . . . That is where the joy of the "festival," the joy of living, is born.

࿊

There has never before been an age when it has been so impossible to have a festival. Every corner of our lives is overflowing with illusions of festivals, with sliced and diced little bits of fake festivals, scattering our spirit. . . . Yet somehow it all seems meaningless. . . . Society today has lost the shared rhythms of a human community. All alone, cut off from others, the individual is deprived of the richness of the whole. In other words, we ourselves are no longer perfectly ourselves. The more organized modern society becomes in the future, the finer the mesh of the System's net becomes, the more human beings will become just components, and will lose the wonder and the grandeur of the unity, of the whole.

∾

Our vast production capacity has raised our standard of living. But if you ask if that has truly made our lives richer, or if that truly signifies human or spiritual progress, I think it highly doubtful.

∾

The Tower of the Sun is a symbol of life-force erupting from the fountainhead of existence and springing toward the future. . . . That is why I kick aside both the Western modernism and its flipside of traditionalism that are the only two value standards the average Japanese possesses today. . . . I want [the Tower] to be something that makes the gathering crowds first cry out in astonishment, "What the hell is that?" but then suddenly feel so wild and recklessly happy that smiles stretch across their faces. . . .

If this kind of *Entwurf* project can call out to and awaken the vitality sleeping deep in the hearts of the Japanese people, such that a new spirit begins to color their image beginning here in 1970, a spirit that can open itself to the world without a care, a spirit full of wild, unbridled energy, then even if that is just the tiniest, faintest first blush . . . my gamble on the World Fair [Exposition] will have been a great success.[6]

This declaration, as one might expect from someone as deeply influenced by Nietzsche as Okamoto is, gives voice to the scream at the heart of modern man. At the same time, however, we can also hear it as announcing the arrival of Japan's third-stage consumer society, and predicting the coming of the fourth.

Progress versus Harmony

Nowadays many seem to think of Japan's second-stage consumer society, the postwar period of high economic growth, as a time bursting with glowing expectations, the last era when everything was going well in Japan.

In fact, however, the reality of those days was quite different. Looking at the Cabinet Office's annual "National Survey on Lifestyle Preferences," the percentage of respondents saying they were "unsatisfied" with their present life ran between 30 and 34 percent from 1959 to 1963, but rose to a much higher 38 to 41 percent in 1971–73. These numbers indicate that many Japanese were actually feeling less happy about their lives during the high growth era than they had been before (fig. 4-3). Accelerating pollution, increasing traffic accidents, "commuter hell" congestion far worse than even the crowded public transportation and highways we have today, homes far from work, overcrowded cities, even alienation from their own humanity stemming from repetitive, routine labor, all likely contributed to this rising discontent.

According to the polls, this dissatisfaction peaked in 1974–75, and then gradually declined until 1995, after Japan's economic bubble had burst. Unhappiness has risen gradually again since then, yet in 2003, the year people were the most dissatisfied they have been in recent memory, the number of poll respondents saying they were unhappy with their lives was still just 39.6 percent, the same level as in the early 1970s.

I imagine most Japanese today—and especially young people who never actually experienced those times—would be astonished to hear that the nation's general sense of malaise was as high in the era of the Osaka Expo as it has been recently after many years of recession.

Another Cabinet Office survey, the annual "Public Opinion Survey on Social Consciousness,"[7] specifically asks respondents to evaluate the impact of economic growth on the country. In 1971 only 27 percent of respondents picked the answer: "It (economic growth) has had more

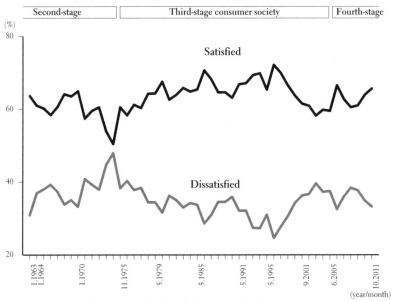

FIGURE 4-3 Satisfaction With One's Currrent Life

Source: Cabinet Office, "Kokumin seikatsu ni kansuru yoron chōsa" (National Survey on Lifestyle Preferences).

positives than negatives." By 1974 that had sagged even further, to only 18 percent. During that same period the percentage of respondents saying growth had "more negatives than positives" jumped from 14 to 24 percent.

Again, when asked in the same survey to rate how good economic growth had been for their own life, those replying "very good" fell from 15 to 7 percent in 1971–74, while those replying "bad" rose slightly from 8 to 11 percent. Those replying "both bad and good" stayed steady at 46 percent.

NHK, Japan's public broadcasting service, also conducted a number of interesting public opinion polls during this time. In one survey asking whether it would be desirable or undesirable for economic growth to continue as it had before, the percentage of respondents choosing "undesirable" rose from 45 percent in 1970 to 53 percent in

1972. The NHK pollsters concluded that 1970–72 marked a turning point. "The stresses and strains of high economic growth intensified," they wrote, "and the very economic growth that had been so celebrated before now lost the support of the Japanese people."[8]

In this way, the era of high economic growth and second-stage consumerism was not as rose-colored as one might have thought, at least not in its final stages. If anything, some Japanese even perceived those years as a kind of "end of the world."

Japan's noted science-fiction writer and futurist Komatsu Sakyō had already pinpointed the problem in 1967:

> As mankind's scientific and technological civilization, begun but two centuries before, continued to accelerate and expand at an ever faster pace, such that its very breadth and velocity had begun to plunge humanity into anxiety and dread, there now arose within the advanced societies a need to "predict" and "forecast" the future as a means of at very least surviving within that rapid current, and at best to in some manner control it. . . . For the first time it became possible to pose "scientifically" the question, "What, ultimately, will become of the human race, now that we have come so far?"[9]

So armed, Komatsu argued, mankind must now return to the key question:

> Does the value of life on this planet derive from its [potential for] further evolution, or does it derive intrinsically from life as it is? . . . It may be that a balanced circulation will yet arise between evolutionary value and the value of life in its own right, and that from that balance shall emerge a vector for a more harmonious evolution.[10]

Here Komatsu has identified the great question of progress versus harmony. Second-stage consumer society constituted the first mass-production, mass-consumption society in the history of the human race, and it had accordingly been a time that left us questioning many things. Those questions would continue to persist through Japan's following third-stage consumer society, until they are finally left standing before us today as the great themes of our fourth-stage consumer society.

Chapter Five

Splintering of the Masses and Harbingers of a Divided Society

From Mass to Micro

In 1984 the same Fujioka Wakao who had brought Japan the "From Driven to Beautiful" and "Discover Japan" ad campaigns once again telegraphed a changing of the times. This time it was with a provocative book, *Sayonara, taishū* (Farewell to the Masses).

In *Sayonara, taishū* Fujioka proposed a new word to describe society: *shōshū* 少衆, or the "micro-masses." This is how he opened his argument:

> Nowadays "the masses" is sounding like a relic leftover from the past. Put simply, nowadays nothing sells. No matter what we produce, no matter what new products we create, nothing catches on. Even when someone does get a hit, it's never more than a single. This has been going on for so long now that you have to wonder where the masses have gotten to.[1]

Observing (based on statistics of unknown provenance) that "starting in 1965 more than 100 million miniskirts sold in Japan in just a few years," Fujioka declared that the days of hits like that were gone forever. He then proceeded to challenge the assumption underlying the traditional marketing strategy of segmenting consumers by their shared characteristics, namely, the belief that the "masses"—once sorted out by gender, age, education, profession, and income—would prove to hold shared values and shared needs.

Not any more, Fujioka declared. Japan had entered a new age, an age that would demand not segmented marketing but "*kansei*" marketing, the marketing of sensibility, of taste.

Fujioka explained himself as follows:

> If we agree that the typical postwar image of affluence was based on an abundance of possessions, then once people are saturated with *having*, they will have little choice but to seek out a private and uniquely personal affluence of their own design, an affluence derived not from having but from *being*, from the way they desire to be in the world.[2]

In this age of being, he suggested:

> It will become intolerable to walk about with the same face as everybody else. . . . Even people with similar social and personal attributes will still want to at the very least alter their mode of self-expression, their way of living. In the past people thought that if their neighbors bought something, they should buy it too. We all thought we should buy because everyone else was buying. Now it is almost the exact opposite. "If everyone's buying it, I don't want it." "If that's what's popular, then I reject it."

> . . . . The value of "*mono*" (material possessions) will decline . . . [and] the center of gravity will tilt toward hobbies, toward self-improvement, toward sports, in short, toward finding fulfillment and purpose in the way we spend our "living time," the free time we have in our lives . . . [and] since that, too, will prove unrewarding should we find that everyone else wants to do the same things that we want to do, then finding the best way to "be ourselves" in those pursuits will become the highest priority of us all. It is for this reason that I believe "*jibun rashisa*" (being oneself) will be the keyword of the coming Age of Being.[3]

With *Sayonara, taishū* Fujioka had clearly articulated the Age of Being. It was nearly ten years since Parco's prescient "be-yourself" slogan,

"Don't look at nudes. Be nude!" (*Hadaka o miru na. Hadaka ni nare*), and the self-expression once championed by only a small handful of Japanese had finally been recognized as a shared trait of all consumers.

Parenthetically, I would like to note that *Across* published a special section titled "*DO no jidai kara BE no jidai e*" (From the "Do" Age to the "Be" Age) in our April 1982 issue.)

Toward an Age of Sensibility and Self-expression

In *Sayonara, taishū* Fujioka cautioned that "expressing oneself must wait upon the workings of one's own personal 'sensibility.'" Nonetheless, he added,

> I believe that this desire to actualize a self different from other people, be it in your sensibilities, in your hobbies and interests, or in the way you live your life, can almost always be seen as a "sensibility/taste demand."[4]

In short, "being oneself" and "sensibility" were to be the new core concepts of consumer society. Yet Fujioka did not say that the coming of this individualized age and the splintering of mass into micro meant that consumer demand was going to dry up and products no longer sell.

> A growing hunger for sensibility means that the products of old will be rejected and no one will want to be like everyone else—consumers will be thinking "I want something new." Therefore it is safe to say that this will create in essence *unlimited demand*.[5]

In Fujioka's eyes, the brand consciousness of third-stage consumerism, the shift from quantity to quality, even "From Driven to Beautiful" itself, were all signs that Japan's consumers were no longer making purchasing decisions based solely on functionality or performance. They were now also choosing goods for their semiotic value and in accordance with fleeting whims of the moment.

In short, consumption was no longer rational or for logical reasons alone. It had become a way for consumers to satisfy their sensibilities and aesthetics. Even picking home appliances was no longer simply about convenience or reducing housework: it was also about the consumer's own self-image, be it that of a refined sophisticate, an indulgent rich girl, or a driving career woman.

Of course, products had semiotic value in Japan's second-stage consumer society as well. But third-stage consumerism had imbued those values with a new importance, to the point that they now trumped all other attributes. By the early 1970s even the home appliances sold in Japan came in bright colors that had nothing to do with practicality. And by the 1980s some companies were selling products that deliberately played up the extraneous, the so-called *omoshiro-shōhin* (fun products) like beer cans in the shape of space shuttles or penguins.

One frequently cited advertising campaign from those days was Seibu Department Store's quirky "Delicious Life"[6] campaign. These print and television ads featured American comedian and movie director Woody Allen doing little more than looking quizzically into the camera next to the slogan "Delicious Life" created by Itoi Shigesato.

おいしい生活。

Woody Allen in an Oishii seikatsu *(Delicious Life) ad (1982–83).*

They can be read today as a symbol of the time when consumption flipped from a rational act into an aesthetic one. Of course, that aesthetic was the aesthetic of third-stage consumer society. It was a sensibility that could only exist in a time of rising living standards when people can meet all the necessities of life and still have money to spare.

The Best-selling Kinkonkan

When consumer behavior begins to diverge based not only upon income but also upon sensibility and aesthetic, it is inevitable that consumption will begin to stratify by class. Ironically, the first person to point this out in Japan was neither a sociologist nor an economist, but an illustrator: Watanabe Kazuhiro, the creator of the 1984 bestseller *Kinkonkan*.[7]

Kinkonkan (literally, "Picture Scrolls of Wealth and Soul") plucked people from thirty-one different professions, classified them as either "Maru-Bi" (for *binbō*, or poor) or "Maru-Kin" (for wealth and money), and introduced their lifestyles in text and witty illustrations. Watanabe explained his analysis in the preface:

> The strength of the Maru-Kin is the happiness that comes with having too much money. The Maru-Kin is always smiling. Since this makes him look like a good fellow, he is always well liked by others. He and his fellow Maru-Kin come together to further solidify the status of the Maru-Kin. Meanwhile, the weakness of the Maru-Bi is that he pines to be a Maru-Kin. Falling for things like "luxury" instant coffee, tanning salons, and handmade Comme des Garcons fashions produced by domestic industry and sold in shops along Harajuku's trendy Takeshita Dōri, the Maru-Bi is undone by his own longings. . . . The world overflows with the goods of the Maru-Kin. And as a result, the Maru-Bi's struggle to make ends meet becomes ever more difficult, and he blindly charges ever further down the path of Maru-Bi-ness.[8]

In the end, Watanabe concluded, "What makes this all so sticky is that once you take your first step down the road to Maru-Kin or Maru-Bi, it is all but impossible to change course."[9]

Kinkonkan called out to a Japanese public who had persuaded themselves that they were all part of an *"Ichioku sōchūryū"* (100-million-strong middle class), and forced them to face the fact of increasingly rigid class differences in Japan. It exposed the fact that the possessions, the foods, the hobbies, indeed virtually everything about the Maru-Kin and the Maru-Bi diverged.

The classic sociological text on class difference in consumption and taste is French sociologist Pierre Bourdieu's *La Distinction: Critique sociale du jugement.*[10] *La Distinction* was published in 1979, but the Japanese translation did not come out until 1990. When I finally did get to read it, I found that it had nothing particularly new to tell me. That was not just thanks to Watanabe's *Kinkonkan.*

Beginning around 1985 much was occurring that was inconsistent with a 100-million-strong middle class. One was the so-called *"Ojōsama* Boom"—a rash of reports in the mass media on the extravagant lifestyles of *ojōsama,* the daughters of Japan's wealthy elite. What with the publication of new magazines for and about *ojōsama* (today's popular *Classy* [Monthly Classy Magazine] went to press in 1984), it was obvious that tastes differed by class.

Nonetheless, it would take Japan's uncompromisingly precise scholars of social class some time longer to acknowledge the existence of class stratification in consumption and taste in their own country. The only papers I can find on the subject from the time are studies by Kataoka Emi beginning around 1996. It was not until 1998—when we were already seeing the first signs of fourth-stage consumerism in Japan and a clear gap had opened between the lifestyles of the country's regular employees and its growing ranks of poorly compensated nonregular employees—that class stratification in consumption and taste finally came in for academic attention.

Birth of the "Divided Masses"

In 1985, the year after *Kinkonkan,* two influential books came out in Japan addressing class and the social stratification of consumption. One was *"Bunshū" no tanjō* (The Birth of the "Divided Masses")[11] published by the Hakuhodo Institute of Life and Living (HILL). The other was *Shin "kaisō shōhi" no jidai* (The New Era of "Stratified Consumption")[12] by Ozawa Masako, then with the research department of the Long-Term Credit Bank of Japan (today's Shinsei Bank).

Class and social stratification is an important field of study in sociology, and the National Survey of Social Stratification and Social Mobility (SSM), conducted by a team of Japanese sociologists every ten years since 1955, had shown that the Japanese public increasingly perceived itself as middle class between 1955 and 1975. The 1985 survey, however, found that this consensus was beginning to falter, and identified signs of widening class divisions.

I find it very interesting, by the way, that 1985 was also the year that the Hakuhodo advertising agency and a bank research department began writing about the stratification of consumption in Japan. It is a testament to the private sector's strengths in research and forecasting compared to traditional academism.

The preface of *"Bunshū" no tanjō* had this to say about the changing landscape:

> In recent years the number of hit "monster products" has been on the decline. . . . If you try to make a product that will appeal to everyone, you are conversely setting yourself up for failure. . . . You can only stir consumer interest with either expensive quality products or extremely low-cost goods. The [Japanese] market has long been described as 90 percent middle class, but is it possible that this "middle class" has begun to polarize from within?[13]

HILL proposed a new coinage to describe the change: *bunshū* 分衆, or the "divided masses." The backdrop for these new divides was the diversification of consumer tastes and a growing income gap. Declared *"Bunshū" no tanjō*:

> Today people have begun to live true to their sensibilities, their tastes, their likes and dislikes. Having lived through an era of mass behavior, of seeking a life like that of those around them, of desiring to be on the same level as everyone else, people have once again begun seeking out different ways of living, different lives. . . . They are no longer content to be like everybody else.[14]

This reading of consumer sentiment was identical to Fujioka's, but HILL's analysis added an important new element. The change, HILL argued, was not only the result of diversifying consumer sensibilities, tastes, likes and dislikes, but also of a widening inequality in household assets.

In the course of its research, Hakuhodo conducted a consumer survey that produced two enduring terms for discussing Japan's bifurcating middle class: the New Rich and the New Poor.

The survey posed two linked questions: "Do you consider your household to be poor (*binbō*), or not poor?" and "Do you feel you have leeway in your life (*yutori ga aru*), or do you feel like you are just getting by (*yutori ga nai*)?" Based on the responses, HILL concluded that 34 percent of survey respondents could be called "New Rich," people with a sense of comfort and leeway in their lives, but that a majority 52 percent were "New Poor," not actually poor as traditionally defined yet still feeling like they were just hanging on. It was these New Poor, HILL said, who were the true leaders of Japan's "divided masses."

In short, the days when any Japanese could reasonably expect to achieve a similar level of affluence as his or her peers were over. That expectation might have been justified in the country's second-stage consumer society, but in the new third-stage consumer society Japan's middle class was beginning to separate out into the comfortably affluent and the barely affluent. In particular, HILL said, it was the rise of the latter, the New Poor, that was rewriting Japan's old social equation in which the middle class was equivalent to the masses.

"The New Poor," argued "*Bunshū*" *no tanjō*, "are in the process of creating a new lifestyle within the constraints of their financially pressed lives based upon a new life consciousness." For example, just because their household budgets were tight, New Poor consumers did not necessarily buy cheap, low-taste goods. Quite the contrary, it was low-cost but high-taste goods, goods created by chipping away some of the quality of more expensive items but retaining their sophistication, that were the New Poor purchases of choice.

The ultimate in low-price, high-taste products were the offerings of Mujirushi Ryōhin—the sleek "no-brand" furniture and household goods private brand that went on sale in 1980.[15] At *Across* we wrote about Mujirushi in our February 1984 edition, arguing that the brand had jettisoned the excess flash and finish of more expensive brands to compete based on the quality of its raw materials; Mujirushi left it to the consumers to "spice" those materials according to their own tastes and sensibilities.[16]

We also published a special report on "Chūryū gakai" (the collapse of the middle class) in the October 1983 edition of *Across*. The basis for that story was the Cabinet Office's annual Survey on the National Life-style. The survey results showed that the percentage of Japanese who identified as "middle-middle class" had actually been dropping since 1979. True, the decline was modest. But class divisions were beginning to widen in formerly middle-class Japan.

Stratified Consumption

The evidence for HILL's assertion in *"Bunshū" no tanjō* that economic inequality lay behind these widening divisions in Japan could be found in an earlier report by Ozawa Masako in the July 1985 edition of the Long-term Credit Bank of Japan's *Chōsa Geppō* (Monthly Research Report).[17] Ozawa would later develop these ideas into her important book, *Shin "kaisō shōhi" no jidai*.

According to Ozawa's report, wage differentials had begun to open throughout Japanese society as the high-growth era came to an end. That was true whether viewed by industry, company size, gender, or profession. In 1965, average wages in the highest paying industries had been 1.65 times higher than average wages in the lowest paying indus-tries. Until 1980 the gap had actually narrowed: wages that year were only 1.41 times higher at the top than at the bottom. But by 1982 the gap was widening again, with wages in the top industries now running 1.52 times higher than those in the lowest paying ones.

More specifically, the wage differential between small companies and large companies had been steadily widening since 1965, but Ozawa found that the pace began accelerating in 1975. The gender wage gap, too, which had been shrinking until 1975, had been widening again since 1976. It was the same story for wage differentials between white-collar and blue-collar workers.

Moreover, Ozawa found a commensurate divide opening up in household assets. Up until 1968 or so, the net financial assets of farming households and white-collar households had remained nearly the same. By 1979, however, the financial assets of farming households nationwide were twice that of white-collar households.

The widening gap was even more pronounced in the greater Tokyo metropolitan area. There, farming household assets were already 1.8 times larger than white-collar household assets in 1968. In 1979, just eleven years later, they were four times bigger.

And that was just the beginning. Ozawa found that divisions were opening up among white-collar households as well. There was a divide between those who bought homes back when land prices were low, and those who bought them when they were high. There was, not surprisingly, a divide between people who purchased their own homes and those who inherited homes from their parents, but there was also a gap opening up between homeowners who purchased before 1977 and those who purchased in 1978 and after. I will not detail every case, but as Ozawa herself pointed out, it went without saying that these expanding gaps in wages and household assets were also fueling a widening divide in consumer spending.

The Inequality Debate Deflated by the Bubble Economy

However, the emerging debate about the New Poor and economic inequality was abruptly extinguished by the rapid expansion of Japan's bubble economy on the back of a strengthening yen and soaring land prices beginning around 1986.

In reality, the Bubble exacerbated economic inequality. After all, people who had done nothing more than inherit land from their parents were now instantly far more wealthy than their compatriots who could only afford a home with a grueling two-hour commute to work. Yet the talk in marketing, advertising, and the mass media was all about the frothy consumption of Japan's new boom times. Of course NHK and other media televised debates on the problem of soaring land prices, but theirs was a minority voice in the overall clamor of the times. Even after the bubble burst there was an optimistic assumption that the economy would bounce back in short order, at least in the beginning. Certainly no one revived the discussion about the New Poor.

Sociologists and economists continued to take notice. A number of important books came out at this time, including Tachibanaki Toshiaki's 1998 *Nippon no keizai kakusa* (Confronting Income Inequality in Japan),[18] Satō Toshiki's *Fubyōdō shakai Nihon* (Japan, Land of Inequality),[19] and Yamada Masahiro's *Kibō kakusa shakai* (Society of Unequal Hope).[20] Yet even these works were not enough to restart the debate in society at large.

It took the sobering realization that the much-ballyhooed economic recovery during the administration of Prime Minister Koizumi Jun'ichirō was in fact a jobless recovery, and a growing awareness of the plight of Japan's under-compensated, under-protected nonregular employees, to bring attention back to the New Poor. In this new environment the author's own 2005 book, *Karyū shakai* (The Underclass Society),[21] became a bestseller. Incredibly, it had taken the Japanese public two whole decades since the publication of *"Bunshū" no tanjō* and *Shin "kaisō shōhi" no jidai* to turn their attention back to social inequality.

In 1999, Watanabe Kazuhiro published a new set of *Kinkonkan* "picture scrolls" in the May 5/12 edition of *Weekly SPA!* magazine. For some reason, the new *Kinkonkan* did not receive the attention it deserved, but it is still profoundly interesting for the way Watanabe's subjects had themselves changed over the fifteen years since the original *Kinkonkan*.

In 1984, Watanabe's wealthy Maru-Kin are flashy and his struggling Maru-Bi are plain. By 1999, however, the wealthier his subjects, the plainer—or perhaps I should say the more subtle—and casual they are, while the poorer his Maru-Bi the flashier and more formal they have become. In the wake of the Bubble—with even Maru-Bi-class middle school girls flashing Louis Vuitton wallets and Maru-Bi high school gals making up their faces with Chanel—flaunting brand products was no longer any proof of Maru-Kin-ness. Far from it. The new Maru-Kin women were wearing understated, timeless fashions in subdued hues that might have gone unchanged for decades.

Even when you wear a Uniqlo cashmere sweater, wear it so everyone will know that you're Maru-Kin. Thereabouts lay the new Maru-Kin woman's mode of self-expression. And thus post-Bubble Japan arrived at a place the exact opposite of third-stage consumerism: the higher your status, the more likely you were to wear Uniqlo and buy Mujirushi.

Chapter Six

An Age of Amorphous Desire

From Needs to Wants

D uring the first half of the 1980s one of the most commonly heard phrases in Japanese marketing was "*Niizu kara wontsu e*" (From needs to wants). In English "needs" indicates latent desires while "wants" indicates desires that have already surfaced. In 1980s Japan, however, "From needs to wants" was used to describe a shift in purchasing behavior from items that consumers needed to items that they wanted. That is, consumers were moving away from the daily necessities of life to items that were not necessarily essential but whose possession made them feel good. The phrase "*Hitsujuhin kara hitsuyokuhin e*" (From objects of necessity to objects of desire) was another variation on the theme.

Consumers have a very clear sense of what their daily necessities are, but even the consumers themselves do not always know what their subjective must-haves might be. Rice and bread, butter and detergent, you always know if you need more of these. When you leave home to live on your own for the first time, you know that you will need a refrigerator or a washing machine. But ask most consumers what they want to buy besides these necessities and you put them on the spot. Not even the consumer knows for sure what he or she will want most next.

An advertising slogan that perfectly captured the feelings of Japanese consumers in these transitional days was, once again, the work of copywriter Itoi Shigesato in his famous 1988 ads for Seibu department stores: "*Hoshii mono ga, hoshii wa*" (I want something to want).

Mizuno Seiichi, Seibu's President and CEO and at the time the man in charge of the 1987 launch of the company's new Loft stores, discusses this period in his 1990 book, *Loft Graffiti*:[1]

> These days we often hear that customers are maturing, but in reality not many people understand at the gut level what this "maturation" of the customer really means.[2]

Mizuno continues:

> The Oil Shock [of 1973], coming as it did just when everyone had finally secured their food, clothes, and shelter and were ready to step back and catch their breath for awhile, in one sense was the trigger that ended [Japan's] "*Shoyū no jidai*" (The Age of Possessions) . . . I am not saying this is the same as Maslow's[3] fifth-stage "Self-actualization needs," but once people have acquired all they need at one level of possession, they advance to the next level. This is, at the same time, a form of flight, an escape from the emptiness of clinging to possession itself.[4]

I like that "escape from the emptiness of clinging to possession itself." A department store president tasked with fanning people's lust for possessions declares the hollowness of possession itself. It's just what you'd expect from the unorthodox Saison Group.

Lest there be any misconception, let me make one thing clear. While it's correct to describe the transformation from second-stage to third-stage consumer society as a shift from "needs to wants" or from "necessities to must-haves," it is important to remember that not all the products on the market suddenly switch from daily necessities to must-haves.

Take the automobile, the product that symbolized second-stage consumerism in Japan. In Japan's second-stage consumer society cars were not a necessity but a must-have. While people longed for an automobile, absolutely wanted to get their hands on an automobile, often they could not afford one. Someday, these consumers swore, they would have a car.

Yet nowadays—as we can see from the declining number of young people who say they want to own their own automobile—cars are no longer a must-have product. If anything, they've become another basic necessity, like water and electricity. Love them or hate them, you'll buy an automobile if you need one to get by. In Japan cars have gone into reverse: from must-haves to a daily necessity.

Stereo systems are another classic example. The stereo was an object of desire back in Japan's second-stage consumer society. Yet if you were to ask my own father how often he actually played a record on his own stereo system, his answer would be not very often at all. For my father, the goal was to possess a stereo system, not to use it. It was enough for it to be sitting there in the house. Stereos were the perfect symbol of the age of "having."

Nowadays, of course, stereos are a niche product. Almost everyone in Japan today listens to music on cell phones and smart phones. And it is these new devices that have become one of the necessities of life.

So one should not take "From needs to wants" or "From objects of necessity to objects of desire" too literally. A more accurate way to put it is that consumer needs have diversified, so that when one of today's individualized consumers shops for a product she or he will look for colors, shapes, or images that match her or his own taste before concluding, "I want it." This is the real transformation from second-stage to third-stage consumer society.

Large Specialty Stores for the "Age of Being"

In *Loft Graffiti* Mizuno essentially agrees with Fujioka Wakao in his analysis of the transition from the "Age of Having" to the "Age of Being." However, he importantly inserts one more word between Fujioka's "having" and "being": the word "doing"

Mizuno's "doing" is the "doing" of sports like tennis and skiing, the "doing" of overseas travel, of taking classes at the local culture center.

In short, Mizuno identifies "doing" as the higher-level pursuit of "play" and "knowledge" in addition to the basic necessities of food, clothes, and shelter. But it doesn't stop there. Mizuno's "doing" goes even further, becoming another means of achieving the greater goal of "Being." As he explains in *Loft Graffiti*:

> Even when consumers engage in the same sport, one may be swimming for health, another going to the health club to make herself beautiful, and another playing golf with new-met friends to deepen communication. In this way, even knowledge and play [are means to satisfy] the Be ("This is how I wish to be") demand for health, beauty, social interaction, and security.[5]

In Mizuno's eyes, Japan had moved from the "have" age of possessing the same things as everyone else to a new age that challenged people to think of how they wanted to "be" in the world.

However, consumers do not always know who or how they want to be, either. And because they don't necessarily know their own goal of who and how they want to be, they likewise don't know what kind of goods to buy as their means of reaching it. Thus the real meaning of Seibu's "I want something to want" campaign was "I want to know for myself what kind of self I want to be."

Or to flip it yet again, we can say that by searching for something they really wanted to buy, consumers were not just discovering products, but were also trying to discover themselves. And as Japan entered this new age, companies—particularly retailers—were left trying to somehow respond to this wavering, wandering demand. That was what the 1980s were all about.

Nowadays when the subject of the '80s and Japan's bubble economy comes up on television, the stations usually run stock footage of girls in miniskirts waving huge fans as they dance on the elevated dance platforms of Tokyo discotheques. Even serious-minded NHK does this, almost without fail (So much so that you have to wonder if it's staffed with old disco dancer fans).[6] Yet you cannot possibly represent the entire 1980s with imagery like that. It's a classic example of oversimplification.

Just looking at those clips and the girls on the dance stands, it would be easy to dismiss that decade as a simple, even a foolish, boom time. Yet examining the 1980s today from a consumer psychology perspective, we find that they were in fact the start of a complicated time indeed for consumerism in Japan.

During this complex era, department stores began finding it harder and harder to sell goods that one might have imagined all consumers would want or need. Consumers had moved on: they were now buying those kinds of items at cheaper discount stores.

As a result, Japan's department stores were forced to follow the example of Parco and other farsighted business models, and stock products that they hoped would appeal to the customer who thought that only he or she, and perhaps a small minority of other people in the know, would be so discerning as to buy. Inevitably, that forced them to cut back on the range of product categories that they handled in order to increase the variety of items they stocked per category. In the end, this process gave rise to a new business model: the large specialty store.

Tokyu Hands and Consumer Creativity

When speaking of big specialty stores in Japan, we cannot forget Tokyu Hands, the self-styled "creative life store."

Technically speaking, the first Tokyu Hands was not its famous Shibuya store but a Tokyu Hands store that opened in Fujisawa City in neighboring Kanagawa Prefecture in 1976, at the very dawn of third-stage consumerism in Japan. Yet from the outset the Fujisawa store was designed to be a test case for opening a store in Shibuya, Tokyo's youth shopping Mecca. The first Tokyu Hands in the form we know it today was the Futako-Tamagawa store on the Tokyo-Kanagawa prefectural border that opened in 1977. It was only the next year, 1978, that Tokyu Hands finally came to Shibuya.

Shibuya Hands instantly won the favor of young consumers. As its name suggests, the store's key concept was *"Te no fukken"* (Returning power to the hands). Hamano Yasuhiro, Japan's retail guru, played a key role in creating this concept. His Hamano Institute (Hamano

Shōhin Kenkyūjo) was responsible for everything from corporate strategy, store concept, core product mix, and store naming to the design of the store's logo.

Hamano, who himself engages in sports and other outdoor leisure activities at a near-professional level, redefined do-it-yourselfism as the joy of creating your own lifestyle with your own hands. The result was Hands' famous core concept: "creative life store."

Thanks to this positioning, Tokyu Hands' reach goes far beyond that of your average DIY shop or home improvement specialty store. Hands created a sales floor where even basic materials like styrofoam are put out on the shelves as products for sale, stirring consumers' desire to create their very own way of living and stimulating their imagination about what kind of life would be the most fun to live.

There is an excellent book analyzing the Tokyu Hands method published by the Tokyo Marketing Research Society in 1986, titled *Hanzu genshō* (The Tokyu Hands Phenomenon).[7] This is what it has to say about the Tokyu Hands revolution:

> In order to call forth people's imagination, there must never be any imposed preconceptions. . . . That kind of approach can only make people's imagination wither. . . . In order to stir the imagination it is necessary for material objects to exist [simply] as another raw material. . . . When the material object calls out to you, saying "use me any way you want," that is when the imagination is pricked, envisioning how one might use it. A nail in an [average] hardware store or supermarket hardware department is just a nail, yet at Hands that nail, even the very same nail, becomes an imaginative object that lets the people who see it there think of various things they could do with it. . . . [Hands] transforms every product into "raw material," from laboratory beakers to metal drums to flowerpot racks, even outdoor lighting for construction sites.[8]

In other words, Hands granted consumers the joy of imagining how to use its products for purposes other than what was originally intended. Perhaps you will use those laboratory beakers not for experiments but to store your food. Maybe you'll use that outdoor flowerpot rack as an interior stand for your accessories and bric-a-brac. Or maybe you'll take those construction-site lamps and use them as bedroom lighting. In that sense, in the words of the Tōkyō Marketing Kenkyūkai:

> [Hands] can be said to sell no material as simply material, nor any finished product as simply a product. . . . Any and every product (object) is a "half-material" or a *han-seihin*, a "half-product." . . . Since they are all only half there either as materials or as products, the users are able to fill in the missing half in any way they desire.[9]

Mujirushi Ryōhin and the "Half-Product"

The philosophy of the *han-seihin* (half-finished product) also applies to Mujirushi Ryōhin, a case study of which is included in the Appendices. The Mujirushi Ryōhin brand first appeared in 1980, right around the same time as Tokyu Hands. We can think of this period as the time a new kind of demand first arose in Japan, a demand that turned its back on the passive acquisition of mass-produced goods and established brands, and instead viewed products as raw material that the consumers themselves could decide how best to "finish."

Tokyu Hands and Mujirushi Ryōhin have thrived for more than thirty years now, outliving Japan's third-stage consumer society to occupy an important place in today's fourth-stage consumer society as well. The reason for their longevity is that they have never stopped responding to the demand for consumer creativity in its truest sense, the demand for—as Parco would put it—*sōhi*: creative consumption.

This Tokyu Hands, Mujirushi philosophy of *han-seihin* strikes me as distinctly Japanese. It is the kind of thinking that turns garden rocks into mountains, and raked pebbles into oceans. Tiny teahouses representing the entire cosmos. Finding beauty in even a chipped teacup, and turning it to another purpose. I feel that this Japanese aesthetic shares deep roots with the notion of *han-seihin*. It also seems to intersect with *mingei*, the influential "Folk Crafts" movement started by the philosopher and art critic Yanagi Sōetsu (Yanagi Muneyoshi), who celebrated the "*yō no bi*" (the beauty of function) in the sundries and tools created and used by ordinary people in their daily work.

The Age of Accessories

As shown by the success of Loft, Tokyu Hands, and Mujirushi Ryōhin, Japan's third-stage consumer society could also be called the age of *zakka*, or "accessories."

Once consumers begin to express their *jibun-rashisa*, their individuality based upon their own aesthetics and sensibilities, they quickly lose interest in uniform, mass-produced products. No one would think of expressing their individuality with their refrigerator or their washing machine. Similarly, while you can express some of who you are with your choice of car or home, these are very expensive purchases of a kind you can only make a few times in a lifetime—they have limited utility as tools of self-expression. Moreover, the time lag in developing new cars and housing makes it hard to keep up with demand in terms of consumer self-expression.

No, the products best suited to casually expressing "the real you" are not home appliances, cars, houses, or other *"jūkōchōdai"* (heavy, thick, long, big) products, but accessories and sundries, the ultimate in lighter, thinner, shorter, smaller *"keihakutanshō"* goods.

Japan's so-called "Interior Boom" began in the 1970s. It was supported by very simple impulses, like those of a housewife unhappy with her cookie-cutter buy-and-build home who decorated the windows with her own pick of curtains to make it feel like her own home.

Or it might not have been mom, but her son and daughter who began to find their mother's classic "My Home," "New Family" interior shaped in her own image hopelessly old-fashioned. So off they went to Tokyu Hands to buy plastic lamps in the shape of ducks (a remarkably popular product at the time) to give their own rooms a whole new personality. Therein lies the interest and allure of *zakka* consumption: it's just so easy to do.

Of course, you can also express yourself with fashion. Indeed, from Chanel at the turn of the last century through to miniskirts, jeans, and designer brands like Issey Miyake, Y'z, and Comme des Garçons, fashion has been the ultimate means of self-expression. That power explains why fashion became so important to Japanese consumers as the demand for self-expression soared during Japan's third-stage consumer society.

Yet fashion is almost too blunt a tool for giving voice to yourself. Fashion can define you too sharply; you can go overboard in defining yourself as a person with your own particular style. There's something about it that's just not playful enough.

No wonder, then, that more and more consumers began to somehow feel that there was an inherent contradiction to using pre-existing fashions to demonstrate how free of convention, how unfettered by conventional style they were. From that awareness arose a new demand to play with juxtaposing different styles to give your look a slightly edgy, off-kilter vibe. And there again, the most effective tools were accessories.

In the end, it was the consumers' own sensibilities, their new aesthetic of adding just a dash of their own personality to a life surrounded by mass-produced goods, of adding a little twist to their fashions, that gave rise to the Age of Accessories. That's why the designs of the accessories and interior goods of those days so often have—like those aforementioned duck lamps—nothing to do with their actual function. Under the influence of the French sociologist Jean Baudrillard, the author of the 1970 *La Société de Consommation: Ses Mythes, Ses Structures* and the leading theorist on consumer society at the time, these products were called *gajetto* in Japanese, from Baudrillard's "gadget," one of his metafunctional objects. There were even some at the time who positioned *gajetto* as the defining symbol of an advanced consumer society.

At the same time, however, this all suggested how difficult it actually was to express your personality and individuality through material things, through possessions. The pursuit of *jibun rashisa* was turning into something very like tumbling down Alice's rabbit hole.

Chapter Seven

Consumer Society
at Saturation Point

The "Nightmare" Of Differentiated Consumption

The longing to find the "real me" only strengthened as Japan entered the 1990s, and a finding-oneself (*jibun-sagashi*) boom going far beyond mere patterns of consumption spread throughout the country. Japanese were increasingly asking themselves what kind of people they wanted to be but could find no ready answer. More and more people simply no longer knew which self was their real self, and which was the self they wanted to become.

In truth, this was very much a problem of the so-called modern ego. Had Japan still been a premodern society, society itself would have predetermined who they were going to be, and they would have accepted their roles with few reservations; in fact, to doubt them would have been frowned upon. Individuals fundamentally lived in small, regional societies, and their places within them were stable and fixed (indeed, they were not "individuals" at all). People only needed to perform their fixed roles within these microcosms and, conversely, that was all they could do.

But with the coming of modernity the kind of person you are becomes a matter of free will. You the individual decide for yourself how you will live, and it is considered a good thing for people to live by their own power in accordance with their own beliefs.

As society becomes more affluent, however, and consumption becomes more diverse and individualistic, people start to view their own beliefs in relation to those of the people around them. They begin to worry about how they are seen by others.

The new freedom thus results in great insecurity for consumers who are out to find themselves. One of the first people to point this out was the playwright, scholar, and philosopher Yamazaki Masakazu, whose ideas we will consider in greater length later in this book. Another was Ueno Chizuko.

Ueno's "*Watakushi*"–*sagashi gēmu* (The "Find-Myself" Game),[1] published in 1987, is a collection of papers and essays from the early to mid-1980s. It came out when she was still an assistant professor at Kyoto's Heian Jogakuin (St. Agnes) Junior College, a point so early in her career that it is hard to even visualize her in such a lowly role. Yet "*Watakushi*"–*sagashi gēmu* stands the test of time. Its observations are as fresh today as they were then. Indeed, it might be considered one of her leading works.

Today, Ueno is Japan's foremost scholar of feminism, but she is also an outstanding student of consumer society. She is even on record in a series of conversations with the author as saying she could easily have wound up at a marketing firm.[2] *The "Find-Myself" Game* includes a provocative study on consumption titled "Shōhin: Sabetsuka no akumu" (Products: The Nightmare of Differentiation). Here is some of what it had to say:

> In an age [like Japan's second-stage consumer society] when an individual product could still become a hit, people thought that "convenience" was what made a product sell . . . [They thought] everyone without exception would want any product that was "convenient to have."[3]

However, she noted, if people were to want these products, there had to be conditions in place to *make* them want them, and all kinds of mechanisms were put in place to that end. One was urbanization—as the number of people living urbanized lifestyles increased, so, too, did the amount of *mono*, of material possessions, that everyone wanted to have. But, Ueno argued, another key mechanism was a sort of forced normalization. Here is how she explained it:

> Up through Japan's high-growth period, products were the status symbols of "normalization," of being just like everybody else. People stampeded toward uniform goals. . . . The ultimate consequence was the creation of a vast bourgeoisie on a national scale, the very goal of "normalization.". . . [However] having achieved this goal, the people no longer had any models left to strive for. . . . That was because even if they aspired to be like others, the "others" had all become something very much like themselves. . . . [In the end,] consumers could no longer even see themselves.[4]

Once society has reached this state, said Ueno, what becomes important is no longer "normalization" to improve your life, but rather "differentiation" to make clear the differences between you and others. She warns:

> There is no limit to being "a little different from everyone else." . . . As long as there is differentiation, there can be no end to desire.[5]

Ueno had identified much the same thing as Fujioka Wakao had in *Sayonara, taishū* (Farewell to the Masses). As noted in chapter five, Fujioka wrote that "a growing hunger for sensibility means that the products of old will be rejected and no one will want to be like everyone else. . . . [I]t is safe to say that this will create in essence unlimited demand." But unlike Fujioka, Ueno did not think "normalization" had gone away. Instead, normalization and differentiation now existed in parallel:

> Even as they long to be different from others, people at the same time continue to want to be the same as others, so long as there is just enough of a difference for it be noticeable.[6]

≈

Trapped between being different from others and being the same as others, they find themselves stuck between facing mirrors infinitely reflecting back their own image. Even when they do make choices, those choices are no longer sufficient to explain whom they are. No one understands anymore his or her own desires.[7]

In describing this state, Ueno evoked the words of the sociologist Inoue Shun to call it a "nightmare choice."[8] An age when consumption had become a nightmare. That, too, was 1980s Japan.

Unlike Ueno, I never called consumption a nightmare. However, by that time I had been editing a monthly marketing magazine nonstop since 1982. Every month it had been my job to identify dozens of trends large and small and convert them into usable data. Moreover, I was thoroughly burned out on the decadence of Japan's bubble era consumption, when people were eating sushi topped with real gold foil. And thus it was that we titled the 1989 year-end double issue of *Across* "Epitaph for the 1980s." This is from the introduction to that issue:

> We now send off the 1980s—a decade during which consumer society achieved an extremely advanced state—with a sense of almost dumbstruck astonishment. It has been a time when countless phenomena have burst forth, been converted into information at lightning speed, differentiated into a plethora of designs, and greedily consumed. It has been a time of people pouring vast quantities of information into their stomachs without time enough to chew, then reaching out to shove even more into their mouths before the last helping is even digested. How will the 1980s be recorded in the pages of history? What kind of era will they say it was? It is still too soon to tell.[9]

Finding Oneself: The New Pathology Of Consumer Society

In this way Japan's consumer society—which was already sinking into a kind of *fin-de-siècle* degeneracy—gave rise to a new, almost pathological phenomenon. In response to the uncertainty born of "nightmarish" differentiated consumption, the *jibun-sagashi* search for self-discovery accelerated even more.

Beginning in the 1990s, Japanese companies took heed of this hunger for self-discovery and started using it in their marketing and advertising. Mass-produced goods and individuality are by nature contradictory. However, as the technology for small-lot manufacture of products improved, it had become possible to respond in a more tightly targeted way to the tastes and preferences of each individual consumer.

Advertising and magazine articles began to overflow with phrases like *"jibun-rashiku"* (true to oneself) and *"watashi-rashiku"* (true to myself). "Being oneself," "being myself" were promoted as the ultimate value that anything could have, not just in regard to clothing or cosmetics, but also to cars and home appliances, condominiums and travel, even credit cards and universities. A credit card that was "true to oneself"? What on earth was that supposed to mean? Yet Japan was awash with ads like that.

For a company, it is a form of defeat to have to appeal to the consumer's identity instead of promoting one's own corporate identity and presence. But if what Japanese consumers were seeking was not some definition of beauty or femininity or masculinity or can-do businessman machismo offered up by a corporation but rather a unique identity of their own creation, then there was nothing the companies could do but say that they were standing by to help in that process.

In this way, consumer aspirations for a unique individuality and corporate appeals to that desire became "partners in crime," complicit in endlessly propagating the myth of self-expression. People soon came to believe that not just the things they consumed, but their work, their marriages, everything in their lives had to be uniquely their own. In short, they wanted to live every aspect of life "my way."

The growing numbers of unemployed young people and young, perpetually part-time "freeters"* became a major social issue in the late 1990s, and one factor in this development was so many young people now wanting to express their individuality, their *jibun-rashisa*, through their work. These young Japanese had a new value system, one that would not tolerate any job that alienated them from their "true selves," even if it paid a lot of money. Indeed, one of the reasons Japanese are

---

* Freeters are young people who do not have regular employment but who work at one or more part-time jobs or at one short-term job after another. The term was coined by combining the English word "free" and the German word "Arbeiter" (laborer).

marrying later and later in life is that young people now want a marriage that "reflects the real me," and dream of meeting up with a partner perfectly suited to them. That kind of person does not come along every day. And marriage keeps getting put off.

What turned young Japanese into such individualism ideologues? Beyond a doubt it was consumer society. The experience of having their own private possessions—their own private bedrooms, their own private stereos, their own private televisions, their own private telephones, their own clothes that perfectly suited (or so they were told) just them—that was the wellspring from which their individualistic quest sprang.

If you were to snatch away from today's young people all of their private possessions, they would likely be shaken by the shallowness of this "self" they concern themselves about so much, and be plunged into anxiety. Without their things, their individuality has no basis. Instead of having a pre-formed individuality that shapes what they choose to buy, their individuality (for such they feel it to be) is created by the very act of choosing what to buy. Just as in the past one's role in the greater community supported one's sense of self, today's individuality is undeniably supported by the things one owns.

In fact, numerous studies have found that not a few people become quite anxious when they forget their cell phones. A cell phone is not just a physical possession, but a splinter version of yourself by virtue of all the saved telephone numbers and communications from your friends that it contains. Take it away, and you panic. Are there any other items out there that have such an ability to throw us into a panic? Perhaps for some women their makeup kit is another. It's essential to creating ("making up") who they are.

A Yearning for Permanence and Self-improvement

Secondly, anxious consumers show a certain longing for permanence, epitomized by the hunger in Japan for foreign luxury brands. Such brands refuse to adapt to the consumer's own individuality, instead demanding that the consumer adjust to them. They lord it over the marketplace as absolutes, transcending the "wish-washy" level of "doing it my way." The uncertain consumer is drawn to the powerful narrative of permanence born of luxury brands. The domestic "Japan Boom" that I will be discussing later, in Part Three, is likely another example of this longing, as may be the recent popularity of visiting Japan's traditional Shinto shrines. Modern man is drawn to things with a history that can be counted in millennia.

The retro boom that has swept Japan is also closely related to this longing for permanence. The objects of revivalism are varied: nostalgic Glico caramel candy, discotheques, *Heibon Punch* magazine, the Beatles. It has long been thought that popular culture is by nature characterized by ebb and flow—even if something sells well for a time, it will inevitably vanish and be replaced by a new product someday. But the "revival boom" has proved that popular culture can also be a resource that accumulates over time. In other words, now even if you do not create a new product/narrative, consumers can still be quite satisfied with the old. I have called this the transformation of popular culture into cultural "stock."[10]

For example, if you already have a billion yen salted away, you can live off your investment income and no longer need to keep working yourself to the bone. Likewise, if culture were truly all about ebb and flow you would need to constantly come up with new popular entertainments and hit products. But if you have a stock of cultural "products," all you need do is keep switching them out. From a corporate perspective, it is thus safer to market a product that leverages off a past brand name with high brand recognition and consumer trust than it is to put out something completely new. That has the additional advantage of being able to project sales with some certainty. It's enough to just recycle the old narrative.

A third characteristic we can identify of the anxious consumer is a hunger for self-improvement. This is the feeling—arrived at after the realization that, be it luxury brands or anything else, one can never truly achieve a self-identity through consumption alone—that one must change one's self.

Self-improvement comes in two dimensions: internal transformation and external transformation. The classic example of internal transformation is the pursuit of various forms of self-enlightenment, of certifications in different skills and activities, of training in the arts, in short, study driven by a hunger for learning. Examples of external transformation include a literal physical transformation, be it dyeing your hair, getting piercings or tattoos, even cosmetic surgery. However, the more common forms of physical transformation include fitness, weight training, yoga, and dietary supplements. Here indeed is the Age of Being foreseen by Fujioka Wakao and Mizuno Seiichi so many years before!

"Multiple Identity" Megahits

The consumer in search of the "real me" and the corporations offering a host of alternatives for how to be "yourself" are clearly acting in tandem. Consumers take in the message sent by the corporations, and take it as feedback about their own choices. This creates endless doubt among consumers about their own unique identity, and drives them to keep on searching for an even more individualistic self. In this way, the cycle of searching for oneself grows and grows.

This cycle never ends in the achievement of a single secure, individualistic self. Instead, consumers ultimately come to accept that they have any number of authentic selves. No matter how hard you try, they realize, you can never achieve a true and totally individual self. Chase too hard, and you wind up surrendering yourself to some seeming absolute, like religion or the state. If that's unpalatable, then you have no choice but to accept that you can only achieve a partial individuality. Acknowledging that there is no such thing as complete and total individuality in every aspect of your life, you continue to add on little fragments of "self"—some of them even contradictory—until you have pieced together a composite mask that you will treat as the "real you." Yes, it may be a mask. But at least it is not a false you. And in this way is born the multiple identity that is a characteristic form of self-identification today.

For corporations, too, the self-expression strategy was no surefire way to manipulate the consumer. In all criminal conspiracies, the co-conspirators will always suspect one another, will always be betrayed by one another. These new consumers with their multiple identity were evolving into something that was harder for corporations to grasp than ever before.

During the 1990s, in the closing half of Japan's third-stage consumer society, this proliferation of consumers with multiple identity gave rise to a mysterious new phenomenon, of which the music CD is a classic example. You could have a few megahits selling millions of copies. And you always had your subculture music that only sold a few hundred CDs. But the good old reliable hits you could count on to sell in the tens of thousands had disappeared completely.

Let us say that you start with a million consumers. And let us posit that each one of them has a consistent, single identity. If 25 percent of them share the same orientation, you can look forward to selling them 250,000 CDs.

But now let us say that each of these consumers is splintered into four "selves," four alter egos. Now, even though there are only a million consumers, there are actually four million selves. If you secure the support of just 25 percent of those selves, you can sell a million CDs. In fact, you could conceivably sell the same CD to every single consumer. That, I suspect, is the mechanism behind the megahits of today.

In short, today's consumers (especially younger consumers) have multiple selves, one of which will always be a conforming self that wants to be in step with everyone around them. At the same time, however, they will also have a discriminating self that wants to be different from other people. Appeal to the conforming self and you get a megahit. Appeal to the discriminating self and you get pocket change. Conversely, it has become much harder to get the solid mid-range hits of the age of the single ego, the single self.

One important background factor behind all of this is the rise in living standards, and the relative decline in the cost of products like CDs. If the price of a CD (or LPs before them, and now increasingly an online download) is high relative to a young person's disposable income, then he or she will buy just the one album she or he likes best. If the relative price of CDs to disposable income is low, however, young people can buy a CD they really like, and then throw in another that everyone else is saying is good to see if they like it, too. This made it even easier to get megahits. And we also should not forget that, in the 1990s in particular, a very large generation joined Japan's consumer base, the so-called *dankai* juniors, the children of the baby boomers.

119

The Scattered Self

I remember reading an observation by a researcher at one of Japan's lifestyle think tanks that surprised me. The researcher was studying the eating patterns of high-school students, and reported frequently hearing from high-school teachers that their students did not seem to enjoy eating anymore; in fact, some kids even found it a bother.[11]

When I mentioned that to an acquaintance in the prepared food industry, however, I was shocked again. My friend told me that it had been conventional wisdom in the industry for years now that more and more people thought eating was a pain.

But why would people lose interest in food? One possible explanation is that, what with all the information out there about diet and nutrition, more and more people want to lose weight. I wonder though if it is not because there is such a huge overabundance of food in Japan today that people are simply losing their appetites?

The fundamental source of desire is scarcity. People want what they don't have enough of. When they have more than enough of something, the desire is not so urgent. If you have it in your head that if you don't eat right now, who knows when you will ever eat again, then you will happily eat whatever you can, even if it tastes terrible.

But today our modern lives overflow with food. You can find food anywhere, any time, at convenience stores, at family restaurants, at fast-food outlets, at the specialty food counters in department store basements, even on train station platforms. And when you know you can always get your hands on something to eat, it's only natural not to feel quite so hungry as before. Even though there is a cornucopia of food laid out before you in vast quantities and variety, free for you to pick from however you please, that very overabundance is turning eating into a chore.

It is a state that closely resembles another in today's information society. Unable to process today's flood of information, we are reduced to simply gaping at it as it flows by. We never said we wanted it, yet there is a constant discharge of highly packaged but ultimately pointless information flowing past us twenty-four hours a day. No, not just flowing by. It's being shot out at us under incredible pressure.

In this kind of information environment we conversely lose our desire to know more. And now a similar situation has arisen around food. Considered dispassionately, our appetites are being subjected to truly abnormal levels of stimulation. In the midst of all that, how is anyone to maintain a normal appetite, or observe a normal diet?

I recall an interview I had with one young man who told me that it had become impossible for him to stock up on groceries in advance. He simply could never predict when and what he was going to want to eat next. So even if he did go to a supermarket and loaded up on affordable food items, in the end he never finished it all because he would find himself wanting something else before he'd eaten what he already had. In his case, it was apparently less wasteful for him to run out at two a.m. in the morning to buy something at a convenience store when hunger struck. Young people (of course not just young people, but especially the young) increasingly no longer eat when their stomachs tell them they're hungry; they eat when their hunger has been stimulated by the omnipresent food information in their environment.

Once we reach this state, however, satisfying one's appetite becomes divorced from any sense of happiness. And conversely, "hunger" itself becomes something that can never, ever be truly satisfied, no matter how much one eats. It is possible you might come to see your hunger as something unpleasant, even weird or uncanny, assaulting you at any time of day or night. Could this be the reason so many young people today have come to regard eating as a nuisance? And at the same time, these same young people may now also feel burdened by a self with unpredictable wants that suddenly erupt when they least expect it. In short, they may no longer understand themselves.

This state might sound similar to the feeling of "I want something to want" that we discussed earlier. However, it is also subtly different. In that era of wanting to find something that you really wanted, you never doubted the self that had those feelings. You thought that you liked this "you" that was so hungry to want something. And when you finally did find that special something that you wanted, you thought that you were happy.

In contrast, might it be that today's young people (and not just young people)—so overburdened with needs and desires that could overcome them at any time—are finding it harder and harder to believe that they understand this self that has such needs, much less to like it, or even to believe they are happy?

That sense of knowing who you are, of knowing that there is a "you," is likely the feeling that comes with successfully integrating your many needs and desires, be they "what I want to have" or "what I want to do" or "who I want to become." When you have an integrated self, it is possible to begin planning your own life, be it as simple as thinking, "I love music, so I want to do work that involves music." We could even call this the feeling that comes with a secure identity.

In contrast, saying that you don't know yourself is the same as saying you cannot integrate your own desires. Your desires are so scattered, arise so suddenly, that it is not even clear if they really are your true desires, or something more fleeting. It is hard for you to even know who you are. You are no longer a single, integrated self, a single identity. Instead of having a single, integrated identity at your core, you can feel other peripheral identities on the outside that you scarcely know. Truly, you have multiple "selves." And it is precisely this multiplicity that makes it impossible for you to know who you are.

From Differentiation to Uniqlo

Another problem is that the shift to "sensibility" consumption that we see in the third stage of consumerism can serve over time to widen the gap between individual consumers in society.

Back in Japan's second-stage consumer society, when consumption was driven by factors like quantity or convenience, the consumption gap was essentially proportional to income. Moreover, since it was the period of Japan's rapid economic growth, everyone's income was rising. It was possible to quickly close any consumption gap, and everyone felt able to entertain the fantasy, encapsulated in a 1983 Toyota catchphrase, that "Someday I'll own a Crown."*

It was also still possible during Japan's second-stage consumer society to be indifferent to things like brand image and design. The kind of value system that decrees a Toshiba television cooler than a Matsushita

---

* "Itsuka wa Kuraun." The Crown is Toyota's top-of-the-line luxury sedan.

Denki television because of Toshiba's "brand image" was foreign to second-stage consumerism. If anything, people were more likely to make choices based on function, like concluding that a Toshiba washing machine would have superior performance because, as a heavy electric machinery maker, Toshiba built its own motors.

With the coming of third-stage consumerism, however, and with the increasing individualization of consumption, differences in personal aesthetics and sensibilities began to affect product choice and consumption behavior. Which brand you bought in which store in which shopping district became an indicator of good or bad taste. If you don't like the words "good" or "bad," let's just say "diversity."

In other words, whether you bought Comme des Garçons at the Shibuya Parco or Burberry at the Shibuya Tokyū Tōyoko department store was considered to show not a difference in income, but a difference in taste. Of course we soon had a situation where people wearing Comme des Garçons looked down on people wearing Burberry, while people wearing Burberry thought the people wearing Comme des Garçons were weirdos. Both camps were at the very least indifferent to each other, and sometimes openly hostile. At *Across* we called this phenomenon the *"takotsubo-ka"*(octopus pot-ification) of fashion.[12] The term refers to pots used to catch octopus, which normally live alone in small caves or rock piles and will take shelter in fisherman's octopus pots on the ocean floor). It was much the same phenomenon that sociologist and subculture researcher Miyadai Shinji would later label *"shimauchū-ka,"* or "Island Universe-ification."[13]

The "octopus pots" of fashion and lifestyle still exist today. However, I feel that they have weakened compared to how it was in Japan's third-stage consumer society. In fashion, at the very least, the ranks of those who would discriminate against one another based on their fashion choices have been shrinking the younger their generation. Among these younger generations it is now quite common for even high-income consumers — perhaps especially high-income consumers — to preferentially buy the mass-market priced clothing offered by Uniqlo or the at-first-glance plain designs of a Muji store.

A survey by the author's own Culturestudies think tank (table 7-1) found that among the *shin-jinrui New* Generation (defined in the survey as those born between 1960 and 1964), 60.6 percent of those identifying as "lower class" liked Uniqlo products, compared to only 37.9 percent of those identifying themselves as "upper class." However, among the post-baby boom *dankai* junior generation (born between 1970 and 1974) there was no class difference at all; if anything, those identifying as "upper class" were slightly more likely to prefer Uniqlo. For Muji (Mujirushi Ryōhin) products as well, while they were preferred by only 17 percent of *shin-jinrui* generation respondents of any social class, they garnered some 35 percent support from both upper- and middle-class-identified *dankai* junior respondents.

TABLE 7-1 Brand Preference by Generation and Social Class Identification

	Class identification	Sample size	Muji	Uniqlo	Gap
	Upper	270	35.3 %	26.3 %	8.8 %
Generation Z	Middle	527	33.9	29.1	8.4
	Lower	316	34.6	27.9	9.2
	Upper	29	37.9	48.3	6.9
Dankai Junior	Middle	92	34.8	45.7	20.7
	Lower	79	25.3	44.3	19.0
	Upper	29	17.2	37.9	20.7
New Generation [*shin-jinrui*]	Middle	100	18.0	54.0	19.0
	Lower	71	16.9	60.6	11.3
	Upper	27	25.9	11.1	7.4
Baby-boomer [*dankai sedai*]	Middle	106	9.4	25.5	5.7
	Lower	66	12.1	33.3	3.0
	Upper	23	0.0	13.0	0.0
Shōwa First Decade (born 1926–34)	Middle	123	8.1	22.8	2.4
	Lower	52	13.5	23.1	0.0

Sources: Based on Culturestudies and e-FALCON Co. research report, "*Shōwa yon-sedai yokkyū hikaku chōsa*" (Comparative Study of Needs Across Four Shōwa-period Generations), 2005, and Culturestudies and Standard Tsūshinsha research report, "Jenerēshon Z sedai" (Generation Z), 2007. Culturestudies and e-FALCON Co. research report.

In contrast, support for the global American casual wear brand Gap was high among upper- and middle-class *shin-jinrui* consumers but low among *shin-jinrui* who identified as lower class, while for *dankai* juniors it was strong among the middle and lower class but low among the upper class. By the time you reach Generation Z (born between 1982 and 1991), class-based preference differences disappear completely among consumers for Uniqlo, Muji, and Gap.

Interestingly, however, when you reach Generation Z, support for Gap in particular does not reach even 10 percent among any class. It appears that there is a growing consciousness among the generations following the *dankai* juniors that—at least so far as basic food, clothes, and shelter are concerned—it doesn't matter if you have the same things as everyone else. At the same time, however, this seems to be accompanied by an aversion for product lines like Gap that push a powerful brand strategy but whose clothes themselves are not particularly superior.

As we have seen, consumption became increasingly complex over the course of Japan's third-stage consumer society. As a result, consumers and corporations alike had reached a state where they were literally exhausted by it. On the consumer side in particular, people were feeling that a mode of consumption that forced them to constantly question who they were and what it was they really wanted out of life was an aggravation, and they wanted to put it all behind them. And thus it was that, as we enter Japan's fourth stage of consumerism, they began to find themselves drawn to cheap and well-made products like Uniqlo, or the simple, unadorned offerings of a Muji store.

PART THREE

THE TRANSITION FROM THIRD-STAGE TO FOURTH-STAGE CONSUMER SOCIETY

To create a new value system and aesthetic born of simplicity and the raw materials themselves while continuing to search for the ideal materials, manufacturing processes, and forms. To thoroughly simplify all wasteful processes while still sampling and incorporating a rich range of materials and processing technologies. In short, to work to achieve not the lowest possible price, but a "rich" low price, the most "rational" low price range. . . . That is the value system that the world is bound to need today and in the future. I would like to call it "Global Rational Value."

Hara Kenya, *Dezain no dezain* (The Design of Design)

Chapter Eight

Fourth-stage Consumer Society: An Age of Sharing

Contradictions of Third-stage Consumerism and the Shift to Fourth-stage Consumer Society

F ive transformations mark Japan's evolution from third-stage to fourth-stage consumer society. Simply put, these transformations are:

1. From self-oriented to society-oriented, from egoism to altruism.
2. From possessiveness to sharing.
3. From name brands to simple and casual.
4. From Western, urban, and individualistic to Japanese and regional (from centralization to decentralization).
5. From goods to services, to an emphasis on people.

When we take a broad overview of the shifts in public consciousness from Japan's first-stage consumer society through to today's fourth, we can see that there has been a series of major reorientations, from the national (an emphasis on the state) to the family (an emphasis on the family and on the company as an extension of family), then on to the individual (an emphasis on the self) and now finally the social (an emphasis on society).

As we saw in the preceding chapter, Japan's third-stage consumer society was often described as an advanced consumer society. Supported by a strong economy, the nation experienced the effects of both an appreciating yen and an economic bubble. The Japanese people succeeded in creating a reality for themselves where they could enjoy, at least on the surface, virtually all of the material affluence and Westernized consumer lifestyle that they had been aspiring to throughout the postwar years, without ever leaving Japan. They also obtained greater freedom to choose for themselves individualized products more closely tailored to their own sensibilities in place of the uniform, mass-produced goods of the past.

Yet, as was also noted in the last chapter, these developments spawned new contradictions. An individualism based on personal sensibility served to split people apart. And the class stratification hovering behind consumers' increasing individualization served to divide and isolate people even further.

Japan's advanced consumer society also fostered a chronic, out-of-control materialism. It made Japanese forget the ecological consciousness and concerns about energy conservation that had bloomed briefly in the 1970s, and swept away the anti-nuclear power sentiment that had bubbled to the surface as far back as the 1980s.

Now, however, Japan's fourth-stage consumerism is moving in a new direction that promises to resolve the contradictions of third-stage consumer society. Rather than that hyper-individualistic, isolated mode of consumerism, fourth-stage consumerism strives to create a society where connection can arise naturally between individuals.

The Latin root of "society" is *socius*, meaning comrades, companions, and acting together. Yet when capitalism, consumer society, individualization, and the primacy of private life run rampant it is easy for people to lose touch with their connections with others. In Japan this gave rise to a peculiar situation: even though they were embedded in society, people could no longer feel their ties to others. Now Japan's fourth-stage consumer society is moving in directions that should resolve that contradiction.

The Information Society and Altruism

In place of the egoism that gave first priority to maximizing one's personal fulfillment, fourth-stage consumer society fosters the spread of a new altruism that takes into account the satisfaction of others, a new consciousness that seeks to contribute in some way to the good of other people and to society. In that sense we can call it society-oriented.

One can enjoy the fruits of material affluence by owning things for oneself. Taken to the extreme, one could achieve even greater satisfaction by monopolizing them. It feels good to have bigger things than other people do, to have more expensive things, rarer things. One can show them off and flaunt them. In the marketing world, this is called differentiation.

However, information is not the same as material goods. It makes no sense to simply keep information to oneself, to monopolize it, hoard it. One cannot savor the joy of possessing information until it is transmited to others, shared with others. Information piled up like gold ingots generates no value. Even if information were to be hidden away like one of those buried pots stuffed with gold coins in the fairy tales, it would bring no joy.

This is the compelling difference between information and material goods. As the digital revolution advances, people do not so much boast about how much information they hold, but instead seek pleasure in exchanging it with others. It may be the most trivial little occurrence in your daily life, but put it up on Facebook and everyone sends you "Likes." You receive "Happy Birthday!" messages from complete strangers. The digital revolution has made altruistic behavior, in the broadest sense of the word, much easier than it ever was before.

The spread of both altruism and the new orientation toward society shows up clearly in the Cabinet Office's Public Opinion Survey on Social Consciousness.[1] Since 1986, there has been an overall increase in the percentage of people saying that they would like to contribute to society. Likewise, the percentage of respondents saying one should put the interests of all ahead of personal interest has also risen since 2005. These trends coincide perfectly with the start of Japan's fourth-stage consumer society.

Survey responses indicating a stronger societal orientation ("Going forward, I should pay more attention to other citizens and society") also began to rise in the closing days of the economic bubble, and have been running above 50 percent since 2005 (fig. 8-1). Meanwhile,

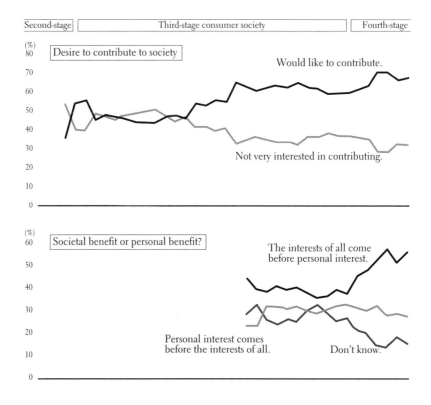

| Second-stage | Third-stage consumer society | Fourth-stage |

(%)

Desire to contribute to society

Would like to contribute.

Not very interested in contributing.

Societal benefit or personal benefit?

The interests of all come before personal interest.

Personal interest comes before the interests of all.

Don't know.

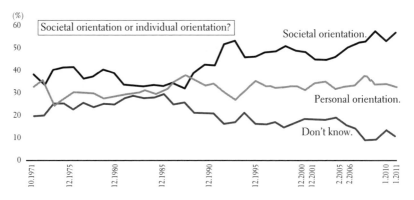

Societal orientation or individual orientation?

Societal orientation.

Personal orientation.

Don't know.

10.1971 12.1975 12.1980 12.1985 12.1990 12.1995 12.2000 12.2001 2.2005 2.2006 1.2010 1.2011

FIGURE 8-1 The Rising Orientation toward Society

Source: Based on Cabinet Office, *Shakai ishiki ni kansuru yoron chōsa*(Public Opinion Survey on Social Consciousness).

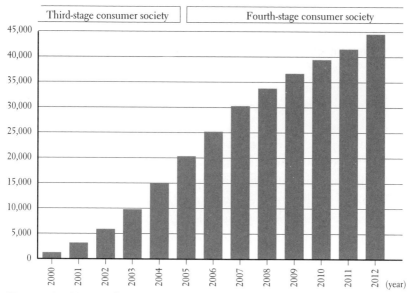

FIGURE 8-2 Nonprofit Organizations in Japan
Based on Cabinet Office website, *Naikakufu NPO Hōmupēji.*

the number of officially recognized nonprofit organizations in Japan surged between 2000 and 2012, reaching 40,000 in just twelve years and underscoring the increased number of citizens interested in activities that contribute to society (fig. 8-2).

A Consumption "Budget Screening"

The shift from egoism to altruism can also be seen as a shift from possessing to sharing. In place of the old "My-Home" emphasis on possession and one's private life—when people could only find happiness by acquiring more and more possessions for their own exclusive use—fourth-stage consumer society will see the spread of an ethos of sharing as people derive happiness from the very act of creating connections with others. Indeed, it is that ethos of sharing that forms the foundation of consumption in fourth-stage consumer society.

Before examining these trends in more detail, let me explain the broad historical flow from private ownership to sharing as depicted in the accompanying charts (fig. 8-3). The charts use a vertical "private-public (shared)" axis and a horizontal "utilization-possession" axis. Since private ownership means possession for one's own exclusive use, it would appear in the upper right-hand quadrant.

Back before the start of high economic growth—in other words, back during Japan's first-stage consumer society—only a very limited upper class could afford to own a car. Even mid-level salaried employees for the most part still lived in rental housing, and it was common for people to finally buy their own home only after they received their retirement payment.[2] Almost the only significant furniture people had in the house was the large paulownia *tansu* wardrobe that was part of the wife's dowry.

Most of the populace had no private property to speak of. They went to public bathhouses to bathe, and for entertainment they went

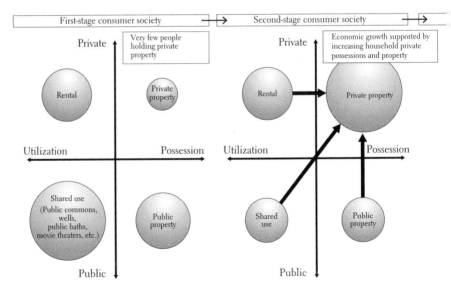

FIGURE 8-3 Transformations in Japanese Consumer Society: Public/ Private and Possession/Utilization

with everyone else to the movie houses. On our charts, the weighting of the upper right quadrant then is much smaller than it is today.

With the coming of Japan's second-stage consumer society, however, home appliances spread throughout the country, and many people could afford their own "My Car" and their own "My Home." The weighting of the upper right quadrant increased dramatically, and it was this shift that became the motive force for economic growth.

This lifestyle founded on private ownership reached a saturation point at the start of today's fourth-stage consumer society. And it was the young people in particular—young people who had grown up surrounded by private possessions—who began to think that maybe it was all right if they didn't personally own everything they wanted.

It was, in a sense, the beginning of a "budget screening" for consumption in Japan. As in a famous phrase of the time—"Do we really have to be first? Is there something wrong with being second?"[3]—consumers began to ask themselves, "Do I really have to own this? Can't

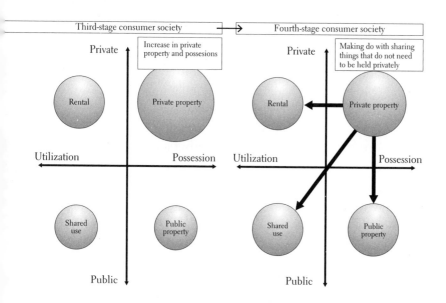

I rent it? Or share it?" Thus ended the age when everyone wanted the same thing as everyone else, when everyone bought one of everything per household or even one per person. The end, in short, of the age of standardized consumption.

The psychology behind the new consumption is straightforward. I will still buy the things I really, really want, fourth-stage consumers think, but if it's something I don't particularly need then there's no reason I should buy it just because the neighbors did. I'll buy things I absolutely want for myself, but I won't buy anything else. I won't buy anything I don't really need.

In other words, if you can get by renting something, just rent it. And if it's something you can share, then share it.

Of course, Japan's fourth-stage consumer society is not a blanket repudiation of personal possessions and private life, but it does seem that more and more people today are realizing that certain of their aspirations can never be satisfied by possessions or in their private lives alone. The idea of sharing is a way of addressing that discontent.

This trend appears to have gained momentum after the disastrous earthquake and tsunami that struck the northeastern Tōhoku region of Japan on March 11, 2011. Watching the footage of homes and cars being swept away by tsunami waters, many Japanese no doubt felt the risk and the futility of private possessions, symbolized by their precious "My Car" and "My Home." There had been similar trends before—like the yoga-inspired *danshari* (decluttering) boom[4]—but it is safe to say that the Tohoku disaster accelerated the trend away from private possessions.

However, the movement toward sharing and shedding personal possessions did not just suddenly begin with the 2011 disaster. Some time earlier observers started noting that young Japanese were not buying as many automobiles or houses as their predecessors. It would be more accurate to say that the March 11 earthquake and tsunami threw this trend into sharper relief.

Indeed, with young people's disinterest in owning automobiles accelerating on top of the overall decline in the country's population (not to mention more and more elderly Japanese simply throwing away their driver's licenses), the total number of licensed drivers in Japan is predicted to begin declining by around 2015. In parallel with that,

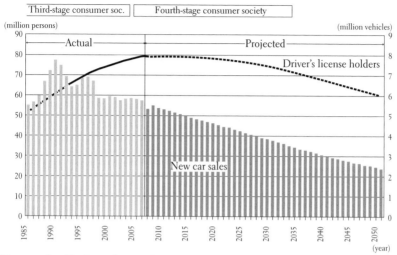

FIGURE 8-4 Projected Trends in Driver's Licenses and New Car Sales

Note: Figures for driver's license possession after 2007 are based on the Ministry of Internal
    Affairs and Communications Statistics Bureau projections for Japan's population of
    eighteen-year-olds and above. The ratio of driver's license holders to new car sales is
    estimated based on 2007 actuals. New car sales projections assume that recent trends for
    fewer people to purchase automobiles and for car owners to retain their current vehicles
    longer than before will continue.
Based on a study by Fourin, Inc.

annual domestic car sales are forecast to plunge to the 2.4 million range
by 2050 (fig. 8-4). Old-style business models predicated on getting people to acquire ever more personal possessions are losing their viability.

Ecology, Nativism, Regionalism, and the "From Money to People" Paradigm

Sharing-oriented consumers share a single item among several people,
and use it jointly. Since they also meet their needs by renting some
items instead of owning them and by recycling and reusing old goods,
they are almost by definition ecologically minded. They are spreading
a lifestyle that eliminates waste and aspires to simplicity.

Then, once you start putting your ecological, simple lifestyle into
practice, you might stop using an air conditioner and hang reed or

bamboo *sudare* blinds over your windows to let the air through. Or you might splash water on the ground around your home in the old style of Japanese *uchimizu* to enjoy the cooling effect. This will lead you to re-evaluate traditional Japanese lifestyles. It all works to strengthen today's growing interest in doing things the Japanese way.

The desire to live a more Japanese way of life will naturally connect to a desire to seek out the richness of a life lived close to nature, away from the urbanized lifestyles that are the symbol of materialistic affluence. This will strengthen the orientation toward regionalism, and living outside of Tokyo and Japan's other big cities.

The ethos of sharing at the same time connects with the trend toward decentralization, which ties in again to a rising regionalism. It all runs in parallel with a shift in orientation away from large urban concentrations, centralized authority, autocratic management, and all the other vestiges of the centralized lifestyle, and toward regional decentralization, regional political devolution, and networked management. "Sharing" consumers also value person-to-person communication; whenever possible they want direct, face-to-face interactions.

If I were to take this even further—and admittedly this is still at a nascent stage—we are also beginning to see signs of a quest for ways to organize human relationships without using money. It seems the next shift—from money to people—may have already begun.[5]

The Impact on Consumption

Once people have learned the pleasures of exchanging information, it seems inevitable that they will start buying fewer things.

After all, in many cases the pleasure you derive from buying something is greatest at the moment of purchase, and fades as time goes by. Buying inevitably brings with it a tinge of futility. But when you exchange information, the pleasure is not necessarily greatest at the moment the exchange takes place, nor does it fade with time. The exchange increases your pleasure, and those good feelings are sustained over time.

Consumers who have discovered the joys of information exchange will very likely discover that the standards that they use for making purchasing decisions are beginning to change. They will start looking for things to buy where the satisfaction is not greatest at the moment of purchase and shrinks over time, but that continue to give them satisfaction long after they have bought them. They will come to want things that actually bring them more and more satisfaction the longer they own them, things that exert an ever more subtle and powerful attraction as time goes by. And in fact the "Simplicity Tribe," which I will discuss in greater detail later, is already seeking out things like old furnishings dating back to the prewar period, craft objects, folk handicrafts, and old, traditional houses.

One reason the digital revolution has reinforced the new sharing ethos is that the Internet has made it so much easier to share information, in turn making it easier to share physical goods, be it through swaps, buying and selling used goods, or other means. Information has become the infrastructure for propagating the sharing value system.

When we consider the impact of the digital revolution on consumption, one of the first things that comes to mind is the decline in the sales of department stores and other brick-and-mortar outlets as more and more consumers do their shopping online at Internet shopping sites. But that is not all.

For example, if you tweet or post a notice on Facebook about an event you are holding at 3 p.m. tomorrow afternoon at a venue in Asakusa, you can probably get thirty or so people to come. If there are one hundred events like that being held around Tokyo—be it in Kōenji or Asagaya or Sangenjaya or Kitasenju or Kanamachi or Koiwa or anywhere—that means some three thousand people will be coming together tomorrow in places all over the map. Without Twitter and Facebook, those three thousand might have been drifting around Shibuya. But thanks to these Internet services they have all come together in scattered knots of thirty. Indeed, when I gave a talk at a bookstore in Tokyo's Aoyama district not long ago, there was a student in the audience who had come all the way down from Sendai, more than three hundred kilometers away, to hear me. I am not some superstar singer. But in this day and age, you no longer have to be a celebrity to bring together people over great distances using social media like Twitter and Facebook.

This presents a huge problem for retailers. If those three thousand people had all gathered at an event space in one of Shibuya's big department stores, perhaps a thousand of them would have stayed on and bought something in the store before going home. But instead they were spread all over the city in clumps of thirty. You simply can't do business that way.

So today's consumers no longer gather in a single place but, thanks to media like Twitter and Facebook, are scattered all over the place. Moreover, instead of just aimlessly wandering around the streets of Shibuya with no particular goal in mind, they are participating in events they are strongly interested in. That means they have a much higher degree of satisfaction than before. They may be getting to know other people who share the same interests and making new friends. And if that is the case, then more and more consumers are going to change their behavior. Instead of strolling aimlessly around the old, big shopping districts they are going to turn more and more to the information they get from Twitter, Facebook, and all the rest to find events that are perfectly suited for them.

Altruism Through Individualism

The new ethos of sharing does not work to differentiate you from other people. Rather, it establishes connections with others. Instead of seeking out and then flaunting a version of yourself that is different from everyone else, it helps you find commonality with others and to thereby create new human connections.

Having said that, however, I should add that sharing is not about seeking assimilation and homogeneity. The spread of a value like sharing is predicated upon individualism having already taken root and spread throughout society. This is not the old model of socialistic, collectivist sharing that said everyone should be given exactly the same share as everyone else, nor is it an aspiration for assimilation that insists everyone should be exactly the same. No, the great precondition for this sharing is individualism itself, the kind of individualism that says it is natural for everyone to be different, and that we should all respect each other's differences.

Indeed, one could say that both the new sharing and the new altruism itself are, ironically enough, predicated on material affluence. Today everyone has at least one and maybe more consumer durables per person. We all have more clothes and accessories and gadgets than we know what to do with. As seen in the recent phenomenon of so-called "Tiger Mask" anonymous giving,[6] it is exactly our excessive consumer society that has made it possible to let other people who really need it take some of our excess "stuff" and make better use of it.

Chapter Nine

The Sharing Lifestyle

The Growing Popularity of Shared Living

We can see in concrete terms both how sharing behavior works and how the value system of sharing is spreading in Japan in the growing popularity of *shea-hausu*: quite literally, "share house," or communal shared housing. "*Shea-hausu*" in Japanese can refer to a range of shared accommodations, from single houses to entire apartment buildings, that have been retrofitted so single people, both friends and strangers alike, can have the privacy of their own rooms while sharing communal facilities like common rooms and kitchens.[1]

There are four main advantages to living in a "share house": (1) economy, (2) security, (3) community, and (4) individuality.

First, economy. The up-front investment for moving into a share house is very small. There is no "key money" to pay to the realtor. There is either no security deposit, as there is for regular rental housing, or when there is, it is no more than about one month's rent. Unlike the standard Japanese apartment, share houses come with pre-installed refrigerators, microwaves, and other household appliances, and the kitchens are as well equipped as in your average single-family home. Every bedroom already has a bed, table, and chair. In short, it takes only a minimal investment to start living there. And since residents share baths, toilets, kitchens, and other common facilities, overhead costs, like electricity and heating, are also low (and often are bundled into the management fee).

Hence share-house living is both ecological and economical. And with residents divvying up the cleaning and other housekeeping chores among themselves, and in some cases leaving it to management, shared living is also highly economical of time—perhaps especially so for working women—in that one does not waste days off on housework.

Next, security. There is less worry about break-ins and other crime when living with other people instead of on one's own. It is also safer than living solo in times of disaster, especially earthquakes. In fact, after the March 11 earthquake and tsunami in northern Japan the authorities reported hearing from many people that they were glad they had been living in a share house when it happened. In case of illness, too, share-house living is more reassuring than living alone, since the residents can help each other out with cooking and other essentials.

Third, community. This, too, may be especially true for women, but having other people around to talk to lowers stress and makes life more enjoyable. There is also the pleasure that comes from meeting people from all kinds of professions and walks of life. But unlike the dormitory-style group housing of the past, share houses give the privacy of one's own room. In other words, one can still have connections with others, while at the same time keeping a certain distance from them.

And lastly, share houses are not all based on the same concept but have different interiors, exteriors, and floor layouts, making shared living more individualistic than housing in Japan's third-stage consumer society. People hearing about share houses often imagine a bland, characterless place with no privacy, but nothing could be further from the truth. No two share houses are alike, be it their floor plans, the year they were built, the number of residents, their interiors, or their exteriors. In that sense, at least some share houses are a little reminiscent of theme parks in the way they are built around different themes. You could move from one "one-room mansion"[2] to another and the interiors would all look the same. But the more you move from share house to share house, the more you can enjoy the variety they offer.

Once you've gotten used to this kind of shared living, in fact, you might well start finding life in a one-room mansion—almost all of which are two- or three-story high stacks of ten to twenty units with identical floor plans spaced precisely the same distance apart down featureless corridors—more akin to sitting in front of a factory conveyor belt.

Of course, not everyone will be living in shared housing in the future. In fact, residents of "share houses" are still a tiny part of the total population. However, a 2010 Culturestudies survey of unmarried Tokyo metropolitan area women in their twenties found that nearly 30 percent of them thought they might like to give share houses a try (fig. 9-1).

The rationale for such share houses is clear. As Japan's population ages and contracts—and particularly as the population of young people who have traditionally fueled the demand for new housing declines together with Japan's falling birthrate—the number of people seeking homes where they can raise their children is going to fall. No matter how you parse it, the demand for new housing construction is about to drop.

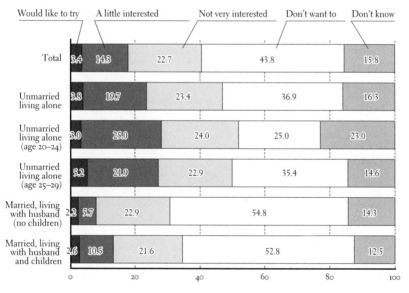

FIGURE 9-1 Would you like to live in a "share house"?

Based on Culturestudies survey, "Gendai saishin josei chōsa" (Newest Survey of Modern Women), 2010, a survey of women aged 20–39 in greater metropolitan Tokyo executed by NetMile, Inc.)

Moreover, Japan's existing housing stock already far exceeds the total number of households. In 2008 there were approximately eight million unoccupied housing units around the country. The ratio of unoccupied housing units to total housing was 13 percent in 2008, but this could soar to around 40 percent by 2040 according to some forecasts (fig. 9-2).

Therefore, from both an economic and an ecological perspective, making use of these increasing numbers of unoccupied residences rather than building new housing is the correct choice in these uncertain times. One can get a higher return on a smaller investment by retrofitting old homes into share houses.

As latent demand for shared housing rises, there will increasingly be people who want to live in a share house but cannot get in. That will fan the discontent of people who find themselves stuck in one-room "mansion" and other traditional housing.

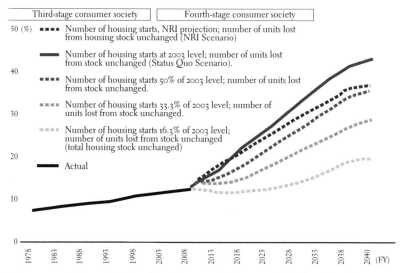

Figure 9-2 Projected Housing Starts and Unoccupied Housing Rates

Source: "Jinkō genshō jidai no jūtaku, tochi riyō, shakaishihon kanri no mondai to sono kaiketsu ni mukete (ge「下」)—2040-nen no Nihon no akiya mondai e no taiōsaku an" (The Dilemma of Housing, Land Use and Social Capital Management in an Era of Declining Population and the Search for Solutions (Part Two): A Proposed Response to the Vacant Housing Problem in Japan circa 2040). *Chiteki shisan sōzō* (Knowledge Creation and Integration). Nomura Research Institute, Vol. 17, No. 10, October 2009.

Ironically, back in Japan's third-stage consumer society people dreamed of living in a one-room mansion instead of an old wooden apartment building. Now the fourth-stage consumerism dream is to live in a share house created by retrofitting an old wooden home.

So what will become of these people brooding in their one-room mansion, or of married couples that do not think a share house would be quite right for their situation? Naturally, they will start demanding share house-like elements in their other housing options, be they one-room mansion, regular apartment buildings, or single-family homes.

One such element would be the freedom to put up different wall-paper or paint the walls as they please even if they're just renting — something traditionally forbidden by Japanese landlords. Or they might demand fancier kitchens, toilets, and baths. If they own their own housing, even units in a condominium, they will want to be able to redo the wall coverings, the floors, the doors, and the like to make their homes exactly the way they want them.

Secondly, they will be looking for at least the minimum sense of community necessary to provide security in time of earthquake, fire, or other disaster. In concrete terms, that means they will want housing that offers some degree of interaction and kinship with neighbors. Rental housing owners will likely find they have no choice but to offer additional incentives to their renters, be it more flexibility in the duration of rental contracts, or reduced security deposits and "key money."

Farewell to Private Possessions

I have been discussing this new orientation toward sharing among Japanese consumers for many years — back to when almost nothing like "share houses" even existed[3] — as well as a growing desire among Japanese consumers to move beyond personal possessions.[4]

In my 1999 book on family and happiness, I took note of the rising popularity among young people of districts like Tokyo's Kōenji, known for its used and vintage clothing stores and other counterculture shops, and the increasing numbers of young people who were wearing used clothes themselves and selling their personal belongings at open-air flea markets. The value system at the root of this kind of behavior among youth, I noted then, is "a rejection of postwar mass consumer society's ideology of private ownership."[5]

I am a little surprised when I reread this book today at how prescient I was back then. Let me quote at more length:

> Land, houses, cars, electric appliances, furniture, private rooms—the notion that you can own all of these things for yourself was the value system that defined Japan's suburbs (and with them, mass consumer society). . . . However, today's "suburbs generation" has begun to separate itself from those values. If you can get by without owning something, then there's no need to own it. If there's something you need, then borrow it. Or put more bluntly: "We don't need anything you can buy with money." Or yet again: "We don't want to kill ourselves over money." This new value system, it seems, is spreading fast. Owning things, having more and more private property, living in bigger houses, driving fancier cars, slaving to achieve these things, sacrificing your individuality to get them, that entire postwar value system is losing its power. . . . What we are witnessing is the rise of a new generation that finds no value in the first place in private possessions, in luxury, in rising in rank and status. Even if they had a hundred million yen they still wouldn't buy a house. Even if their income rises, they still won't buy big automobiles. They will never compromise the personal style they find most comfortable for themselves. This is the value system being born today, and in the years ahead it will spread to more and more young people. In time it will likely overtake and transcend Japan's postwar dream of "family and suburbs" that was created by climbing the ladder of consumption and private possessions.[6]

"Is It Really Consumption?"

It was a set of experiences I had the previous year, in 1998, that led me to realize way back in 1999 the limits of Japan's postwar affluence, an affluence founded on private ownership.

I happened, for some reason or other, to come that year to Kōenji, a neighborhood I had not visited for thirteen years. Walking around the town again I felt an indescribable sense of liberation on its streets overflowing with vintage clothes shops. Again, it was also right about that time that young people started setting up flea markets in Inokashira Park, not very far from my own home in Tokyo's Kichijōji district. Once again, I found myself thinking how free and happy they looked, how perfectly fine they seemed without brand-name fashions or shiny new products. And lastly, still in 1998, I had the experience of working on a project with a group of young architects and designers. Seeing the way they worked, I felt for myself the pleasures of living without being beholden to a single company. All these encounters had a powerful impact on my thinking.[7]

I later had the opportunity to meet up again with one of the young architects from that project, I think it was in 2001. It was something he said when we met that launched my research into sharing.

In *"Kazoku" to "kōfuku" no sengo-shi* and in my earlier 1995 book *"Kazoku to kōgai" no shakaigaku* (The Sociology of Family and Suburb),[8] I had argued to the effect that consumption worked to bind families together and make them function as joint consumption units. While it might no longer be as intense as it had been during Japan's second-stage consumer society, even now consumer behaviors like a family eating *temaki* sushi rolls together on a Saturday or going camping on a Sunday in the family minivan served to bring together, in one place and at one time and however temporarily, all the members of the family who were essentially living separate lives. In short, I argued, it was consumption that created their sense of togetherness.

However, when I shared my pet theory with this young architect he muttered, *"Shōhi na no ka naa?"* (Is it really consumption?).

The instant I heard his words, I had a realization: *No. It's not!* To this younger generation, I realized, the proposition that consumption held families together, the notion that buying brand goods could make you happy, in short, that entire value system, simply no longer applied.

An Age of "Shared Consumption"

But if not consumption, then what? What does work to bind family members or other groups of people together? At the time the answer still eluded me. Of course, I thought, the love between them brings them together. But even the expression of love often requires some kind of external intermediary. What could that be?

Observing the young freelancers I had been working with, I saw how they cooperated with each other, how flexibly they negotiated and shared their tasks, and how they got their fun from the work itself. Using cell phones and e-mail to the full, they were able to be in as tight communication with each other as they wanted, even without belonging to the same firm.

These young people had no interest in filling their "My Home" or their "My Room" with stuff. No, they were into sharing ideas, working together, playing together. And in that lay a value system that took joy from the act of doing things together. My coinage *kyōhi* 共費, or shared consumption, emerged from that realization. It is a term that has much in common with those other words we now hear so often, *shea* (sharing) and *tsunagari* (connection).

Fourth-stage consumer society no longer places much stock in whether consuming a product or service leaves you feeling satisfied or not. Instead, it values the social dimension. It puts value on consumption that helps build connections with others or, taking consumption off the table completely, on whether the things you do will help you get to know and have interchange with other people or not.

Just as I was arriving at that conclusion, Hakuhōdō's Research and Development Division contacted me for a joint research project into new consumer behavior. In the end, *kyōhi* became the keyword for our research, and the title of the resulting 2002 report.

Flaunt-free Consumption

When you buy an item of clothing at Uniqlo, you don't expect to derive that much pleasure from owning it. You can hardly boast to others that you are a "Uniqlo shopper," nor flaunt the things you buy there. Yet even so—or more to the point, exactly because this is so—people buy Uniqlo. Shopping there can even be a statement that you are not one of those people who obsesses about possessions.

For this reason, it may actually be more appropriate to think of Uniqlo as providing a service rather than products. For just a thousand yen or so each you can buy all the basic clothes needed in daily life. Like the famous "tap water philosophy" of Matsushita Kōnosuke—the legendary founder of consumer electronics giant Panasonic Corporation who argued that a manufacturer's mission "is to create material abundance by providing goods as plentifully and inexpensively as tap water"[9]—Uniqlo provides clothes that are inexpensive yet attractive and functional enough that you don't feel uncomfortable wearing them. Moreover, Uniqlo takes those clothes back when you no longer want them, and donates them to developing countries. In this way the Uniqlo business model comes not just with a public water system but with a public drainage system as well. It offers its customers not only clothes but also an opportunity for altruistic behavior.

In this Uniqlo model, we can feel at a gut level how, as discussed earlier, the goals of consumption, and indeed the goals of life itself, have changed in Japan over the course of the shift from first-stage consumer society to second-stage, third-stage and now fourth-stage consumerism.

It has been a transition from the family to the individual and on to the social. Evolving from a time when they consumed to create an affluent family (up to and through second-stage consumerism) and then to consuming for an affluent personal life and expressing their own individuality (third-stage consumerism), Japan's consumers have today reached a point where they seek to use consumption as a way of building connections with others and contributing to a better society. Indeed, the popularity of fair trade products in Japan today is quintessential fourth-stage consumer society behavior.

The Changing Nature of Happiness

The generation that grew up used to the private-ownership values of Japan's high-growth period often doubt whether today's young people can really be content without owning things. But one thing has not changed: people want to be happy, no matter what decade it might be. Although there was a time in Japan when happiness meant having "My Car" or "My Home, now we are in an age when people no longer think such material things will make them happy.

If you were to ask them, then, what is happiness, their answer would probably be *tsunagari*, or "connection"; this could also be defined as "communication" or "community." Consumption in this new era is not the old consumption of buying things and boasting about them to others. Instead, the consumer psychology spreading today is a desire to consume in such a way that one is spurring communication with others, giving birth to community. It is exactly because today's society—through the growth of nonregular employment and like trends—treats people like throwaways that consumers have come to value human relationships that are nondisposable.

As mentioned earlier, it was around 2002 that I myself noticed this trend, and *kyōhi*—"shared consumption"—was the word I came up with to describe it. Actually, today's young people are just fine as long as they have more communication and community with others, regardless of whether that involves buying things. Frankly, though, putting it that way was a bit problematic from a marketing perspective, so I added the "*hi* 費" from "consumption" (*shōhi* 消費) to the "*kyō*" of "shared" (*kyōyō* 共用) to create *kyōhi* (共費) in order to better express the concept of a consumption that gives rise to communication and community.

Semantics aside, however, it is safe to say that today's young people are fast losing interest in actually "consuming" anything in the traditional sense of "*tsuiyasu* 費やす" or "using something up."

Everyone a Single

Another factor behind the spread of the sharing lifestyle in Japan today is the rising number of singles. According to a forecast by the National Institute of Population and Social Security Research, the "lifelong unmarried rate" (the percentage of women who have never been married by age fifty) for Japanese women is increasing, and is set to reach 23.5 percent for the cohort of women born in 1990.

Meanwhile, the "divorce experience rate"—in other words, the ratio of women who have been divorced at least once to women who have been married at least once—has been rising steadily. For the cohort of women born in 1955, this divorce rate was 18.4 percent at age fifty. But for the cohort born in 1970, 18 percent had already experienced divorce when they were only thirty-five. If this trend continues, the study suggests, the divorce rate at age fifty for women born in 1990 could be a full 36 percent (fig. 9-3).[10]

In short, by the time women born in 1990 have turned fifty, 23.5 percent of them will never have been married at all, and of the remaining 76.5 percent who did marry, 36 percent—or 27.5 percent of the entire cohort—will be either single or single mothers. If we add in everyone who has been widowed by fifty, the percentage is even higher. And then, of course, by the time these women reach their sixties or seventies even more of them will have been widowed or divorced. In short, singlehood will have become pan-generational.

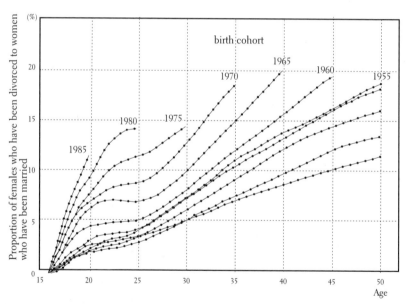

FIGURE 9-3 Proportion of Females Who Have Been Divorced to Females Who Have Been Married, by Birth Cohort

Source: Iwasawa Miho, "Shokon-rikon no dōkō to shusseiritsu e no eikyō" (Recent Trends in First Marriage and Divorce and Their Effects on Fertility Rates in Japan). *Jinkō mondai kenkyū* (Journal of Population Problems), 64-4 (2008.12), pp. 19–34

Clearly the number of women who cannot (or in some cases may not wish to) depend financially on a man is going to increase. In that sense, the sharing lifestyle will in time come to function as a social safety net. It will be an essential source of security not just against crime or in time of disaster but across all aspects of life.

Of course, men are no exception to these trends. We can expect both the ratio of single males to the total population and the ratio of men in nonregular employment to the total work force to continue to rise, especially so among younger generations. Males, too, will increasingly need to adopt a sharing lifestyle to get by.

Yet another pressing problem in Japan's future will be the aging of the so-called "parasite singles" still living with their parents. Only 8.1 percent of males thirty-five to forty-four fell in this category in 1990. By 2010, that had more than doubled to 19.9 percent, while the percentage of "parasite" single women had surged from 3.3 percent to 12.2 percent (fig. 3-2, page 45). In absolute numbers, there were just short of 200,000 male and somewhat less than 200,000 such female singles aged thirty-five to forty-four in 1980, but by 2010 their ranks had leaped to 1.8 million men, and over one million women (fig. 3-3, page 46). Taken together, there are nearly three million singles aged thirty-five to forty-four still living in the family home in Japan today.

If this huge cohort remains mostly single in the future, and if we add to it those men and woman who are currently married but might return home and "parasite" off their parents after a divorce or other separation in the future, then there is a strong possibility that thirty years from now there will be another huge bump in the number of singles in their late sixties and seventies living alone as the parents of the "parasite" singles start to pass away.

In 2010, half of single households (i.e., households of just one person) in Japan were aged fifty or older. By 2030, the number of single households is projected to rise to 18 million, of which 67 percent will be individuals aged fifty or older (fig. 9-4). That would herald the arrival of an unprecedented state of pan-generational singlehood in Japan. Instead of the famed "100 million middle-class" nation, we will be a "100 million singles society."

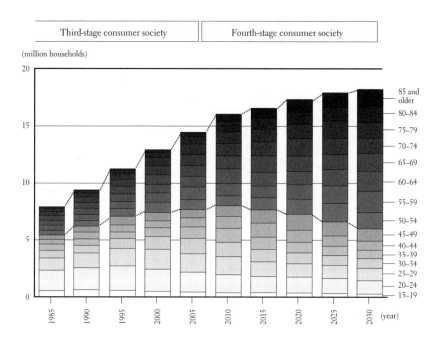

FIGURE 9-4 Single Households by Age Group

Source: Ministry of Internal Affairs and Communications, "Kokusei chôsa" (National Census)
& National Institute of Population and Social Security Research (IPSS), "Nihon no
setaisû no shôrai suikei" (Household Projections for Japan), March, 2008 projection.

The Increase in Nonregular Employment

But that is not all. Today we are witnessing a decline in the number of
regular employees in Japan, as nonregular employees (part-time and
contract workers) are coming to account for more and more of the
labor force. Accordingly, it has become harder and harder for companies to play their traditional role as the platform for people to create
social connections.

Here is yet another factor making a shared lifestyle more essential
than before. In 1990 nonregular employees accounted for only 20 percent of all employees. By 2000 that had risen to 26 percent, and since
2005 it has climbed to between 33 and 34 percent today (fig. 9-5).

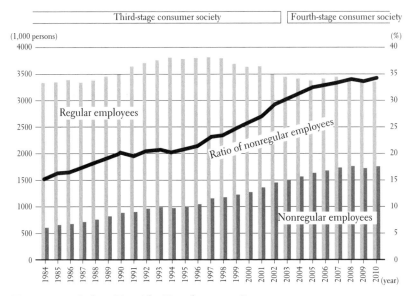

FIGURE 9-5 Labor Force by Employment Status

Source: Ministry of Internal Affairs and Communications Statistics Bureau, "Rōdōryoku chōsa tokubetsu chōsa" (The Special Survey of the Labour Force Survey) prior to 2001 and "Rōdōryoku chōsa shōsai shūkei" (Labour Force Survey [Detailed Tabulation]) since 2002.

Looking only at workers aged twenty-five to thirty-four, in 1988 the ratio of nonregular employees to all employees was just 3.6 percent for men, and 25.9 percent for women. By 2010 it was 13.3 percent for men and 41.6 percent for women (fig. 9-6). This destabilization and casualization of labor will be one of the core factors defining Japan's fourth-stage consumer society.

Of course, the primary cause of this increase in the number of non-regular employees was Japan's protracted recession. Another reason, however, lay in the characteristics of Japan's third-stage consumer society itself.

One of those characteristics was the shift from mass production to high-variety, low-volume manufacturing, the small-lot production of a much larger variety of products discussed earlier in chapter seven. Companies have to respond nimbly when consumers with diverse tastes find that those tastes are changing along with the times. In the

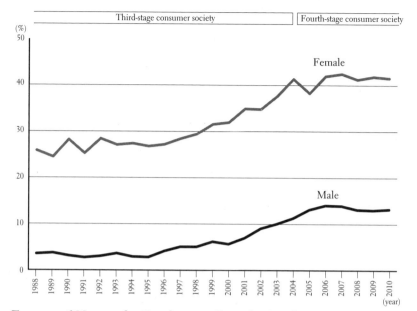

FIGURE 9-6 Nonregular Employment Rates by Gender (Ages 25–34)

Source: Ministry of Internal Affairs and Communications Statistics Bureau, "Rōdōryoku chōsa tokubetsu chōsa" (Special Survey of the Labour Force Survey) from prior to and including 2001 and "Rōdōryoku chōsa shōsai shūkei" (Labour Force Survey [Detailed Tabulation]) since 2002.

era of low-variety, high-volume manufacturing, it was almost unheard of for a product to suddenly stop selling. But in a time of high-variety, low-volume production it is much easier for, say, Product A to be selling well and to have Product B suddenly stop selling overnight.

This changed production environment led to new inefficiencies. For example, if you hire one permanent employee and keep him at the same post, there will be times when the products are practically selling themselves and he has almost nothing to do, and other times when, as fads suddenly change, you need to come up with new products fast and find yourself with a labor shortage.

That being the case, as the variety of products and their turnover accelerated during Japan's third-stage consumer society, companies began to think it made more sense to switch to nonregular employees that they could hire quickly when they needed them and dismiss when they didn't. The surge in nonregular employees that began in the closing days of Japan's third-stage consumer society was a direct product of the nature of third-stage consumerism itself.

In practice, however, it is almost impossible for a nonregular employee to get a loan to buy a house. Indeed, there is a good chance that he or she will not even be able to pass the background checks required to get into most rentals. "Parasite singles" can keep on living in their parents' old home indefinitely—putting aside whether or not they can afford to maintain it as the years go by. But other nonregular workers are at real risk of not being able to find housing. True, they might clear the background check for some decaying old wooden apartment. But in that case it might be simpler just to move into a share house, and much more comfortable as well.

In this respect, too, share houses seem singularly suited to Japan in the present age. And that is not limited to housing. For people in today's unstable work environment, there is real merit in switching to a lifestyle based on sharing.

Chapter Ten

Simplicity, Localism, and the Japanese Way

From "One Grade Up" to Simplicity

As we have seen, sharing-oriented consumers are more likely to jointly own things with others, to meet their needs by renting rather than owning, and to recycle and reuse old goods. Given such behavior, they are almost by definition ecologically minded, seeking a simple lifestyle that expunges excess from all aspects of their life.

I have examined this in more detail in my 2009 book *Shinpuru-zoku no hanran* (Revolt of the Simplicity Tribe).[1] But to quickly summarize here, the lifestyle that consumers are seeking today is not the "bigger and bigger" lifestyle of second-stage consumer society. It is not third-stage consumerism's more luxurious, more fashionable, "one-grade-up" lifestyle predicated on climbing the social ladder and expressing the self. No, the lifestyle that is emerging today is simple, tranquil, and environmentally friendly.

The publishing world was quick to pick up on these new aspirations. *Sotokoto* magazine—which describes itself as a magazine for "LOHAS people"[2]—appeared in 1999. Similarly LOHAS-inflected lifestyle magazines *ku:nel* and *Ten'nen Seikatsu* (Natural Life) both went to press in 2003. Meanwhile *Chiruchinbito,* a natural living and home-making magazine, has been on sale since 1997. From this publishing boomlet, it would seem that there has been a building interest in Japan in an alternative to materialism going back at least to 1997. Nowadays, even run-of-the-mill mail-order catalogs imitate the tastes seen in these LOHAS and lifestyle magazines.

Thinking back on it, Japanese marketing in the 1980s constantly trotted out the phrase *"Wan ranku appu"* (One rank up). If consumers got to feeling too satisfied with the homogenous lifestyle their nation's second-stage consumer society had given them, then corporate earnings would stagnate. Hence, Japanese companies were constantly suggesting to consumers that they needed more luxury in their lives, more products that were one step up, to give full expression to their individuality. But as we have seen, consumers eventually tired of that "nightmare of differentiation" and from that disillusionment was born a new longing for simplicity.

Does this mean that simplicity-seeking consumers no longer feel a need to express their individuality? Anything but. The desire for self-expression is still there. But whereas the "individualism" of third-stage consumer society consisted at least in part of consumers selecting brands they thought were more "like themselves," fourth-stage consumers do not want to buy products that come with a distinct coloration of their own. They choose products that are neutral and unadorned. Their thinking is that individuality comes from within, and they prefer that the medium for expressing it be as colorless and transparent as possible so as not to interfere with the self.

Of course there is no such thing as a product without some distinct identity of its own, but consumers are doing their best to approach that sort of ideal.

A Love of Japanese Culture

Another salient characteristic of fourth-stage consumer society is a renewed love for things Japanese.

For example, in recent years fewer young Japanese are traveling abroad, while more are visiting Kyoto. The ancient Kumano Kodō pilgrimage route, the historic Ise Jingū shrine, and other cultural and historical sites are growing in popularity. Magazine specials on Shinto shrines and Buddhist temples are popular with readers, and when you do in fact go to a shrine these days you will find lots of young women there. Interest in Japan's traditional culture is clearly on the rise.

I analyze this phenomenon in my 2010 book *Aikoku shōhi* (Consumption as Nationalism).[3] In brief, however, according to the 2010 Cabinet Office Public Opinion Survey of Social Awareness, the percentage of Japanese males in their twenties who said they felt "strong" love for their country had risen 15.2 percentage points over the preceding ten years. Among females, the increase was most striking for women in their thirties: up 10.4 percentage points over the same period. We might expect a survey to find the Japanese to be more Japan-oriented the older they are, but in fact, there is now very little difference in nativist sentiment among the young and the old.

What do we actually mean by "Japan?" In a sense, we can think of Japan as a vast narrative, and for most Japanese it is their greatest narrative. That is especially true for today's younger generations.

Why is this? For one thing, the younger the generation, the more likely they are to have experienced life in many different parts of Japan as their parents were transferred by their company from city to city; some may even have lived for a time overseas. They do not actually have a hometown or area that they strongly identify with. Just because they were born in such-a-such a prefecture, it no longer follows that they have any particular personality or traits reflecting that place.

In my case, I was born in Takada in Niigata Prefecture, and grew into young adulthood in the same region. My ancestors are said to have lived there for eight centuries, and I feel that I really am a Niigata person, a son of Takada.

When you look at the generation where many were children of the *tenkin-zoku*, the so-called "Transfer Tribe," they have little awareness of their characters having been formed by where they were born, or the localities where they grew up. They are, in a sense, the generation of the "homeland-less." The ranks of this generation have been swelling among Japanese born beginning in the 1960s. If you were to ask any of them where they are from, it is likely they would not answer Niigata Prefecture or Kumamoto Prefecture, but "Japan." This could well be one of the factors behind the growing love for their country among younger Japanese.

At the same time, could it also be—now that Japan has surrendered the title of the world's second largest economy to China—that the Japanese people as a whole are seeking in their traditional culture a new source of pride to replace the pride they used to have in economic superpower Japan? To my eyes, at least, most Japanese hardly seem to be in despair over their country's fall from second place. If anything, it strikes me that many are actually glad to find some value other than economic power that all Japanese can share together.

Globalization may also be playing a part. As the impact of globalization threatens to homogenize lifestyles the world over, it is easy to imagine a growing hunger among many Japanese for a stronger sense of their own Japaneseness. Trips abroad can conversely bring home the virtues of the clean and peaceful homeland they left behind. All these factors could be coming together today to drive the growing interest in Japan among the Japanese themselves.

One interesting suggestion comes from the NHK Broadcasting Culture Research Institute's annual "Survey of Japanese Value Orientations."[4] According to the survey, the number of young Japanese responding that they feel "a strong affinity for Japanese tradition" at the sight of old temples or traditional-style houses has actually been rising since 2003. In 1988, the response rate was 63 percent for Japanese aged sixteen to nineteen, and 71 percent for Japanese aged twenty to twenty-four. In 2008, that had grown to 69 percent and 87 percent respectively.

Old traditional houses should have no direct place in the nostalgic life experiences of Japan's younger generations, yet even so—or perhaps because that is so—the image of these old houses has become part of the shared primal landscape of the Japanese people.

Love of Japan and the Simple Life

We should also note that this reorientation toward things Japanese ties very naturally into the desire for a simpler and more ecological lifestyle discussed earlier; there is a natural affinity with such trends toward ecology and simple living.

Generally speaking, the American way of life founded on mass consumption is incompatible with ecology. (The Quakers living their frugal and pious lives and others like them are exceptions, of course.) The traditionally Russian, French, or Chinese way is indifferent to ecology. No doubt premodern societies everywhere lived in coexistence with nature, but if one is talking about societies that did not simply coexist with the natural world but that sought to elevate that coexistence into a sophisticated lifestyle and culture, then there is clearly something about Japanese culture that has led so many people to regard premodern Japan as a model ecological society. We cannot say there was nothing else like it in other countries, but at very least it was clearly an integral part of the Japan of the past.

A green consciousness is not simply a scientific issue in Japan but a cultural one as well, tying into pride in Japan's traditional way of life. In fact, simple living is now seen as a new goal for the country's future, in place of the economic superpower aspirations of the past.

When you think about it, Japan's transformation into an economic superpower was none other than turning into a Western state. This is why, as I see it, there has always been a place in the heart of the Japanese people that could not find it in itself to fully rejoice when their country did become such an economic powerhouse. I believe this conflicted consciousness goes all the way back to the 1960s. There was an awareness even then that we had sacrificed and destroyed much of what had been good about the old Japan. It is that sense of loss that wells up from Fujioka Wakao's passage about his Discover Japan advertising campaign discussed in chapter four.

This is why even as China overtakes Japan in GDP and the country falls to third place in the world's economic pantheon, the Japanese people are not really that stricken. That high-flying GDP itself is, after all, just a quantitative indicator, a measure of the affluence of just a single era in Japan's history, the era of modernization.

Japan's brand consciousness was, in the end, all about Western brands. But no matter how many brand-name goods you may own, you cannot buy authenticity.

Compared to buying things, the simple and ecological lifestyle present in Japan since the days of old does confer cultural legitimacy. In fact, in our Culturestudies survey of modern Japanese women 41 percent of women who expressed an interest in environmental issues also replied that they "strongly liked" Japan. For women expressing little or no interest in the environment that figure was only 15–16 percent (fig. 10-1). There seems to be a high correlation between a concern about the environment and positive feelings toward Japan.

The survey also suggested that the more people were concerned about the environment, the more likely they were to engage in traditional Japanese behavior (fig. 10-2). They were also more likely to buy "designs that can be worn in future years, instead of following current fashion," "products that are well made and look like they will last a long time," and "products with good basic functionality" (fig. 10-3).

I suspect some corporations may not like the thought that replacement demand will shrink in Japan as this green consciousness takes hold. However, simple-life consumers are willing to buy quite expensive products if they know that they will last. And it is, after all, the job of business to respond to changing demand.

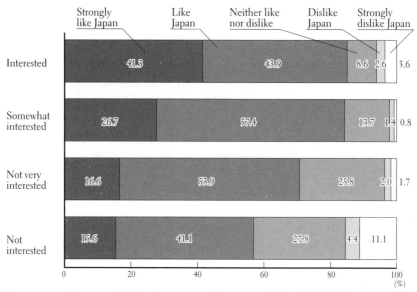

FIGURE 10-1 Interest in Environmental Issues and Positive Feelings Toward Japan

Based on Culturestudies, "Gendai saishin josei chōsa" (Newest Survey of Modern Women), 2010, a survey of women aged 20–39 in greater metropolitan Tokyo executed by NetMile, Inc.

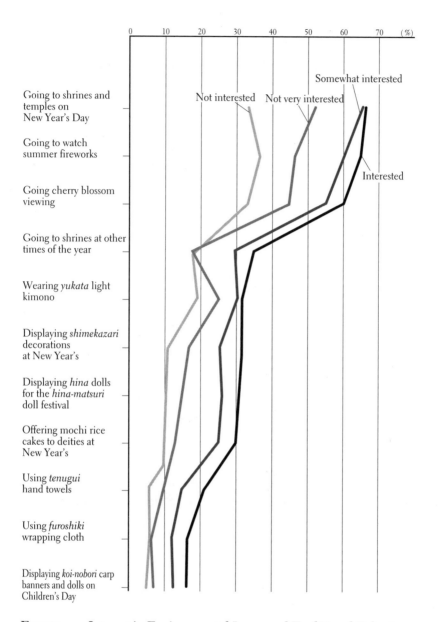

The chart shows percentage scale across the top from 0 to 70 (%), with markings at 0, 10, 20, 30, 40, 50, 60, 70.

Categories listed along the left axis:

- Going to shrines and temples on New Year's Day
- Going to watch summer fireworks
- Going cherry blossom viewing
- Going to shrines at other times of the year
- Wearing *yukata* light kimono
- Displaying *shimekazari* decorations at New Year's
- Displaying *hina* dolls for the *hina-matsuri* doll festival
- Offering mochi rice cakes to deities at New Year's
- Using *tenugui* hand towels
- Using *furoshiki* wrapping cloth
- Displaying *koi-nobori* carp banners and dolls on Children's Day

Line labels: Not interested, Not very interested, Somewhat interested, Interested

FIGURE 10-2 Interest in Environmental Issues and Traditional Behavior

Based on Culturestudies survey, "Gendai saishin josei chōsa" (Newest Survey of Modern Women), 2010, a survey of women aged 20–39 in greater metropolitan Tokyo executed by NetMile, Inc.

■ Buy designs that can be worn in future years, instead of following current fashion.

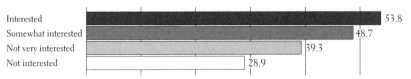

■ Buy products that are well made and look like they will last a long time.

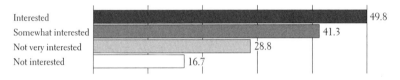

■ Buying products with good basic functionality.

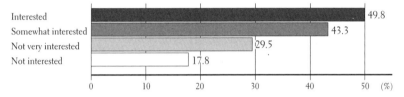

FIGURE 10-3 Interest in Environmental Issues and Consumer Behavior

Based on Culturestudies survey, "Gendai saishin josei chōsa" (Newest Survey of Modern Women), 2010, a survey of women aged 20–39 in the greater metropolitan Tokyo executed by NetMile, Inc.)

The burgeoning trend toward simplicity will mean the demise of the old third-stage consumerism lust for foreign luxury brands. More and more young Japanese have no problem with dressing from head to toe in Uniqlo, with fewer young consumers expressing themselves through brand goods. It seems that today's young consumers have decided that standardized, mass-produced goods are just fine for things that do not impact their individuality.

Let me point out here that I am not saying that this new simplicity is something foreign to the thinking in other countries. In fact, many Japanese have had their eyes opened to the simple lifestyle by their experiences overseas.

The lifestyle of the average European, for instance, could be called frugal compared to their counterparts in Japan or the United States. No European high-school girl would carry around a Louis Vuitton wallet. Many Europeans live in houses built hundreds of years ago, and use century-old furniture. In the United States, too, it is quite common, even in big cities like New York, to renovate hundred-year-old buildings instead of tearing them down.

When Japanese who have witnessed these practices on vacation or while working overseas look at the lifestyle of their compatriots back home, they notice with fresh eyes that houses and buildings in Japan are torn down after just forty years, that almost all the furniture is discount store furniture that no one would dream of using a century from now, and even architecturally distinguished buildings are usually demolished as soon as they get old. Driven only by market principles, Japan's cities and buildings alike are in a continual cycle of scrap and build, making it almost impossible to live a calm and simple life. Not a few Japanese international travelers and expatriates must come home full of doubts about the modern reality of their country compared to the ecologically-friendly lifestyles of its past. So while it is true that today's trend toward simple living owes much to Japan's traditional culture and way of life, in some instances the trigger that opened people's eyes to the virtues of simple living may have come not from within Japan, but from overseas.

The End of Modernization and the Comeback of Regional Japan

There is another important aspect to this growing nativist sentiment—a turning away from Tokyo to regional cities and the countryside. This trend is particularly strong among younger generations. According to a Cabinet Office survey, some 30 percent of urban Japanese in their twenties would like to relocate permanently to rural Japan (fig. 10-4).

Why are these young people so set on leaving the cities? I do not have a definitive answer, but if we subscribe to community designer Yamazaki Ryō's analysis in my interview with him in this book (Appendix

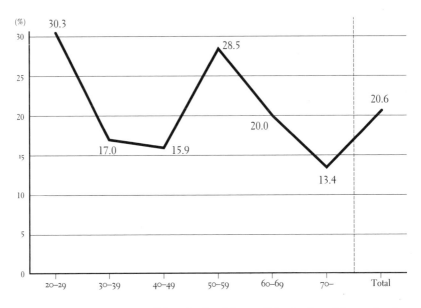

FIGURE 10-4 Percentage of People Desiring to Live in Rural Japan by Age

Source: Cabinet Office survey, "Toshi to nōsangyoson no kyōsei-tairyū ni kansuru yoron chōsa" (Public Opinion Survey on Complementarities and Interrelationships between Urban and Rural Areas), 2006.

II) it begins with the environmental education that young people receive today beginning in elementary school. When as adults they ponder how to follow a greener lifestyle, they naturally find themselves drawn toward life in Japan's hinterlands rather than the big city. This appears to be one important factor.

We can also speculate that young people, with no expectation that their incomes are going to rise significantly in the future after Japan's long years of recession, are attracted to life where the cost of living is lower than in the big city. And a third factor could be the positive coverage of countryside Japan in today's mass media. Nowadays, even magazines like *Brutus* that would normally be introducing cutting-edge urban lifestyles to their readers are running specials on agriculture and other aspects of the country life.

From a longer-term perspective, I would point to a larger shift in values. The new fourth-stage consumer society does not subscribe to the value system that has dominated Japan in the past: modernization at all costs. Up through Japan's third-stage consumer society, there was a hunger for modernization, for Westernization. Those cities and urban districts that had been quick to Westernize—like Yokohama, Kobe, and Tokyo's downtown Ginza district—were considered fashionable. Cities themselves were thought to be "advanced," while Japan's regional and rural districts were "backward" and "behind."

Yet in today's fourth-stage consumer society, Japanese society and lifestyles are already highly advanced wherever one lives. Naturally the hunger for modernization—now defined not as modernizing but as making Japan even more modern that it already is—has weakened. And once that happens, the value the old mindset placed on big city living will weaken as well, while, conversely, a new value system will emerge that values life outside the big cities in communities in regional and rural Japan.

Chiba University professor Hiroi Yoshinori, one of Japan's foremost scholars of regional and rural Japan and the Japanese welfare state, has argued that societies founded on a drive for modernization give greater priority to the temporal axis than the spatial axis. This is how he explains it in his book, *Sōzōteki fukushi shakai* (The Creative Welfare Society):

> In the age of growth and expansion, the temporal axis of "advanced versus backwards" (for example, industrialized nations are advanced; cities are advanced, etc.) was in the ascendance as the world advanced in a single direction. Once a society reaches a steady state, however, it rediscovers the local traditions and cultural landscape, the geographical diversity and the unique value of its many regions.[5]

Connections: From Vertical to Horizontal

If we follow Hiroi's model, a modernizing society devalues and rejects its own premodern society. It thinks that today is better than yesterday, and tomorrow will be better than today—more advanced, more correct, more cultured. A modern country is considered to be superior to a nonmodern one, and a more modern metropolis superior to a nonmodern farm village.

However, in fourth-stage consumer society—a "steady-state society," to borrow Hiroi's terminology—modernization is viewed relatively. It is no longer a given that today is better than yesterday was. People can once again see good things about the past. Once that happens, the spatial axis becomes more important than the temporal axis, and the unique culture of regions and rural districts—dismissed as backward by the value system of modernization—suddenly becomes very important.

I personally believe that human connections—*tsunagari*—can also be positioned along Hiroi's spatial axis. If the temporal axis and the spatial axis are, in a sense, the axes of vertical connections and horizontal connections, then the vertical connections are the connections encompassing history and tradition. And the horizontal connections are the connections of human relationships.

When I was explaining this concept of vertical and horizontal connections one day, one of those present proposed that in Japan the vertical connections were traditionally the province of Buddhist temples, while the horizontal connections were the province of Shinto shrines.

I instantly got the point. Buddhist temples are places of ancestor worship. They are where you go to reconfirm your present-day existence being tied to the generations of your ancestors that came before. In contrast, the Shinto shrine is the nucleus that brings together the *ujiko*, the members of the regional society in which the shrine is located, through *matsuri* festivals and other events and rituals. In other words, Buddhism and Shinto traditionally divided up vertical and horizontal connections in Japanese society.

This is where the green consciousness we discussed earlier comes into play. Once an awareness of ecological issues takes hold and people begin to give greater importance to the natural world, then places rich in nature, regional communities where people live in coexistence with the natural world, will be accorded greater value than the cities.

This will mean the end of another old way of thinking, the ranking of the culture of one region as superior to that of another. Instead, people will come to see the cultures of every region and locality as having their own distinct value. The renewed nativism we discussed earlier is a case in point: Kyoto is no longer seen as the one true source of traditional Japanese culture. Rather, the local culture of every region of

Japan is given its own, equal value. When I wrote at the beginning of this chapter that young Japanese today have a renewed love for things Japanese, I was not talking about the stereotypical version of old Japan symbolized by Kyoto culture. In fact, today's Japan-oriented youth seek to honor and enjoy the cultures of all Japan's many regions, regardless of whether it was where they were born and raised themselves.

Regional Identity and the Re-evaluation of Handwork

For the above reasons we can say that the appealing and distinctive culture of regional Japan will be key to product development in the future. Japanese life today is saturated with the same mass-produced products wherever you go, of which Uniqlo is a sterling example. It is an absolutely workaday, "*ke*"[6] mode of consumption, but consumers have long since stopped feeling bad about wearing inexpensive clothes.

In times like these it will be goods that are the polar opposite of mass-produced products—traditional crafts made by local craftsmen, handmade folk craft produced by countless nameless people for their daily use—that will have the greatest value.

In fact, in recent years there has been a growing trend toward reevaluating the traditional crafts created across Japan. Go to the bookstore and you will find many magazines like *Kāsa Burūtasu* (Casa Brutus) and *Pen* that promote an urban lifestyle. In recent years, however, they have all featured specials on the history of Japanese design and the traditional designs of regional Japan. Articles have taken a close-up look at the folk crafts of different regions like the Nambu cast-iron kettles of northern Iwate prefecture, or been written on topics like Yanagi Sōetsu (Muneyoshi) and his *mingei* folk crafts movement.

There has also been a new readiness to value terraced paddy rice fields and other features of Japan's premodern landscape as national cultural assets. Today those landscapes themselves have become the setting for contemporary art festivals around the country, from the Echigo-Tsumari Art Triennial in Niigata Prefecture to Kagawa Prefecture's Benesse Art Site Naoshima on an island in Japan's Inland Sea.

In short, the focus of today's love of things Japanese is no longer just the elegant "*miyabi*" aristocratic culture of Kyoto. It is far broader and,

if anything, more centered on the folk and common people's cultures of
the more remote corners of Japan. That new focus is driven in part by a
sense of crisis, a fear—as symbolized by the term *genkai shūraku*, or "terminal villages," for Japan's depopulated rural communities[7]—that out in
the countryside the nation's unique cultural traditions are in imminent
threat of dying out completely.

Yamazaki Masakazu, one of Japan's most distinguished playwrights
and critics, has put it this way:

> Regional societies were there before the modern state, and existed
> independent of the wielders of power. A feudal lord might be removed
> from his seat and moved to a different domain, but the farmers and the
> townspeople stayed where they were. Premodern local governments
> were clearly inferior to what we have today, yet regional societies them-
> selves were far more vigorous. If you really want to talk about regional
> revitalization, is it not necessary to first go back and reexamine the
> issue from its origins? The healthy villages and towns of the past were
> not simply centers of production. They had their village shrines and
> village temples where the people enjoyed festivals celebrating the four
> seasons. It was the world from which long ago Kanze Noh theater[8]
> was born and where Okuni Kabuki theater[9] was developed, a world
> that gave us scholars and cultural leaders like Ise's Motoori Norinaga[10]
> and Osaka's Yamagata Bantō,[11] and that fostered the foundations of
> Japanese culture. Even if we look only at the production of goods, the
> villages and towns of the past were fiercely committed to generating
> added value and fostering what we now call cultural industries. From
> primary products like rice and vegetables to industrial products like
> textiles, paper, ceramics, lacquerware, and cutting instruments, every
> region had products for which it was famous, generating not simply
> revenue but regional pride. Could it be that what is impoverishing
> today's regional communities is not just a lack of monetary wealth, but
> the knowledge that their cultural power has waned, and the loss of the
> local pride that such a realization brings?[12]

The key point here is Yamazaki's argument about the importance of
regional pride. Thanks to the erection of mammoth shopping centers
all over the country, today the Japanese can enjoy virtually the same

level of consumption wherever they live. Yet even if consumption in regional Japan rivals Tokyo's, its unique local cultures have been eviscerated. If those shopping centers and megastores become unprofitable and pack up shop again as the nation's population shrinks, there will be nothing left behind but shuttered main streets and the empty hulks of abandoned megastores. In other words, ruins.

I doubt that many of those indulging the most in this mall-centric consumer civilization would say they don't care if their communities are left in ruins in the future. When the time comes to try to breathe life back into those ruins, a love for and pride in local history will be crucial.

Could it be that Japanese today are trying to use exactly such regional and local pride as a catalyst for establishing new connections with one another? Compared to the tiny narrative of self-expression and individuality they were pursuing during third-stage consumer society, this is a story having a vastly greater history and one much more grounded in reality. I believe this is the kind of narrative people are seeking today.

Take any region of Japan, and it has its own history, its own stories, its own myths and folklore. It has tradition and culture, unique lifestyles and language. Even if these different and diverse regions continue to adapt themselves to this new age, so long as they do not lose their unique regional identity in the process, there will be a host of distinct and individualistic cultures existing across Japan in the future. That would be a country richer by far than a nation with only one flavor of "Japaneseness."

One Designer's Discerning Eye

The designer Hara Kenya is the man who most occupies the same position today in the re-appreciation and promotion of Japan's—especially rural Japan's—crafts and industrial arts as did Yanagi Sōetsu in prewar Japan. This is how Hara put it in the preface to his 2011 book, *Nihon no dezain* (Japanese Design):

> Japan today is at a historic turning point. . . . A question is rising to the surface, still faint yet resolute, a question that has been unremittingly

173

suppressed since the Meiji Revolution [of 1868] by keeping our economic and cultural rudder turned toward Westernization: Would not a more effective way to preserve this nation's possibilities and pride be to take back again in the future . . . our own Japanese sensibility brewed over a millennium and some-odd hundred years of time?"[13]

Hara identifies the elements of this sensibility as the ability to create physical objects and environments with delicacy, precision, detail, and simplicity. It is exactly this aesthetic and sensory "resource," he argues, that Japan has to contribute to the world. You can feel in his words the strength of Hara's desire to find a new source of pride for Japan when it will no longer be an economic superpower.

Hara points to industrial designer Yanagi Sōri's iconic stainless steel kettle,[14] as one example of contemporary design that manifests this Japanese aesthetic. He has praise for this age when a quiet design like this can receive such wide support: "the minds of we who pursued 'newness' with such fevered eyes have returned a little to normal, and we once again have the leeway to look squarely around us at our everyday surroundings."[15] In other words—if I may borrow Hiroi's terminology once again—that is

Yanagi Sōri's iconic stainless steel kettle

a shift from a Western-oriented era emphasizing the temporal axis to an age when the spatial axis is coming back into ascendance.

No doubt many background factors have contributed to the emergence of a theory of design like Hara Kenya's in today's Japan Over the short term, however, the March 11 Tohoku earthquake and tsunami must surely have played a part. Those who felt the emptiness of material possessions as they watched "My Homes" and "My Cars" swept away on the tsunami waters must have felt the desire for a simpler life—a life not of buying or making things they did not really need, but of treasuring things they had long used.

In such times, the purpose of design should not be to excite people's lust for things they don't really need. Instead, suggests Hara, it should be to bring out "ethical aspects shared by society as a whole."

The challenge for design today, he suggests, is to ask "not how to create alluring things, but rather how to rebuild a way of life where people can savor things in an alluring way."[16] His approach goes far beyond a simple theory of designing the physical to what could be called a philosophy of social design, and has much in common with the ideas of Yamazaki Ryō in his interview later in this book. What we need today is to design not things, but the connections between human beings.

Regional Pride Tying People Together

Hara's observations intersect as well with my own critique of the destruction of Japan's traditional-style shopping districts by the suburban invasion of giant box stores, articulated in what I call my *"fasuto fūdo-ron."*[17] My book *Fasuto fūdo-ka suru Nihon* (The "Fast-*fūdo*-ification of Japan), published in 2004, has sold well and been read all over Japan. Since its publication I have found myself invited to lecture on the subject of preserving and restoring local communities from snowy Hokkaido in the north to semi-tropical Okinawa in the south.

Now, I am still a marketer by trade, and in my talks I always point out that it is only natural for consumers to choose to shop at stores where they can find the same product for less and where it is more pleasant to shop. I tell my audiences that they can never win back consumers' sympathies just by haranguing them about how they should buy at the old mom-and-pop stores.

What I tell them instead is that the bigger issue is that when old shopping streets turn into "shutter streets," with all the stores sitting empty and their metal shutters locked down tight, the community loses not just sales but its very history. I ask if their shopping district simply sells products. Of course not. It built up a town over hundreds of years. It raised people. To do that it held festivals, created firefighting brigades, worked hard in every way. The shopping district played a huge role in the history of this town, didn't it? Is it really all right for these streets to be lost? If they are, then the history of your town will go with them.

That is the gist of my message, and when I deliver it the shop owners who up until that point had only been talking in the short term, about how angry they were seeing their customers snatched away by the megastores, suddenly catch fire with pride. "That's right!" they say. "This isn't just about short-term profitability. Our ancestors built this town over generations. They created us!" That is the new consciousness that takes hold within them.

Once people start seeing the problem from that perspective, it becomes possible to consider the challenges facing the community's shopping district from multiple angles. And when you do that, it becomes clear that the issue is not just about sales. Attention turns to the latent functions of the shopping streets, to the town's history, to its culture. The spark to revitalize and rebuild their community begins spreading through the population, from the educators and cultural figures who live there to parents and local activists. In short, new connections are forged among a diverse host of people, all centering on their shared sense of crisis that the present situation cannot be allowed to continue, that something must be done to save their community. (For more on this process, see my interview with Yamazaki Ryō in the appendix.)

You will not be able to find any local shopping district which has regained the full vitality of its golden days once it has been reduced to a "shutter street." Even if a community succeeds in driving out a suburban shopping center, it is highly unlikely that it will be able to restore all the energy of its most flourishing years in a country where the population is currently shrinking.

However, the correct question to ask is not whether or not a shopping district or a town can be revived as a place for commerce. The real goal of revitalization efforts is going to become the creation of towns and districts with multiple functions, streets for community life.

Of course towns are places for doing business and for people to reside. But they must also be appreciated anew as centers for welfare, eldercare, education, childrearing and culture. This will require new, more flexible approaches to town planning, replacing the previous "modernist" urban planning model built around business, commercial, and residential districts. And above all, fostering attachment, memories, and pride in local communities will be increasingly important. (See also my interviews with performer and self-described "everyday life editor" Asada Wataru, the architect and University of Tokyo assistant professor Naruse Yuri, and the architect Nishimura Hiroshi in the appendix.)

Decentralization and New Connections

As we have seen, fourth-stage consumer society is, by virtue of being Japan-oriented, also locally oriented, and that local orientation in itself makes it anti-centralization and pro-decentralization. Even as globalization blankets the world with uniform products—and indeed because that is happening—fourth-stage consumer society values the distinctive products of different regions and localities.

By extension, the arrival of fourth-stage consumer society in Japan also signals the demise of the nation's centralized mass media. The media that really demonstrated its power during the March 11 disaster and the Fukushima nuclear power plant catastrophe were the so-called social media like Twitter and Facebook. Useful information was flowing over these networks almost as soon as the earthquake struck (of course, there was misinformation as well). The information circulating over these networks helped survivors and brought individuals back together again.

In comparison, the numerous press conferences held by the government, the Nuclear and Industrial Safety Agency, and the Tokyo Electric Power Company (Tepco) and transmitted by big media were as unbelievable as the announcements from Imperial Headquarters during World War II and only made us angrier. Japan's mass media will have to work hard to restore the trust it lost during the March 11 crisis.

By its very nature, communication via the mass media is one-way. Information flows in only one direction, from the information provider to the information recipient. The greater bandwidth of terrestrial digital broadcasting makes some interactivity possible, but so far no one has demonstrated an effective way to use it.

In contrast, social media are interactive from the start. There is no distinction between sender and receiver. Multiple independent actors are constantly exchanging information. Of course there is some garbage in the mix, but the amount of useful information is boundless. It is obvious that the media of fourth-stage consumerism will not be the traditional mass media, but new media where the individual is the actor, and can connect interactively with other individuals.

The rise of social media will also impact urban structure and national land use policy. Instead of gathering in giant downtown shopping districts full of large commercial establishments, people will follow their own individual interests, dispersing and regrouping at the stores and event spaces that most match their own interests, no matter how large or small.

This new urban landscape will not be the urban structure of the past, with the urban functions concentrated in the city center transmitting goods and information outward in concentric circles. Rather, it will become possible to bring together at least a certain number of people virtually anywhere you wish, be it in the outer suburbs or the inner suburbs, or even little pockets in the urban core.

This is already happening. In recent years we have seen phenomenon like the street demonstrations against nuclear power, poverty, and other issues popping up in Tokyo's counterculture Kōenji district being broadcast over YouTube and watched by people all over the world. It may not be the Arab Spring, but it is clear that Japan's centralized media can no longer control the flow of information even if it tries.

In another example, community designer Yamazaki Ryō, mentioned above, has already moved a portion of his company's operations to the mountains of Japan's rugged Mie Prefecture. Using the Internet, he can work from there without a hitch. Even if you live on a remote island, nowadays you can shop and buy things online little differently than you would in the big city, just so long as you have an Internet connection. The urban lifestyle of living and working in concentrated cities is set to undergo a radical transformation in fourth-stage consumer society.

Japan has spent years building little-used freeways and airports out in its hinterlands. Now is the time to use that accumulated stock of public works projects to the full. Someday it may be commonplace to have a work life where you live on an island in the Japan Sea and come into Tokyo once a month for your job. And indeed, that is how it should be.

Chapter Eleven

The Ultimate Consumer Society

What Then Is Consumption?

Having delineated the characteristics of fourth-stage consumer society, let me return once again to the question of what exactly consumption is, and where consumer society will go from here.

When you look up "consume," or *shōhi* in Japanese, in an English-Japanese dictionary, you find a list of words like *tsukai-tsukusu* (use up), *yaki-tsukusu* (burn up), *tabe-tsukusu* (eat up), and *nomi-tsukusu* (drink up). The "con-" in the English "consume" means "all," and "-sume" means "to take or to clear away." And indeed in societies with only limited material goods the primary form of consumption was in fact eating. They ate up what they produced, used up what they produced down to the last bite.

However, over time societies became more affluent. They produced more and more consumer durables, until today even the man on the street is likely to own goods like high-end wristwatches that do not get "used up," that essentially last forever. So what then is "consumption" in a society that no longer "uses up," that no longer "eats up" everything?

Before answering that question, let us return to our dictionaries. It turns out that there is another English word very similar to "consume": the word "consummate." The "con-" in "consummate" means "all." The "-sum-" is the same as the "sum" meaning "the sum of, or to total up" and therefore also implies "all." "Consummate" therefore means "complete." The adjectival form can mean variously "complete, versed, virtuoso, practiced." And the noun form is "consummation."

In French, *consommation* is the equivalent of "consumption" in English and *shōhi* in Japanese. But interestingly enough, *consommation* in the French also carries the meaning of "to complete" and "to achieve, accomplish." The French word that is the closest etymologically to the English "consumption" is actually not *consommation* but rather *consomption*, meaning "exhaustion, emaciation."

In short, the French *"consomption"* is the English "consumption" stripped of the consumption of goods and leaving only the "consumption of the flesh" as in tuberculosis and other wasting diseases. Meanwhile, the French *consommation* can be seen as the English "consumption," with the additional meaning of "consummation" added in.

I am certainly no linguist and so I have no idea how these things come to be. Yet as a result the French *consommation* contains two at first glance contradictory meanings: "to use up" and "to complete, to accomplish." Perhaps your cooking is complete when you have used up all the ingredients?

Consumption and the Consummatory

What is of even greater interest to our discussion is that a derivation of the English "consummate"—the word "consummatory"—is actually a key concept in sociology. In Japanese sociology texts it is usually translated as *jikojūsoku-teki*, or to back-translate again into English, "self-sufficient."

The antonym of "consummatory" is "instrumental," which is readily translated into Japanese as *dōgu-teki* or *shudan-teki*. "Consummatory," however, is a far greater challenge, as Mita Munesuke observes an entry in *Shakaigaku jiten* (Dictionary of Sociology):

> "Instrumental" can be translated into Japanese as *shudan-teki*, but "consummatory" is untranslatable. The [commonly used] *mokuteki-teki* (purposeful) is a mistranslation. *Sokujijūsoku-teki* (immediately fulfilling), for all its pedantic precision, does not adequately convey the meaning. A "consummatory" moment is that moment when, as in [Wordsworth's] "My heart leaps up when I behold/A rainbow in

the sky," your heart actually does leap at the sight of a rainbow. In other words, it is an act, a relationship, a state, a time that is like that instant of unbridled joy, like sexual ecstasy, like the thrill of high art, like religious bliss, that is not an instrument to any end beyond itself. That is what is meant by a "consummatory" act, relationship, state, or time. In contrast, paid labor, profit-making activities, studying for college entrance exams, organized political action—in other words, acts, relationships, states, or times that serve a purpose external to themselves—are "instrumental" acts, relationships, states, or times.[1]

Of course, Mita's "paid labor, profit-making activities, studying for college entrance exams, organized political action" could also conceivably be—depending on the person, on the time, on the circumstance—an "unbridled joy" that is not an instrument to any end beyond itself. In practice, however, such activities are meaningless, are incomplete, unless they do achieve some kind of result (salary, profit, university admission, election).

Consummatory acts are different. Consummatory acts are complete even if they do not yield salary, profit, university admission, election. They are complete so long as they are in themselves a source of happiness, pleasure, and joy.

And thus to my point. If, as seen above, the word "consumption" does encompass within it both the concepts of "using up" and of "achieving and accomplishing," as in the French word *consommation*, then what if I were to assert that the act of consumption encompasses them as well? That "consumption" is not just instrumental—not just buying and gulping down food to fill an empty stomach—but can also be Mita's "unbridled joy" without being an instrument to any end other than itself?

A landmark book that quite consciously makes this point is the 1984 *Yawarakai kojinshugi no tanjō* (The Birth of Soft Individualism)[2] by the playwright and intellectual Yamazaki Masakazu. It is a classic work that, while written in the very thick of Japan's third-stage consumer society, had already picked up on the signs of the next stage of consumerism, and set about giving it a theoretical framework. In it Yamazaki critiques Jean Baudrillard's *La Société de Consommation* as follows:

[Baudrillard's] notion of consumer society is little more than a society that enjoys "excessive affluence" and engages quantitatively in "over-consumption."[3] . . . [He] states that human beings have a fundamental instinct that stands in opposition to the "instinct for self-preservation," and that this is the desire to "consume all of their power," a drive that longs constantly for "ever more, ever faster, ever more often." It is Baudrillard's assertion that so long as modern society is dominated by this instinct, it will always run toward ceaseless overconsumption, and will inevitably give rise both to the flaunting of conspicuous luxury and to hatred and violence directed against it.[4]

Having thus laid out Baudrillard's views, Yamazaki counters with what is almost a "Columbus's Egg" of an argument in its obviousness:

If I were to be slightly cynical, "ever more, ever faster, ever more often" is actually the slogan of the doctrine of efficiency. It should rather be seen as the underlying principle, not of a consumer society, but of a society that puts production ahead of all else.[5]

Is it possible, Yamazaki asks, that the real issue is not overconsumption, but rather that we are, as he puts it, "in fact exhausted by efficiency?"

Certainly in the end stages of industrialization human desire worked in an authoritarian direction, and people raced to flaunt how "ever more, ever faster" they could consume as a way of setting themselves above one another. That tendency still lingers in Japanese society today, and when a not insignificant number of people do try to get their hands on popular products "ever faster, ever cheaper," they are quite literally competing at "efficient" shopping. What we must not forget, however, is that this is a phenomenon occurring at one partic-ular stage in the history of one particular society. It does not necessar-ily indicate the eternal essence of human desire.[6]

Consumption as Self-fulfillment

Before following up on Yamazaki's thoughts on individualism and consumption, allow me to write a little more about myself. My first encounter with Yamazaki was an article he wrote for the *Asahi Shimbun* newspaper titled "Fukigen no taiken" (An Unpleasant Experience)[7] that I clipped in my sophomore year in high school. What left a much more lasting impression, however, was my high-school junior year Modern Japanese textbook. It included a passage from Yamazaki's work of literary criticism on the early twentieth-century novelist Mori Ōgai, Ōgai: Tatakau kachō (Ogai: The Combatant Head of the House). My instructor for Modern Japanese was also my student advisor, and perhaps a Yamazaki fan as well. He used photocopies of other passages from Ōgai in class that had not been included in the textbook. He also used another of Yamazaki's books, Gekiteki naru Nipponjin (The Dramatic Japanese). Listening to my teacher, I too became a Yamazaki fan. This all happened just before my college entrance exams.

Then came the exams. I went to Tokyo to prepare for them in early February, and the first thing I did was to visit the Kinokuniya bookstore in Shinjuku[8] to buy my own copies of both Ōgai: Tatakau kachō and Gekiteki naru Nipponjin and yet another Yamazaki title: Geijutsu gendairon (Modern Theory of Art). I had prepared myself well for the tests and I thought I might only make myself more nervous if I studied too much at the last minute, so instead I spent all my time reading these three volumes. I was particularly taken by Yamazaki's passage on the meaning of handwork in Geijutsu gendairon.

I took my tests at the end of February for the private universities I had applied to, and took just the English and mathematics first-round exams for the then-national Hitotsubashi University in early March. Then it was time for Hitotsubashi's second-round test. There was only one test question for Modern Japanese: read a passage from a text and write an essay on it.

The passage was from Yanagi Sōetsu's Teshigoto no Nippon (Handwork Japan)! Ah! I cried out in my heart. It must be the will of the gods! Perhaps I even did a little jig. I was absolutely confident my essay would get a perfect score for content. Later I read an article by novelist and critic Maruya Saiichi in Shūkan Asahi (Asahi Weekly) magazine where he said that any university that gave its applicants a test question like that one deserved respect. I was overjoyed. You can see why I sometimes think that if it had not been for Yamazaki Masakazu I might never have passed my entrance exams.

To return to point, Yamazaki is at heart a playwright and it is only natural that he would write about literature and the arts. However, when I re-read *Gekiteki naru Nipponjin* and *Geijustu gendairon* today I am struck by how many pages he devotes to advertising, consumption, and industrial design. If a playwright's greatest concern is the human being, our lives, and the ways we live them, it may be only natural to include advertising, consumption, and industrial design when talking about modern man.

"Soft Individualism"

The book where Yamazaki writes comprehensively about consumer society is *Yawarakai kojinshugi no tanjō* (The Birth of Soft Individualism). In retrospect, it is no exaggeration to say that prior to its publication in 1984 there had been no definitive treatise on consumer society in Japan, nor have there been any since. Before *Yawarakai kojinshugi no tanjō* there were only one-sided critiques of consumer society from the Left and marketing-oriented theories of consumption from the very advertising industry committed to promoting it. Baudrillard's *La Société de Consommation*, too, is a left-wing critique. As late as the mid-1980s about all you could find in print were works by left-leaning critics, completely out of step with the times and busy decrying Shibuya's Kōen-dōri as a capitalist controlled society.

It was in this environment that Yamazaki—as brilliant a philosopher and sociologist as he is a playwright—cast a critical eye on the modern ego since Descartes, which he labeled the "producing ego." Quoting from Max Weber, Emile Durkheim (*The Division of Labor in Society*), and Jean Baudrillard, building on David Riesman (*The Lonely Crowd*) and Daniel Bell (The *Cultural Contradictions of Capitalism*), and further deploying not just statistical data but very specific examples of advertisements and hit products as supporting evidence, Yamazaki argued the limits and possibilities of consumer society and pondered where we would be heading now that the overripe decade of the 1980s, the so-called "advanced consumer society," had burned itself out. Here is some of what he had to say:

The greatest misfortune a person can have . . . is not to have even his material wants met. But the second greatest misfortune is not that his desires are infinite, but rather that they can be satisfied so easily. . . . For a person stuffing down his food, the greatest sorrow is the reality that there is a limit to the capacity of his stomach, and that regardless of how delicious the meal may be he can eat no more once he has exceeded a certain amount. . . . Even as his wants are satisfied, the pleasure he takes from them wanes, until at last it transforms into pain.[9]
[This would echo what I was saying in chapter seven.]

As on the one hand the number of our objects of choice has increased, and as on the other the amount of free time available to us when we are supposed to be able to live according to our own choices has also increased, the life of modern man has truly become an endless series of opportunities for us to lose our way. . . .[10] When people ask themselves, "Isn't there anything interesting out there?" they are halfway to confessing that they have no idea what that "something" might be. They are beginning to realize that their existence is incomprehensible even to themselves.[11]
[Here Yamazaki foreshadows Itoi Shigesato's "I want something to want" advertising copy four years later in 1988.]

People are kept scurrying by the extremely ironic structure of our wants, i.e., that satisfying our material wants can only exist as a goal when it has not yet been accomplished, and vanishes the instant it has been achieved.[12]

How do people respond to this dilemma? According to Yamazaki, "materialistic consumption" is to try, even as you pursue the goal of consuming some "commodity" completely, to at the same time draw out the process of achieving that goal for as long as possible. By this, "the goal of 'consuming' is transformed into a way to enjoy the process of consumption." In short, he says, instead of "trying to consume the greatest amount of food possible in the shortest possible amount of time, people instead, quite conversely and in order to maximize their enjoyment, try to take the longest possible amount of time to consume the smallest amount of food."[3] Broadly speaking, concludes Yamazaki:

> . . . the way people behave when consuming is the polar opposite of the doctrine of efficiency. It is a behavior that is far more concerned with the process of achieving a goal than it is in the achievement of the goal itself. . . . In that sense, while its putative goal is the consumption and regeneration of "objects," consumption is actually a behavior the true purpose of which is the consumption of rich and fulfilling time.[4]

In short, Yamazaki predicted that the ultimate mature form of consumption would be the conversion of the "consumptive" into the "consummatory." He wrote hoping for both the limits and the maturation of consumer society, in other words, for consumer society to be "completed by being used up completely." He truly had prophesized the coming of the next, fourth stage of consumer society.

This was a theory of consumption that could only have come from a Kyoto native like Yamazaki. I have to admit that my own twenty-five-year-old self—busy stuffing my face with greasy McDonald's hamburgers and french fries while burning the midnight oil—could not yet appreciate the sophisticated flavor of Yamazaki's Kyoto cooking. But reading *Yawarakai kojinshugi no tanjō* again today I find that his predictions are right on target. It took a playwright who had never stopped thinking about what it means to be human to so accurately read the future of desire in a consumer society. No sociologist of any stripe has presented a theory of consumerism superior to this.

Nonetheless, it has probably only been these last few years that we have been able to feel at a gut level how Yamazaki's predictions are coming true. The swelling of Japan's economic bubble not long after the publication of *Yawarakai kojinshugi no tanjō* served to prolong that period when, as Yamazaki had put it, "human desire worked in an authoritarian direction." We Japanese continued to race to "flaunt how 'ever more, ever faster'" we could consume as a way of setting ourselves "above one another." It delayed until now the coming of the next, new age of consumption.

And yet, it may be precisely because we did live through the Bubble Years that we have finally become so tired of wasteful consumption, and have at last begun to search for new meaning in life.

I might also add that the contrast that Yamazaki draws between self-sufficiency and the doctrine of efficiency strikes me as having parallels with the contrast Komatsu Sakyō drew (cited in chapter four) between the value of life as defined by its "potential for further evolution" and its intrinsic value deriving from "life as it is." Today we are not simply seeking "efficiency" or "evolution." We are beginning to demand that the act of living be considered sufficient unto itself.

From Things to People

Looking back through this lens, it is clear that the consumption of material goods remained central to consumer society in Japan up through the era of third-stage consumerism. However, there can be no doubt that this is going to change with the rise of fourth-stage consumerism. The direction of change will be from the simple consumption of material goods to the consumption of highly developed human services. Moreover, those services will involve more than simply paying money to a service provider and unilaterally receiving service in return. In the future people will be seeking more and more to use consumption as a means to creating human relationships.

What does this mean in concrete terms? For one, it does not mean growth in service consumption defined simply as consuming a service "product." Rather, people will want the consumption of services to be, not "consumptive," but "consummatory" for both the customer and service provider alike. It will not simply be the type of service provided that matters—that part of it is a given. Instead what will have ever greater weight will be who you receive the service from, and what kind of ongoing human relationship you can have with that provider.

Once this shift takes place, it will of course also apply to the buying and selling of physical commodities. Who is doing the selling and how they do it will be key: consumers are going to find increasing meaning in interacting with people who have a deep knowledge of and real love for the products they sell, rather than some perfunctory, by-the-manual sales approach.

Furthermore, given fourth-generation consumer society's emphasis on ecology, consumers will also find particular value in products with a long life. By long life, I mean products that continue to be produced for years without going through incessant model changes. For that to happen, products will have to add truly necessary value to our lives, and have excellent functionality and performance. The emphasis will no longer be on products or stores that sell like gangbusters for a short period of time, but on products and outlets that can continue to sell year after year.

Once this happens, the people who make the goods, the people who choose them, and the people who create the stores will have to maintain a laser-like focus. They will need a discerning eye to pick out the items with substance that can sell for the long haul. It is the stores staffed with such individuals that customers will trust. And when they trust a store, they will come back to it, will want to buy the things it offers, and the store, too, will be able to remain in business for years to come.

In this way, in fourth-stage consumer society it will become extremely important to carefully tend the relationships between stores and the people they serve. The work done by the designer Nagaoka Kenmei—who I will introduce in more detail in the next section—and others like him are concrete examples of what this is going to require.

As fourth-stage consumer society takes shape, consumer attitudes will change. The brand worship that made a fetish of the product itself in third-stage consumer society will wane. Goods and commodities will be seen simply as tools to an end, and the end that will matter most of all will be the human connections that can be created using those tools. In the next section, we will explore this new landscape in more detail.

PART FOUR

THE FUTURE OF
CONSUMER SOCIETY

What we can envision for the future is a modern civilization stripped of the concept of progress, what might be termed an enlightened society no longer predicated upon future aspirations. Of course progress in the sense of mending rips and tears in the fabric of civilization will likely continue forever. Yet we can anticipate the coming of a civilization where people will no longer see progress as a predicate for their present-day lives, and where they can live, be there progress or not, richly and fully in the present.

> Yamazaki Masakazu, *Sekai bunmeishi no kokoromi*
> (A History of World Civilization)

In the previous sections, I have detailed the progression from first-stage consumer society through to today's fourth-stage consumer society. We have seen how in fourth-stage consumer society—the stage arrived at by a fully mature consumer society—there is a lessening of the impulse to seek satisfaction in material possessions and a rising tendency to seek fulfillment through connections with others, with physical goods coming to be perceived as one means toward that end.

In this fourth and final section, I would like to think more concretely about the future of fourth-stage consumer society. Along with looking at a number of real-world examples of what is taking place today, we will consider what the corporate sector can do in the context of this shift from material possessions to people.

Chapter Twelve

The Search for New Ways of Living

A Generational Analysis of Changes in Consumer Society

F irst, however, I would like to briefly consider once again the progression from first-stage to fourth-stage consumer society, this time
from a generational perspective.

Japan's first-stage consumer society beginning in 1912 coincided
with the birth of the Taishō generation. This is the generation that
went off to fight in China and the Pacific. At this time Japan's annual
birthrate was running at two million or more, such that between 1900
and 1940 the nation's total population grew by 64 percent.

Japan's second-stage consumer society began in 1945 with the birth
of the *dankai sedai*, the first baby-boom generation. This is the generation born immediately after Japan's defeat in war, the offspring of the
men who came back from the war. In other words, they are the generation of the children of Taishō. And this second-stage consumer society saw a second baby boom, with the country's population expanding
another 55 percent between 1947 and 1975.

Then 1975 marked the arrival of Japan's third-stage consumer
society with the birth of the *dankai*-junior generation. Since this
term is generally used to indicate the second baby-boom generation
born between 1971 and 1974, it is widely assumed that it was mostly
composed of the children of the preceding *dankai*-generation baby

boomers. In fact, however—and as readers familiar with my own generational theory[1] will already know—the generation that contains the most children of the *dankai* generation, particularly their male offspring, is actually the generation born in the second half of the 1970s after the second baby boom had ended. For this reason it has become more common in recent years to refer to all children born in the 1970s as *dankai* juniors, and that is the practice that I will follow here. Since Japan's birthrate began to decline over the course of its third-stage consumer society, there was only a minor further increase in the nation's population overall.

The fourth-stage consumer society that began in 2005 should by all rights have started with the grandchildren of the *dankai* generation. However, thanks to trends toward later marriages and smaller families, the *dankai* generation's grandchildren were somewhat late off the mark. Furthermore, there have been no more surges in the birthrate that could properly be termed a baby boom. Japan's total population has begun to contract, and it is predicted that by 2035 it will have fallen to approximately 112 million from some 128 million at the start of fourth-stage consumer society in 2005.

Looking back over this history, it is clear that the people responsible for the growth of Japan's second-stage consumer society were the generations born in the Taishō (1912–26) and early Shōwa (1926–89) periods. It is incontrovertible that they propelled Japan's period of high economic growth. The postwar *dankai* generation, in turn, contributed as consumers to the development of second-stage consumer society, particularly from their childhood years through young adulthood.

The generations that shouldered the rise of Japan's third-stage consumer society were the *dankai* generation and the New People *shin-jinrui* generation born in the latter half of second-stage consumer society. However, the attitudes of the *dankai* generation and the New People generation were very different indeed.

The *dankai* generation married, had children, created their "New Families," bought their "My Homes" and "My Cars," and filled their houses to the brim with material possessions. In other words, they supported Japan's economy in full accordance with the principles of second-stage consumerism.

The New People generation which emerged in the late 1980s, however, was already engaging in flagrant consumption worthy of today's so-called "single aristocrats" (*dokushin kizoku*; i.e., unmarried new adults, often still living with their parents, with lots of spending money) when they were still just kids. In this way they contributed to the diversification, individuation, and "luxurification" of consumption. In a sense we could almost say that it was the New People generation that breathed life into third-stage consumerism. But of course, even among the *dankai* generation there was a more advanced strata of consumers who contributed in their own way to the new modes of consumption seen in third-stage consumer society.

Having thus viewed the progression from first-stage to fourth-stage consumer society through the prism of generational change, it is not surprising to find that the generation of the *dankai* juniors is the generation destined to bear the burden of fourth-stage consumer society. This fourth stage began when the *dankai* juniors were around thirty years old and will end when they are around sixty. (In fact, Yamazaki Ryō, who I introduced earlier, and many of the other individuals who I will be presenting here were all born in the 1970s, and thus fall within the *dankai*-junior generation as broadly defined.)

Arriving as they did during Japan's third-stage consumer society, the *dankai* juniors were born into affluence and raised in middle-class households. They grew up seeing their parents buying things willy-nilly and filling their "My Homes" with material possessions. They themselves were bought things from early childhood, owned brand-name goods in middle and high school, and went on overseas vacations with their families.

Yet it was exactly because of these experiences that a host of new trends arose from within their generation. Moving from quantity to quality, valuing artisanal handwork over mass-produced products, seeking not the satisfaction of material possessions but the fulfillment of connections with other people and of the heart, preferring Japanese to Western, aspiring to rural living over big city life, all these trends have gained strength with this generation. It is the changing value system of the *dankai*-junior generation that has created the defining characteristics of fourth-stage consumer society.

Preparing for Fifth-stage Consumer Society

By this point some readers must be asking whether a fifth-stage consumer society is going to follow today's fourth. According to my schematization, they may say, this next stage should start around 2035 and run to about 2064. What will it be like? Will it be based on sharing, like fourth-stage consumer society, or will it be something completely different?

To state my conclusion first, that is all beyond my ability to forecast with any certainty. However, one thing is certain: by the time fifth-stage consumer society does arrive, the *dankai*-junior generation will be around sixty years of age, and when that fifth stage ends they will be entering their nineties (fig. 12-1). Regardless of what fifth-stage consumer society does turn out to be like, it will be the society in which the *dankai* juniors grow old and start passing away.

That being the case, the *dankai*-junior generation should, during today's fourth-stage consumer society, be working to shape the society of their own old age. Yet it seems their preparations will not be enough if they rely solely on personal savings. Even if the government continues to hike Japan's consumption tax and take other measures to meet projected financial shortfalls, it is very likely that the country's social safety net will contract in both quality and scale.

Once that happens, the *dankai* juniors will need an alternative safety net not dependent on government, and financial guarantees alone will not be enough to provide it. It will be necessary to create societal mechanisms that enable people to live securely, safely, and happily—in short, to completely change the way we live. The resulting new society cannot be based on old twentieth-century models predicated on rising populations and economic growth. It will need to be a new model that assumes shrinking populations and economic contraction. In which case I suspect that if this endeavor is to turn out well, fifth-stage consumer society will have to be a sharing society, too.

I do have one small caveat. By the year 2035, the housing stock that the *dankai* juniors will have inherited from their parents will be fifty to sixty years old. The juniors themselves will be coming up on sixty-five. Consequently we can expect an explosion in the number of homes that need rebuilding, and this should revive demand for housing

1920 (First-stage consumer society)

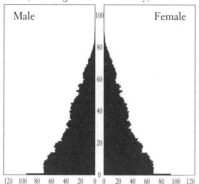

1950 (Second-stage consumer society)

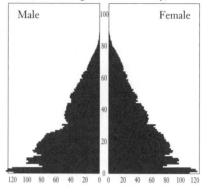

1980 (Third-stage consumer society)

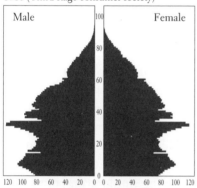

2010 (Fourth-stage consumer society)

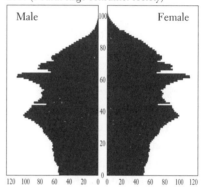

2040 (Fifth-stage consumer society)

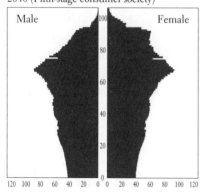

Vertical axis: years old

Horizontal axis: population (10,000)

FIGURE 12-1 Demographic Changes, Historic and Projected

Based on population pyramid data, National Institute of Population and Social Security Research.

construction and for relocating to new residences. While many people will try to get by with simply renovating their current properties, we can nonetheless expect some uptick in various forms of demand around that time. How best to respond to such needs could prove a key theme of fifth-stage consumer society.

Three Elderly Supporting One Youth

Life in Japan's fourth-stage consumer society is going to require many changes in old assumptions. To take but one example, by the year 2035 there will be 10.46 million Japanese in their twenties, while the population aged sixty-five to eighty-nine will have climbed to 32.93 million. That is more than three seniors for each young person. Many people are certain that it will be impossible for Japan's young to support the nation's elderly.

Yet what if we flipped the equation? What if we phrased it as there being three seniors available to support one young person?

Clearly each young person will be effectively supporting three elderly people through their income and contributions to the nation's social safety net. But conversely, three elderly people could do things to support one young person in his or her life. If the different generations helped each other, the burden on the young would even out to zero. Cannot we start viewing the problem this way instead?

We will look at some concrete examples a little further on. For now, however, let us simply suppose that there is a single young man. He does not have much income, yet he has to live in the city for his job. His expensive urban rent is a terrible burden. If he pays all that money just for a place to live, he may not be able to afford to get married, much less have children.

Yet even as he struggles to get by, there are elderly people living alone who have property and homes close to the city center. In fact, we are not even close to the year 2035 yet and there are already many affluent but solitary seniors with homes and property in comfortable districts of Tokyo like Setagaya Ward and Suginami Ward.

Let us now suppose that one of these seniors—let us make him an elderly man—offers the young man an empty room in his house for free. The old lady next door offers to cook the youth's meals. After all, she finds cooking for another person more satisfying than cooking for herself alone. The other neighbor is an old gentleman who used to work at a major corporation. He mobilizes his professional network to help the young person get a better job, and further introduces him to people who will be helpful to him in his new position. If all this helps the young man succeed, the elderly trio will all feel happy.

In exchange, our young man can go shopping for his elderly supporters. He can run errands and help them out in many other ways. He can teach them how to use computers, for instance, or how to Tweet. In this way, all four can overcome the various inconveniences in their lives, find more reasons to enjoy living, even find a job, while using hardly any money at all. By sharing the things they can do and the things they have, however modest those may be, they can fill in the gaps in each other's lives so they can all conversely be more self-reliant together than they were alone.

The image most people have of "sharing" is of large undertakings, like a park that everyone owns and uses together. Certainly this is one mode of sharing, but there is another dimension to sharing as well—laying out all the things that you can do, all the possessions you own but no longer need yourself, and letting people who are in need make use of them. Everyone has more of something than they actually need, and everyone has the leeway to do at least a little more than they are actually doing already. On the other hand, everyone has things that they are short of, or things that they would appreciate having someone do for them. If everyone puts their cards on the table, the surplus possessions can circulate to those without, while those who are able to do more can reach out to those who could use a helping hand. Once all these many people are filling in the gaps in each other's lives, what will emerge will be human connection.

When I discuss these ideas with *dankai* juniors who already have a strong predilection for sharing, they often tell me that they feel a huge gap between themselves and their own parents and others of the generations from Japan's second- and third-stage consumer societies. They say that their parents' generation is totally invested in private possession, and cannot shed the habit of buying bigger and bigger automobiles and televisions. When they tell them that they live in a "share house," their parents just shake their heads and ask why anyone would want to live that way. I am always being asked by this new generation how they can get their own parents to understand the concept of sharing.

The answer I offer is that their parents and others of their generation will probably never truly feel a need to share so long as they are still healthy in body, their spouses are well, and they are comfortable economically. But in the not too distant future, I continue, they will begin to fall ill. Their spouses will start to pass away, their financial cushions will shrink, and they will begin to feel something lacking inside. When that time comes, I tell their children, I expect that even these parents of theirs will realize how important it is to have a circle of friends and acquaintances outside the family who can help fill that emptiness inside and keep them from feeling bitter and alone.

Experiments in Fourth-stage Consumer Society

Armed with this reading of the future, what should companies, government, and citizens themselves be doing in today's fourth-stage consumer society? I believe the following basic rules and principles are obvious:

1. Convert to a sharing society across the board, in lifestyle, business, and community building.
2. Promote the creation of the public sphere by having people open up, little by little, their own private spheres.
3. Work to revive each region of Japan, so younger generations will enjoy living outside metropolitan Tokyo and other big cities.
4. Encourage the shift from money to people, from the economic principle to the life principle.

Looking around us with these precepts in mind, we find that there are experiments already underway steering us toward this vision of fourth-stage consumer society, and the fifth stage of consumer society beyond that.

(1) The Local Community Area Model
One such experiment is the local community area model advocated by internationally renowned architect Yamamoto Riken.

Yamamoto's model[2] derives from his perception that there was, as he puts it, a "fatal flaw" in treating the concept of "one housing unit = one family" that took hold in Japan after World War II, and especially over the course of second-stage consumer society, as the ideal model for housing across the entire country. He is working instead to design regional societies composed of citizens who are not "a conglomerate of family units."

The "one housing unit = one family" model was steeped in "notions of privacy and security," argues Yamamoto in his books on the concept,[3] resulting in housing that "attenuated relations with the outside." The national policy of promoting individual homeownership predicated on one-family housing units made them the core of housing supply in Japan. But now, concludes Yamamoto:

> [Home ownership] is destroying our daily lives. Most of our income is sucked up by our homes, while protecting that asset turns our consciousness ever more inward. Meanwhile, the family itself is breaking down from within.[4]

With this as his jumping-off point, Yamamoto defines his Local Community Area as meeting a set of specific parameters.[5] It is not necessarily premised upon the family. It takes as its core principle the interrelationships among all the people who live there. Rather than being disinterested in surrounding community areas, it is planned together with the surrounding environments. It is not simply a consumption unit, but is designed to be a viable small economic sphere within that area. Whereas conventional housing is simply an energy consumption unit, a Local Community Area produces energy.

In short, says Yamamoto, a Local Community Area does not treat housing as an instrument for economic growth, but gives top priority instead to the lives of the people who actually live there.

(2) The Urban Hunting and Gathering Life
Two other books I have found helpful when thinking about the new forms communities and human connections could take in the future are Sakaguchi Kyōhei's *Zero kara hajimeru toshigata shuryōsaishū seikatsu* (Starting from Zero: The Urban Hunting and Gathering Life)[6]

and *Sumibiraki: Ie kara hajimeru komyunitii* (Open Living: Community that Begins From the Home) by Asada Wataru.[7]

Sakaguchi was born in 1978. He became interested in houses at an early age and decided that he wanted to be an architect. He did go on to enroll in Waseda University's Department of Architecture, but one day he suddenly thought: "Why do we really have to buy or rent our homes?" In the end, his attention zeroed in on life lived on the streets. "If you ask me why," he explains in his book, "it was because I thought that they [the street people] were the only people in the city who were inventing home and work, in other words, their own lives with their own hands."[8] In the end, he began living on the street himself. Writes Sakaguchi:

> You who were living in an apartment before may not have even recognized the faces of the people living next door, but in this life starting today you no longer get to say things like that. . . . If you do not take full advantage of your meetings with other people, your life possibilities will shrink away almost to nothing. To you, all the people living here [on the street] are valuable sources of information.[9]

Where can you go to find people tossing out good food? Where can you find clothes that are still wearable? Where can you pick up things that can be traded in for cash? All this essential information for surviving on the street, says Sakaguchi, is transmitted by word of mouth among the street people themselves.

Is not this the true origin of community?

Street people, Sakaguchi found, even have their own *nariwai*, their own ways of making a living. First there is collecting beer and soda cans for recycling. Then there is *kikinzoku-hiroi*, collecting valuable metals. If you search carefully through those tossed out bags of garbage you might find a ring left inside an old purse. Some people make 200,000 to 300,000 yen ($2,000–3,000) a month this way. Then there is *denkaseihin-hiroi*, collecting old electrical appliances. Apparently there is even an electrical appliance shop somewhere on the floodplains along Tokyo's Tama River that stays in business just selling abandoned items. Sakaguchi's tales from the street are a revelation, but I will stop here lest I get totally off track.

Of course I am not suggesting that the homeless lifestyle Sakaguchi describes should be our prototype for fourth-stage consumer society. What I do want to say, however, is that we can find hints in the lives of these men and women living on the street for the community we have lost in our own lives, and the new kind of community we will need in the future.

The homeless are not trying to preserve and perpetuate a single group comprised of the same unchanging members. However, they do all know one another by sight, know who among them is particularly adept at what things. They swap goods and information among themselves, living without causing problems for anyone else, while working in the interests of them all.

In contrast, how are we all living ourselves? We live holed up inside layers of privacy and security, knowing neither the names nor even the faces of the people next door, increasingly isolated from everyone except the people in our own companies and organizations. Certainly we can find in this lifestyle the freedom of anonymity. But at the same time, we have ourselves thrown away the chance to use the things and information we have to create ties with other people.

This tendency, in turn, is accelerated by our blind belief in private ownership, that we should buy things and use them only for ourselves. If we find ourselves running short of something, we go out and buy more. Yet if we were to change the way we think—if we first tried to make what we needed by ourselves or, if that were beyond our ability, to find somebody else who could make it for us, or, failing that, borrow it from someone else who already has it—then we would naturally and organically be building ties with other people.

(3) "Sumibiraki"

This is one of the lessons taught by Asada Wataru. Born in 1979 and about the same age as Sakaguchi, Asada published his own provocative book *Sumibiraki* (Open Living) in 2012.

What Asada means by *sumibiraki* is for people to quite literally open, to "liberate," to jointly use with other people, the home where they live. For example, he tells us about a garden designer who has built a garden café on the roof of her apartment in downtown Osaka. A picture book library in one room of an Osaka home where local children can gather. A "university" in Osaka using a tiny, two-tatami mat room in a private house for group study. A Tokyo art studio and "share house" created from a former karaoke studio.[10] His examples go on and on. As Asada himself puts it:

> By opening your home just a crack a small community is born, and your own work and pastimes come, surely and naturally, to be shared by other people. Of course this community is not bound together by money, or blood, or company and workplace. Instead, a "third tie" has been knotted that knits all together organically.[11]

I include an excerpt from a dialog I had with Asada on page 253.

Yamamoto Riken, Sakaguchi Kyōhei, and Asada Wataru all offer an antithesis to the nuclear family model that expanded so dramatically during Japan's second-stage consumer society, to homes that are simply boxes to contain those nuclear families, and to the value system locked up inside the privacy of all those homes. Their work, at the same time, marks a clear parting of the ways with the value system that prevailed up through third-stage consumer society, a value system that could only think of where we live—of life itself—in terms of money.

It is, if I were to flip it around, a message—like we heard from Yamazaki Ryō on page 249 when he said that if you help out a farm-wife living in the country you will get a mountain of *daikon* radishes in return—that if we live lives organized around connections with others we can get by just fine even without a lot of money.

Over the course of Japan's second- and third-stage consumer societies we built ourselves a world where it is all too hard to live without money. We could say that it is our soul-searching about what we have done that sounds the keynote of fourth-stage consumer society.

From "Share House" to "Share Town"

In this way, as more and more people open parts of their homes little by little to the outside world, the towns where they live will also become "sharing" communities, a state I call a "share town." And as more and more share towns emerge, I expect a more sharing society to inevitably take hold across Japan as well.

In short, instead of opening a house to select individuals in a shared living arrangement, we are talking about opening it to the community as a whole. People with an empty room, an unused chamber for the tea ceremony, a garden or other space that they feel comfortable sharing with others would make that available to anybody. When that most private of all places—the home—is opened to all, albeit only one small part of it, then private space has been transformed into public place.

There are already movements afoot to create more "share towns" both in Japan and abroad. One example is the Open Garden campaign in Nagano Prefecture's Obusemachi, which I discuss in detail in my book *Kore kara no Nihon no tame ni "shea" no hanashi o shiyō* (Let Us Talk About "Sharing" for the Good of the Future Japan).[12] By opening their gardens to others, including tourists, the citizens of Obusemachi have converted what were once private spaces into a public tourism resource, and by doing so are helping revitalize their entire community.

On the other side of the world, there is now an annual London Open House Weekend organized by the nonprofit organization London Open House. Each year at the end of September more than eight hundred buildings across the city are opened to the public so anyone can tour them free of charge. It does not matter what era, purpose, or type of building it is, nor whether or not it happens to be a piece of distinguished architecture.

One of my own pastimes is to go view homes designed by leading Japanese architects like Maekawa Kunio and Yoshimura Junzō. You can feel an architect's philosophy and personality from his or her work, and I find the experience profoundly interesting. However, there is no reason to limit this to homes designed by the giants. There are many residences dating back to before World War II in places like Tokyo's Setagaya and Suginami wards that I would love to see the interiors of. Having occasional open houses when you could view the interiors of homes of architectural or historical significance would not just be meaningful to specialists and students of architecture. It would generate community pride among all the surrounding residents.

But why stop at just preserving and viewing architecture? These assets could also be used in more proactive ways. For instance, a pre-war residence in Tokyo's Suginami Ward that has been designated a Registered Tangible Cultural Property can now be reserved for dinners, study groups, *haiku* gatherings, and other events. How enjoyable it would be to see more examples like this all across Japan.

Likewise, Tokyo's Setagaya Ward is home to Setagaya Trust and Community Design, an incorporated foundation implementing a wide range of sharing-based activities aimed at creating a "local symbiosis community." One of the foundation's pamphlets[13] is packed with examples of people opening their own gardens, as the people of Obusema-chi did, so others can enjoy them, of turning *yashikirin*, the lush groves of trees that grow up around old homes, into places of relaxation for all members of the community, of opening unoccupied houses to child-care circles, or converting garages into activity spaces for the elderly. In one instance, a homeowner has converted his private library with its collection of thirty thousand books into the community salon libro niwas. In another, a classic Western-style house from late in the Taishō period (1912–26) has been donated to create Dokusho Kukan Mikamo, a privately operated library and reading room.

All of these different undertakings are isolated examples, yet connect enough of them and you have a line, and connect enough lines and you have a web encompassing an entire community. This is not some kind of official public space imposed by bureaucrats and city hall. It is a public sphere born of many individual citizens each opening, little by little, their own private spheres to all.

This is the way a real new public commons begins. There was much talk of a "New Public Commons" during the Democratic Party of Japan's short-lived administration (September 2009 to December 2012), and the phrase has gained some currency since. However, it was never clear how the DPJ's own policies had anything to do with actually creating a commons, and I doubt that many Japanese to this day understand what the phrase was supposed to mean.

In fact, it is these kinds of local-level initiatives that I have been describing here that are what a "new public commons" is all about.

And while we owe it to a terrible human tragedy, I believe the Japanese people as a whole have learned, at a very personal level, the true meaning of a public commons from the 2011 Tohoku earthquake and tsunami and its drawn-out aftermath. Following that disaster, huge numbers of average citizens, volunteers, and many others worked hard to help the communities affected by the disaster, many of them traveling to devastated communities at their own expense to assist. There were countless examples of relief efforts that relied not in the slightest on the power of government.[14] Of the many projects that have been implemented since that disaster, I introduce just one—the Community Living Space Project in Rikuzentakata in tsunami-ravaged Rikuzentakata City—on page 259 of this book.

Consumption in Pursuit of the Meaning of Life

When we look at these kinds of positive examples, and at the work of individuals like Yamazaki Ryō and Nishimura Hiroshi (who you will be meeting shortly), one cannot help but feel that the consumption patterns of second- and third-stage consumerism in Japan, that cycle of creating buildings, spaces, and objects and destroying them once again, really was more about wasting than consuming. Young Japanese who have been taught about the environment in school since elementary school are particularly sensitive to this kind of waste. They no longer have any interest in wasteful consumption. Indeed, they find it criminal.

As I wrote in the previous chapter, the French word *consommation* contains within it both the meaning "to use up" and the meaning "to complete." Throwaway consumption, consumption that uses more than is actually needed, is waste. And a kind of consumption that ultimately leaves you fatigued and worn out is simply exhaustion.

If we recall that "consume" can also refer to physical strength, and even to time, it all becomes clear. We are exhausted when we use too much of our physical energy, until we no longer have any reserves left. When we speak of a "war of attrition," of consuming all of the opposing force's resources, we are talking about wasting resources and time until we are completely worn out, and all in a fruitless cause. When we waste time, we mean that we did not achieve as much as we should have, did not enjoy ourselves as much as we should have, given the amount of time we put into it. In short, wastefulness and exhaustion are not things that anyone would desire.

Yet at the same time, we also cannot have a good time, a fulfilling time, without "consuming" and "using up" some time. If we do not consume an appropriate amount of our physical strength in exercise, we cannot sustain, much less improve, our health. So in that sense, we can also say that the kind of "consumption" we do desire, that we actively want, is consumption that helps us to perfect ourselves, to restore ourselves, to have a fulfilling time in our lives.

When I look at the work of the people who are building a fourth-stage consumer society in Japan, my strong impression is that what they are seeking is the diametrical opposite of a wasteful and exhausting consumption. The consumption they seek is measured and appropriate. It is not done on a whim. These trailblazers are just as attentive to the old and the already owned as they are to the new. They do not throw away things that are still usable; they make skillful use of what they already have. They have broken free of the old value system of the temporal axis, the value system that declared that what is new will always be better than what came before.

That value system always harbors within it an implicit nihilism. If the new is always superior to the old, then you can never be truly satisfied, can never achieve perfect satisfaction, no matter how long and hard you try. And indeed, as can be seen from the marketing term "planned obsolescence" (*chinpuka* in Japanese), one of the iron rules of consumer society for many years has been to persuade consumers that the things they already own are boring and obsolete in order to get them to buy something new.

As is well known, one of the first companies to do this in a deliberate and organized way was the American automobile maker General Motors. Back in the 1920s the reigning car, the Model T Ford, was available in only one model. As long as it kept running, there was no reason to replace it. Faced with this conundrum, General Motors adopted a strategy of implementing model changes every two years, and rolled out a product line that ran from mass-market vehicles to luxury models. In fact, it was this GM strategy that suddenly put such a spotlight on industrial design.

Consumers were brainwashed into thinking that the automobile that they had finally managed to buy and had liked so much was now already obsolete just two years later. In Japan the message was "Someday I'll own a Crown." They bought a Toyota Crown. But then a new Crown came out. And then a Lexus. And in this way they were driven to keep on buying newer and newer things. That underlying nihilism is the destiny of consumer society.

Max Weber once said that a peasant in the Middle Ages died "old and satiated with life" because "he stood in the organic cycle of life," but that civilized man dies "tired of life."[5] And why should this be? It is because in civilized society, in, as Weber put it, "the midst of the continuous enrichment of culture by ideas, knowledge, and problems," the new springs forth ever anew and the old is forgotten and passes away. Nothing is ever definitive, and as a result death itself is rendered a meaningless occurrence. It is because no matter how much you have lived, your life will still be incomplete and end inconclusively. Strip death of meaning, and you strip life of meaning. If our final and ultimate death has no meaning, there was no meaning to our life itself.

Of course Weber was not writing about consumer society in the twentieth century. Yet I think we can safely say that twentieth-century consumer society was exactly the kind of society he described.

If we were to take Weber's analysis and flip it, however, then it should conversely be possible to say that if you are trying to find meaning in life, and if you are trying to find meaning in death, then even if it is not possible to completely escape from today's consumer society so overflowing with new things and information, you would still do well to distance yourself from it. And to take that even farther, I think that most people would also want the act of consuming to be, not an "expending" of their time and even of their lives, but something that enriches both their time and their lives.

When you think about it, the greatest object of human consumption is life itself, and the ultimate form of consumption should be the consummation of that life. Do we waste this life and end it point-lessly? Do we wear ourselves out and pass away exhausted? Or do we have a rich and fulfilling time here and pass away content? This is the greatest choice that faces us as human beings, and I believe fourth-stage consumer society is serving to make us more conscious of that critical choice.

Chapter Thirteen

Creating the Sharing Society

What Should Companies Do?

As we have already seen, the maturation, so to speak, of people in fourth-stage consumer society is bringing a search for ways of living that give us not just materialistic satisfaction, but also a sense that there is greater meaning in life. This is especially true given the rapid aging of Japanese society as a whole.

People have moved beyond simply consuming, and have begun seeking connections with other people. They are finding that borrowing, fixing, and sharing the use and ownership of things they already have with others is a far more effective way to create those connections than the old mode of buying more and more possessions and hoarding them for oneself.

Further, as will be clear from the examples later in this book, once people begin to adopt the sharing lifestyle it will quickly come to extend far beyond just borrowing and lending. Ultimately they should, to some degree, be able to take on part of the responsibility for what has traditionally been considered the public good. Once that happens, the burden on government and public administration should lighten. In an age when constricted finances are driving a push for small government, it is better for Japan's citizens to evolve themselves.

However, there is one party that may feel left in the lurch by fourth-stage consumerism: Japan's corporate sector.

When there are fewer consumers invested in the old cycle of buying the new and throwing away the old, when more and more people are making better use of what they already have and are creating a new set of values, then products are not going to sell as they did before. When I give presentations about these coming social changes at major corporations, what I hear back from my audiences most often is concern that their products will no longer sell.

It is a real concern. The reality is that Japan's population is already contracting. As I have been pointing out for years, even if companies try to cling to the old business model of selling individual products to individual consumers, over the long term their sales can only decline, and their profits with them.[1]

It is my belief, however, that share-style business will in fact enable companies to cover the coming decline in sales. If people say that they no longer want to buy "My Homes," or that they no longer want to live in "one-room mansions" but do want to live in "share houses," then that is a new market right there. If more and more people have no intention of buying their own "My Car" but would consider using car-share services if they were available, then that, too, is a market. If people are concerned that the empty houses in their neighborhood are deflating the value of their own property, then that will create demand for asset management services that enhance the value of the entire neighborhood.

Share-style businesses should not be seen as a threat to corporate sales. Rather, they should be seen as a way of adjusting to the coming inevitable decline in sales and of generating new revenue to take its place. Admittedly, companies accustomed to the old "sell and run" style of business may feel that these share-model alternatives are either too much trouble or too time-consuming for the relatively lower profit margins they generate. Employees, too, may not like the idea of expending such time and effort.

For this reason, I expect that in this new age there will be many more opportunities for Japanese women to shine. It has been my impression over the years that men in general are more partial to the "crank it out and walk away" model of doing business. Women, again speaking broadly, are more likely to take good care of what is already there. Of course there is huge individual variation, and I am in no way saying that women are only caretakers.

What is totally unambiguous, however, is that in share-model businesses the kind of work that involves caring for and maintaining what has already been built, looking out after people, and discovering and responding to new needs through frequent communication with customers and clients—work that we have traditionally labeled as more feminine—will be increasingly important. In that sense we can expect more opportunities for individuals with those qualities to shine. Women and men alike with an affinity for caring work will be particularly suited to the emerging age of sharing in Japan.

The work of these new, share-oriented businesses will often be rooted in local communities, and if you are providing a locally based service it is better to live close to that community yourself. In this sense as well, these new businesses will be tailor-made for working mothers who would rather work close to home where they do not have to commute but can carry out their duties in between raising the kids and keeping up the home.

From "Pleasant" to "Joyful"

Another thing struck me several years ago when I was organizing my thoughts on sharing society. Simply put, it was the realization that what consumers are really seeking is not just something pleasant, but a joyful experience.

Let's, for example, contrast the following two sentences:

1. It was pleasant today because I ran into some of my college classmates downtown and we chatted over tea.
2. It was a joy today to run into some of my college classmates downtown and chat with them over tea.

In the first sentence, it was "pleasant" having a chat. But use "joy" instead, and see what happens? Now the "joy" is all about meeting friends. I personally believe that it is this subtle nuance that makes all the difference between third-stage and fourth-stage consumer society.

Other examples expressing joy are: "I was overjoyed when I was shopping at the local green grocers, and the shopkeeper told me, 'I'll give you a discount, young lady.'" And "I went into this shop and found something I'd been looking for for ages, and I was overjoyed when the shopkeeper told me all about its good points."

The point that I want to make is simply this: communicating with other people is itself a source of joy.

The value system that prevailed in Japan through the end of third-stage consumerism was entirely focused on things. Now, with the arrival of fourth-stage consumer society, the emphasis is squarely on people. What matters today is not what you consume, but who you bought it from, how you bought it, who you consume it with, and who you are able to meet because of it, and how you bought it from whom.

For corporate Japan, the challenge will be to come up with business models appropriate to this transformed consumer society in an era of population decline, with new innovative models that help build ties among people. Let me share some of my own ideas for strategies that I think can succeed in Japan's fourth-stage consumer society.

(1) *Housing and Real Estate: From "Sell and Run" to "Soft" Management Services*

As we have seen earlier, new housing starts in Japan are already less than half what they were at their peak and are clearly going to continue downward. If companies want to make money from selling in sheer quantity, they will need instead to cultivate markets abroad, in countries like India or China.

But what can be done in Japan itself? There is only one answer: stop focusing on selling housing, and instead offer management services for residential neighborhoods. If the image you have on hearing this is of something like today's apartment management services, you would be half right but also half wrong.

I have a good sense of what goes into apartment management from my own experience with buying a used condominium and serving as the director of our condominium's homeowners association. Yet it is surprising to note that in Japan it is still less than twenty years since people began getting serious about condominium management. Of course there had been building managers for many years, but usually they just sat in their offices and only got up now and then to clean up around the premises.

What really got people serious about condominium management was the passage of time. As buildings erected in the 1960s and '70s started passing the twenty-year mark, their walls began to peel and their plumbing to leak. As maintenance needs increased, real condominium management companies began popping up to repair, maintain, and manage the hardware side of condominium living. Complexes with good management were able to maintain their asset value. Back in the day Japanese condominium prices had continued to climb regardless of whether the buildings were kept up or not, but that came to an abrupt end with the collapse of the economic bubble in the 1990s. Once prices began to fall, owners finally began to think seriously about how best to preserve at least some of the value of their assets through proper building management.

Today we finally see this attention to managing the hardware side of condominiums taking hold. However, the situation is different in single-home residential districts, where it has traditionally been the homeowner's responsibility if the walls peel or the plumbing leaks. There has been no reason for anything to change at the neighborhood or subdivision level.

Now, however, Japan's population is shrinking. Fewer people will be buying houses, and prices in residential neighborhoods will sag. There will be more and more homes going unoccupied. Arsonists could target empty houses. Inevitably there will be more single elderly dying lonely deaths in homes where they were living alone. Then it will not matter how carefully you maintain and prettify your own property. The asset value of your entire neighborhood is going to fall.

I suspect that as time goes by, more and more residents will be willing to spend money on property management for their neighborhoods as a whole as a way of supporting the value of their own personal assets. Two decades after the condominium community, we will see a new era of property management for neighborhoods.

Managing a neighborhood on their own is more than most amateurs can handle, no matter how motivated. Owners will need the services of professional management firms with specialized knowledge and skills in preserving townscapes, cleaning, crime prevention, fire prevention, maintaining empty houses, and much more. And all this presents an enormous business opportunity.

However, I personally happen to think that it will not be the upkeep of social "hardware" like condominiums and houses that will be crucial in Japan's fourth-stage consumer society. Rather, the need will be for new business models for managing and operating the "software" of society.

One specific example might literally be services to promote and enhance smoother communication among all the residents of a neighborhood. The need is to keep single elderly people engaged with society so they do not wind up cut off and dying alone in their homes, to enable families with small children to feel secure about raising them in the neighborhood. There will be a growing need for professional management of the soft side of residential neighborhoods that can help build new connections and positive interactions among neighbors.

Let me introduce one example of this kind of resident-participation neighborhood that was planned and implemented on a commercial basis: the Village Homes subdivision in Davis, California, also famous as a model for sustainable communities.

Village Homes is a 28 hectare (70 acre) subdivision designed by Michael Corbett and his wife Judy that began accepting residents in 1975. Nine hectares (22 acres) of the subdivision are given over to fruit orchards, greenbelts, parks, and other commons. The 225 residences are mixed, ranging from 60-square-meter (646-square-foot) row houses to single homes and a nine-room cooperative. Most of the houses are solar. Even the subdivision's drainage system is not built of concrete but uses natural swales and collection ponds.

According to the Corbetts' book, *Designing Sustainable Communities*,[2] when newcomers moved into Village Homes in the early days the residents would hold work parties to help them put up their houses (It sounds like life in a traditional Japanese rural community like the famous villages of Shirakawa-gō[3] in Gifu Prefecture). The Corbetts' goal was to deliberately foster a sense of community among the residents through working together. The swimming pools, playground equipment, and even the bridges over the creeks were largely built by the residents, too. You could call it a do-it-yourself subdivision.

The Corbetts also had Pakistani immigrants work on the housing construction as a way of acquiring skills that could help them get construction jobs later, and set up a system that let them build their own homes in the subdivision once they worked off the value of a down payment. The community is also economically diverse with low-income households accounting for 16 percent of all Village Homes households.

When I first heard about Village Homes residents helping build the houses of new arrivals, I assumed it was a classic example of the American hippie ethic of the time. However, I later learned from an American friend that it was common as far back as the days of the pioneers for everyone in the community to come together to help put up homes for new arrivals. While I do not really expect to see communities cropping up in the Japan of today where everyone will help build a home for a new arrival, this example does offer valuable hints for community-building here at home.

(2) Apartment Complexes: Creating Connections Among Diversified Residents

Let us look at another example: the Urban Renaissance Agency's (formerly the Japan Housing Corporation) Tamadaira no Mori Renaissance Project to renovate and re-envision Tamamusubi Terrace, a section of the Tamadaira no Mori *danchi* housing complex (the former Tamadaira *danchi*) in western Tokyo.

The Tamadaira *danchi* was built in the mid-1950s. In recent years UR has been renovating the old apartment blocks, in the process reducing the original 2,792 rental units to 1,528 units and converting the remaining land into private-sector housing and commercial zones. Tamamusubi Terrace is an experiment using five remaining apartment buildings to see if there is a different, more sustainable way to use them than simply razing them and building anew.

UR started by soliciting private sector proposals for how to re-use the buildings, in the end picking three plans: the Aura 243 Tamadaira no Mori residential-complex garden-house building, the two-building Riento Tamadaira apartment-style share-house, and the Yuimāru

Tamadaira no Mori complex[4] consisting of a dedicated rental building for seniors paired with a multigenerational rental building. The three companies chosen renovated their respective buildings themselves, and residents started moving into them in 2011.

None of the people moving in had lived in the old Tamadaira apartment complex and, except for the tenants of the dedicated seniors building, most were younger people in their twenties and thirties. One of the two share-house buildings was rented out to Chūō University as a student dorm, and houses foreign exchange students as well as Japanese young people.

Wooden decks connect interiors to the outdoors.

The result is a diverse community, where people can interact between young and old, between men and women, and even between cultures. At the same time, there has also been an influx of younger people into neighboring parts of the renovated Tamadaira complex after UR rebuilt the old apartment

Vegetable gardens for the residents.

blocks with more varied floor plans.

As I have long pointed out in my own writing, one major weakness of the *danchi* apartment complexes and the sprawling "new towns" that were flung up in Japan during the postwar era is that they tended to be extremely homogenous, populated by households of the same general age, the same general family structure, and the

A community mochi-pounding event brings together men and women, young and old.
Above three photos by Miura Atsushi and courtesy of blue studio.

same general income level. As the decades passed, this became a serious problem as all the residents aged together. Today, these vast complexes are increasingly full of single elderly people, all living isolated and alone. I have heard that in some sections of the original Tamadaira complex nearly half the residents were sixty-five years old or older.

At the reinvented Tamamusubi Terrace it is not just the population that is now more diverse. Vegetable gardens have been created in the open spaces, and residents can use plots for small-scale agriculture. The building for seniors has a dining hall, but it is open to everyone, not just residents. All the buildings have expansive wooden terraces where residents can relax and commune outside on sunny days.

On the day that I visited Tamamusubi Terrace the residents were holding a *mochi-tsuki* rice-pounding festival. Young people from the share-house were pounding the rice for sticky *mochi* rice cakes that the old ladies from the seniors' building were flavoring. You could see interactions arising naturally among the residents. The old ladies were even inviting women from outside the *danchi* who were strolling along the paths beside the garden patches to join in, and soon their children were pounding rice cakes, too.

In this way, instead of leaving its residents shut up inside their own rooms, the "hardware" and the "software" of Tamamusubi Terrace have been carefully calibrated to make it easy for relationships to spring up naturally among not only the people living in different buildings, but with people from different parts of the Tamadaira no Mori complex and even outside the development itself. Such a concept might seem obvious enough, but the reality is that the countless *danchi* blocks flung up during Japan's second-stage consumer society were cookie-cutter developments that put efficiency ahead of everything else, making it all too easy for residents to shut themselves up in their own private lives. Put that way, you can see how quintessentially fourth-stage consumer society the Tamamusubi Terrace experiment actually is.

As we saw before, as of 2013 some 13 percent of Japan's housing is standing empty, or eight million units in all. Some of these dwellings are virtually in ruins, yet many more would be quite habitable with just a bit of renovation and earthquake reinforcement. From an ecological perspective, it would make much more sense to use these still livable residences, not just as homes but for many other purposes as well, than it is to keep throwing up new houses to no purpose as is being done today.

Nor is that all. Residential neighborhoods could be made much more convenient for their residents simply by building facilities for the elderly and for childcare. And a few cafes and other places where neighbors can comfortably get together and mingle would be all the better.

Certainly there is no problem with having some commercial shops, and if really necessary a convenience store. But it would be better by far to have neighborhood shops selling things that local residents have made themselves, to have galleries displaying art by the people living there, or indeed anything encouraging resident participation. It is in places like these—not in convenience stores or chains and other stores from outside the community—where real interaction and communication among the people who live there will be born.

(3) From Convenience Store to Community Store

How does the omnipresent convenience store, one of the flagship business models of Japan's third-stage consumer society, fit into fourth-stage consumer society? Convenience stores have truly become indispensible, especially for live-alone singles. Yet at least in the big cities most customers interact almost wordlessly with the staff, and the impression you get overall is that, despite their strong presence, convenience stores are not helping foster communication.

Since there are in fact tens of thousands of these stores all over Japan, should they not be used differently? In a way that could make them the nucleus of their local communities?

Convenience stores are where people consume at a very personal level. And since they are located in virtually every corner of the country, it should be more than possible for them to evolve into the institution most closely tied to each locality, one that can communicate most effectively with local residents, thereby contributing to community building. If you will permit me to roll out another of my linguistic hybrids, they can become, not convenience stores, but "community stores," revitalizing both communication and the community itself.

Lots of local residents come to convenience stores. As they are so conveniently located, even the elderly find them easy places to shop.

In fact, quite a few convenience stores have started home food deliveries for their customers.

At present, however, most people go to their local convenience store at different times with different needs, and there is not that much personal interaction. So why not do something to help change that situation? Why not provide a place in the store where people can gather? Just put out a few tables and chairs, and patrons would be able not simply to buy food and beverages and then leave, but to pause there awhile and talk together.

Or it might be possible to add short-term childcare to the list of convenience store services. It would be incredibly convenient for parents if they could drop their children off at the local convenience store for just thirty minutes or so while they run errands nearby.

Or yet again, there is going to be a growing need in the future for people who can help you out just a little bit when you really need it. Changing a light bulb or moving a heavy box or piece of furniture may not sound like much, but it can be a major ordeal for an elderly person. Today people have so little interaction with their neighbors that they often have no one to turn to when they need help, but if the local convenience store had a corner where local residents could post notices asking for that kind of small but critical help, it would put members of the community in touch with one another and help give rise to a greater spirit of cooperation.

In this way, I expect to see convenience stores being called upon in the future to function not simply as a place to do last-minute shopping or pick up concert or movie tickets, but also as a place that provides opportunities for people to come together and interact. Once that happens, more and more people in the local community will start to know each other by sight, and before long silence will be replaced by greetings and conversation.

Then, once people are conversing with one another, community naturally begins to arise, and local citizens begin to feel safer and more secure in their lives. There will be more people in the neighborhood that say, "Hey, I haven't seen Miura for a couple of days. Do you think he's okay?" And thanks to that, there will be that many fewer people dying cut off and alone inside their homes.

Of course, this will also benefit the convenience stores themselves. Once people have more reasons to gather at a convenience store, they will also have more occasions to buy there. Today the key role played by close neighborly relations in creating safe and secure lives is being recognized anew. Helping build those relationships is a role that Japan's convenience stores are eminently positioned to perform.

Actually, in the aftermath of the Tohoku earthquake and tsunami I ran out of rice and went out looking for more. There was none to be found anywhere. The only place that had any rice left at all was a mom-and-pop rice store run by an elderly couple. These old shops, it turns out, buy large quantities of rice at a time and mill just a little each day for sale. They were the only stores left that still had plenty in stock.

Today's convenience stores depend on just-in-time delivery. They keep only small inventories on the premises, not just of rice but of everything else they carry. This means they are largely useless when a disaster disrupts deliveries. Yet it is these stores, with their nationwide networks, that should be the natural strongholds of local communities when disaster strikes, and it would not take much to make them so.

For example, convenience stores could be equipped with reserves of water and emergency provisions for the community. Their inter-store information networks could be designed to handle emergency communications. They could even be built with solar or wind-power systems to generate their own electricity if the grid goes down. If convenience stores cooperated with local government in disaster preparedness, they could evolve into true "community stores," strongholds and supply bases for the communities they serve.

(4) Retail and Fashion: Department Stores By and For the People
Clothing and fashion retailers have seen their sales shrink with the arrival of the kind of low-cost apparel epitomized by Uniqlo. According to the Ministry of Internal Affairs and Communications "Family Income and Expenditure Survey,"[5] average monthly expenditures on clothing and footwear by households of two or more individuals peaked in 1991 and have been falling ever since. In 2010 this spending was just 11,565 yen, on a par with 1973 levels.

Japan's population is shrinking, and especially its youth population, which means that total spending on fashion will continue to fall. How can retailers—especially department stores and other purveyors of high fashion—respond to this situation?

Why couldn't one response be to stop simply selling apparel, and to start creating human connections among people by taking care of every aspect of clothing, from purchasing to cleaning, storing, renting, altering, re-selling, and even recycling? Currently these services are spread out over many different businesses. Could not the department store or apparel industries take care of them all as part of an integrated total system? Uniqlo's practice of taking back its clothes once its customers are through with them, and providing them to developing countries in the form of aid, already approximates this model.

However, a different model that is much more closely aligned with the direction fourth-stage consumer society is heading can be found in the southern Kyushu city of Kagoshima: the new model department store Maruya Gardens.

Maruya Gardens is a commercial center that was created after the big Mitsukoshi Department Store that anchored Kagoshima's core Tenmonkan district closed its doors. The store had been jointly managed by Mitsukoshi and Kagoshima's own locally based Maruya Department Store. After Mitsukoshi withdrew, Maruya turned to Takeuchi Masayoshi of the innovative architectural group Mikan for suggestions on how to re-envision the store, and Takeuchi introduced them in turn to the designer Nagaoka Kenmei, who has been rolling out his own chain of cutting-edge D & Department Project design stores across the country. Nagaoka is friends with the community designer Yamazaki Ryō, whom we met earlier. For the Maruya Gardens project he asked Yamazaki to work on community design while he handled the creative direction himself. Needless to say, including community design as an integral part of a department store revitalization project was unprecedented in itself.

This is how Yamazaki describes the project's conception in his book, *Komyunitii dezain* (Community Design):

> The first thing I proposed was that just because we were talking about
> a department store, we should not simply pack it with tenants like

restaurants and purveyors of merchandise, but also create spaces where communities active locally could operate. . . . Someone with no interest in fashion is rarely going to visit a department store floor filled with fashion tenants, and someone with no interest in gadgets and accessories is rarely going to go to the accessories floor. Yet if they did wind up on those floors, they might find something there that they actually wanted.[6]

For this to happen, however, these people must first have a motive to stop on floors they would usually consider irrelevant. Yamazaki's idea was that by having local groups and organizations hold events and activities inside the department store itself, they would provide that motive, be it a film group screening a little known movie, special classes for children who have refused to go to regular school,[7] an outdoor sports organization that wants to encourage children to play outside more, or even an "eat local" cooking school using locally grown ingredients.

There are not as many today as there used to be, but during Japan's third-stage consumer society with its interest in self-improvement and self-expression there was a rush by department stores to create in-store "culture schools" offering classes in everything from traditional Japanese arts like flower arranging to Western cooking. The people actually planning the curriculum were all department store employees.

The Maruya Gardens model was different. The department store would simply provide already active citizens and citizen groups in the community a venue for their activities. What made this approach possible was the way Japan's citizens themselves had grown and matured through the transformation from third-stage consumerism to fourth-stage consumer society.

We now live in an age when you can do your actual shopping online. If you expect consumers to come all the way into town to your department store just to buy things, more and more often they will not come. However, if there are also events happening at your store organized by local groups, then even people who would normally never set foot in a department store will make a trip there for that.

Based on this concept, Maruya Gardens opened its doors in April 2010 as a department store that offered twenty different public programs to its visitors in addition to its eighty shopping outlets. A department store linked to the activities of citizens in the local community—could there be a more fourth-stage consumer society model than that?

Maruya Gardens provides a venue for public activities rooted in the local community. Here a community presentation about the environment is taking place next to a sales floor. (Photo courtesy of studio-L)

(5) Community Building: Making Full Use of Existing Elements
It may be fine for a conveniences store or department store to serve as a community core, yet it will all be for nothing if the town around them is going to pieces. That may sound obvious, but shopping streets are being shuttered all over Japan. In the worst cases, the shops themselves are being torn down and replaced with a patchwork of parking lots.

Yet today, when residential complexes are springing up in the exurbs and people are increasingly using cars instead of public transit, you can put up all the new stores in the central shopping districts that you want and the customers still will not come. You can pave over your downtown with parking lots, and they still are not going to drive all the way into the town center just to shop.

It is time to abandon the old notion that you have to build more retail shops and more rental buildings that can be filled with retail tenants in your town center because it is a shopping district, and turn our attention instead to the town itself. A downtown does not have to be lined with stores. What needs reviving is not the shopping—it is the community itself.

In the appendix I include a discussion about an innovative experiment in community revitalization underway in Saga City in northwest

Kyushu. Saga is no exception to what is happening all across Japan. Its downtown area has been hollowed out and filled with parking lots where there used to be buildings. Now Saga-born architect Nishimura Hiroshi is trying new ways to revitalize this area. His goal is to turn the empty lots downtown, not into more parking lots, but into open fields that can be used in creative ways to bring vitality back to the town through citizen participation. The key words of Nishimura's project are "come together," "meet one another," and "discover." I talk with Nishimura about his approach on page 265.

(6) Automobiles: From Speeding to Living

Another mainstay of Japan's old economy that is fated to wane in fourth-stage consumer society as the population declines is the automobile. As we saw in Figure 8-4, Japanese car ownership is projected to drop dramatically in the years ahead. If you are fixated on selling cars in quantity, you will have no choice but to do your business in newly rising economies like China, India, or Brazil.

But what can still be done at home?

One thing is clear. In Japan, at least, the question should no longer be how many cars you can sell, but rather how you can sell entire traffic and transportation systems.

In that context, I was particularly taken by the Honda Motor display at the 2011 Tokyo Motor Show. Built around the theme of what makes people feel good, the Honda pavilion offered proposals not just for new automobiles, but also for products that turned the conventional notion of the automobile—"ever faster, ever cooler"—on its head.

Take Honda's collapsible Townwalker electric mobility scooter that could be driven by anybody, including the elderly and disabled. Or the tiny Motor Compo electric moped designed to be useful even when it's not being used for transportation, as a foldable seat, for instance, or even a mobile battery pack. It was a display that, far from focusing simply on getting from one place to another, was already proposing ways that Honda could contribute to a new way of life that values quiet time spent in rest and conversation.

It was an auto show display sure to disappoint people still looking for flash and cool in an automobile. Yet in fact it showed careful thinking about how all kinds of people, male and female, young and old alike, actually behave and connect in their daily lives.

(7) The Travel Industry: Travel that Ties People Together

The travel industry, too, has much to gain from the arrival of fourth-stage consumerism, as long as it is willing to try new models.

For instance, how does this sound for a vacation? You rent a traditional farmhouse in the countryside that has been turned into a new-style bed and breakfast. An older woman from the village does country cooking for your morning meals. In exchange, you help her with things she needs assistance doing. You might also help with the fieldwork or fishing in the nearby farm town or fishing village. Of course the food you eat is fresh from the field or the sea, and if you like to cook you can suggest dishes to your hosts using cooking techniques different from the traditional local dishes. If they like your new recipes, they can market them as a delicious new local cuisine. They could even choose to share some of the profits with you, the B & B guest who came up with them. Personally, I think it would be wonderful to see an approach like this that forges ties between visitors and local residents.

Or how about this? Your town could rent out a traditional thatched-roof house as a "share house" where guests can stay for a whole month for just ten thousand yen each. If you built a hotel in your community, a room would go for around ten thousand yen a night. But at that price most tourists would stay only one night. In the worst case, they might just make it a day trip. So instead of a fancy hotel, create a share house where visitors can get a room for a month for that same ten thousand yen. If they want to cook for themselves, make sure the house is set up so they can. All the guests in the house will share the same kitchen, bath, and toilet. In fact, you can create the share house from anything, not just an empty house but also an abandoned school, even an old *ryokan* inn down on its luck.

Do this, and guests who normally would not stay for even a single night might now choose to stay in your community for a whole month. Of course it could be priced differently, say, two thousand yen a week. The key point is to get people to stay longer by bringing down the cost of lodging. Once you do that, you will have people going out to eat in your town or buying food to cook themselves, purchasing local products and souvenirs, and visiting the local hot spring. And not for a single night but for a week, with all their living expenses for that entire week thus staying in your community.

You might protest that your community has nothing to offer to justify such an extended stay, but you would be wrong. It is precisely the things that the local people consider so commonplace that they have not bothered to turn them into tourist traps that will most delight today's fourth-stage consumers. They will get a lot out of visiting even a rather ordinary Shinto shrine in your town if you use the visit to introduce your local folk beliefs and history. The point is, today's consumers want services different form what they can find at any conventional hotel or *ryokan*, and you will need to pitch your community not simply as a place they can go to consume, but as a place they can experience the true appeal of the countryside as a place where real people work and live.

I can also easily envision ways in which the travel industry could team up with other industries to create new fourth-stage consumer society vacation products. Take cosmetics as one example. As Japan's population shrinks, cosmetic sales will shrink, too. Taking that as a given, the cosmetics industry, too, will need to change course, and start selling cosmetics not as products but—as we discussed earlier—as part of a system promoting beauty and health as elements of a total holistic lifestyle.

The cosmetics tourists would travel to the countryside and stay in a classic old renovated country home. They would be fed healthy meals made from the freshest of local ingredients. Nearby is a hot spring bath that not only gives them beautiful skin, but also refreshes their spirit. That is the kind of "journey" that could be provided by a cosmetics company.

Capitalizing on Regional History and Culture

For the small and medium-sized businesses of local Japan, fourth-stage consumer society presents a tremendous business opportunity. During Japan's second- and third-stage consumer societies, Japan's many regions were reduced to subcontractors in a national system of mass production. But in today's society handwork infused with tradition is prized.

Mass production works to drive product prices down, but the handmade pieces of master craftspeople can always command high prices.

It is exactly because of today's globalization, homogenizing everything in its path, that local products are so highly valued today. Indeed, products that retain a local flavor have, ironically, the chance to go global. It would be a shame to overlook this opportunity.

Hotels just like in Tokyo, restaurants just like in Tokyo, those were the demands of second- and third-stage consumerism. In response, luxurious resorts were flung up all over Japan. Then, when the economic bubble burst, most of them collapsed under a mountain of debt.

Walk through the mammoth shopping malls you can now find almost anywhere in Japan, and you can feel for yourself how the consumption gap between Tokyo and the hinterlands has all but disappeared. Indeed, if you are on the Internet and if you do not mind that it might take a little longer for things to reach you, you can buy virtually anything you want from anywhere in the world, no matter where you live, more easily than you could find them in the big city.

In such an age, there is no point in keeping on building things in Japan's countryside that people can already find in Tokyo. All that will accomplish will be to destroy regional Japan's unique sales points. Fourth-stage consumer society is regional Japan's moment to reevaluate its own history, tradition, and culture, and to create products, innovative designs, and a new tourism rooted in that unique heritage.

The Sharing Workstyle

Lastly, I must point out an inescapable dilemma for the emerging sharing society: the problem of employment, and of what I call "workstyle."

As sharing lifestyles spread across Japan, it will no longer be necessary to create more "big government." Yet having said that, it does not follow that government can be completely hands-off. There are many tasks specific to fourth-stage consumer society that government alone can and should carry out, be it easing regulations that are creating obstacles to more sharing among the citizenry or providing expertise to help citizens expand the circle of sharing with confidence.

Likewise, too, Japan's corporate sector. If more and more people are living happily through sharing, it may mean that more of their own employees will begin to say that the share-house life is so pleasant they no longer need a company dorm or housing allowance anymore. If that happens, companies will be able to save on personnel costs, on employee welfare and benefits, and other expenses. This does not mean, however, that companies will have free license to shift responsibility for all those things that they should be doing onto the public.

As we have noted before, the hiring of full-time, regular employees has stalled since the closing days of third-stage consumer society, while the numbers of nonregular employees with much more limited benefits have surged. Indeed, the problem of the rise in temporary and part-time employment, and the accompanying uncertainties for workers, the scattering of workplaces and declining incomes, is undeniably one of the factors behind the spread of share houses and sharing lifestyles. To take a page from the work of the award-winning Polish sociologist Zygmunt Bauman,[8] I believe there is a real danger that the lives of today's workers, and especially nonregular workers, could in the end simply be used up and thrown away. That would be a far cry from what anyone would call a fulfilling life. If we cannot solve these critical issues of employment and work, we will never be able to achieve a truly sharing society.

Yet simply making everyone a regular employee again is no solution to these problems. Given the severe economic realities Japan faces today, that would be all but impossible in any case. Furthermore, there are many nonregular employees—not to mention freelancers and the self-employed—who are living that way by choice, and cannot be forced willy-nilly into standard, nine-to-five jobs. Yet I doubt that even among the ranks of those who have chosen nonregular employment or self-employment of their own accord, many would say that they do not care if their work dries up, or that they prefer not being able to construct a life plan or prepare for the future.

That being the case, we will clearly need social mechanisms that enable even people who are not regular employees to be able to plan their lives with a sense of security.

Today's new sharing society is a complicated thing. It is a society where people want to create connections with others, but at the same time do not want to be tied down. It is a society that revolves around a value system that wants to avoid entanglements, but also wants connection and a certain measure of security and stability. It is a society in direct conflict with the "corporation man" mentality that demands submission in return for connection.

In my opinion, just because you are a regular company employee it does not follow that you have to sacrifice your whole life to the company, while it is beyond the pale that people should be denied any kind of security just because they are nonregular workers or self-employed. If a share-style fourth-stage consumer society is to work, it will need to be a society where people can feel secure in their lives, and can work happily and with as much stability as possible for as long as possible, regardless of the way they choose to work. There is an urgent need to create a palette of different workstyles, including work shares and beyond.

I introduced a number of examples of different workstyles in my 2008 book *Kakusa shakai no sabaibaru-jutsu* (Survival Skills for an Unequal Society)[9] and elsewhere. Uniqlo, for example, has introduced a "Regional Regular Employee Hiring System" to accord regular-employee benefits to employees who were previously limited to nonregular employment for refusing to accept transfers to other Uniqlo locations. Loft, for its part, has rolled out a system it calls "unlimited employment" (*muki-koyō*) that provides improved job security even to employees who do not want to work more than twenty hours a week.

Putting employees at the mercy of the company, commanding them to work overtime, requiring them to come in to the office or the plant on their days off, expecting them to accept transfers anywhere the company wants to send them and to leave their families behind when they do so—these are the lingering artifacts of the "doctrine of efficiency" that ended with the passing of Japan's second-stage consumer society. Some people who found that rigid way of working unpalatable actually preferred nonregular employment where they at least would not be subjected to transfers. Yet the better employees these nonregulars were, the more the companies themselves wanted to ensure that they only worked for them. It was this reasoning that led to Uniqlo creating its "regular regional employees" system, which guarantees that workers will only be transferred within a specific designated region.

There is a similar backstory to Loft's "unlimited" employment system. It turns out that the same kind of people who are fine with working as "freeters" also tend to be more sensitive to trends in fashion and design than are the people who aspire to regular full-time employment. Bellwether staffers like that are important resources for a trendy store like Loft, even if they only work part-time. You certainly do not want them jumping ship for one of your competitors. So to help them feel secure working with the firm, Loft devised an employment system that gave even employees working only twenty hours a week the job security of full-time employment. It could almost be considered a form of work sharing.

In second-stage consumer society the classic Japanese "salaryman" life was considered a positive thing, something to aspire to. In third-stage consumer society, Japanese began to find that salaryman way of life confining, and more and more of them chose to become freeters instead of looking for regular employment. Each time the pendulum swung too far. Now, in today's fourth-stage consumer society, there needs to be a new way of working that is neither salaryman nor freeter, that strikes a balance between stability and freedom.

We spend so much of our life at work. It goes without saying that it will be better for us all if the way we work is not simply a waste of time, does not just "expend" our time, but leads to more fulfilling times, and to a full and rewarding life.

APPENDIX I. CASE STUDY

Mujirushi Ryōhin: The Evolution from Third-stage to Fourth-stage Consumerism

M ujirushi Ryōhin—literally "no-brand fine products"—is a private brand born in 1980, in the midst of Japan's third-stage consumer society, that has succeeded in sustaining its popularity so that today it has a thoroughly fourth-stage consumer society image. Outside of Japan it is known simply as Muji.

I first became aware of Mujirushi in 1982 when I stopped by a convenience store in Tokyo's Yūtenji district on my way home from work one day and spotted a new sort of product. It was stationary, but it was completely plain, in a neutral color and with no patterns or other embellishments. I thought instantly, "Yes! This is what I've been looking for!" and bought it on the spot. Needless to say, the stationary was by Mujirushi. I developed a strong liking for Mujirushi products after that, and over the years I have bought their bicycles, clothes, tables, cabinets, even lighting fixtures.

As Mujirushi founder Tsujii Takashi (a.k.a. Tsutsumi Seiji), then the chairman of Saison Group and later president of the Saison Foundation, explained when I interviewed him before his death in 2013 (see page 273), the Mujirushi line was proposed as a protest against other brand products. It was conceived as a kind of raw material that consumers could use to create their own personal, individualistic lifestyles free of extraneous values imposed by a corporation. From a *jibun-rashisa* ("being yourself") perspective, this made Mujirushi the epitome of third-stage consumerism.

Japan's third-stage consumer society saw the flourishing of brands that appealed to aspects of people's individuality. Yet despite this, or more accurately, because of this, Mujirushi was created as an "anti-brand." Instead of asking consumers to pick a brand that was more "like you," consumers were invited to treat Mujirushi's products as raw material—as empty containers that they could color themselves, fix up themselves, throw together however they wanted—in a philosophy that shared much with the "half-product" (*han-seihin*) philosophy of Tokyu Hands (see chapter six).

At the same time, Mujirushi eliminated all excess packaging, colors, and patterns, and developed products using items—like shiitake mushrooms with small imperfections—that would previously have been thrown away. In this way they also came to be perceived as environmentally friendly. Mujirushi products were already expressing aspects of Japan's fourth-stage of consumer society in the middle of its third.

Mujirushi goods further incorporated another fourth-stage characteristic in the particular air of Japanese culture that they gave off. Instead of layering on more and more functions and embellishments, Mujirushi products shaved off anything extraneous. It was an aesthetic of subtraction that resonated with Japan's culture of *wabi/sabi*, of subdued simplicity, and gave Mujirushi products an even more fourth-stage consumer society sensibility.

Indeed, when you match up interest in environmental issues with affinity for Mujirushi products, you find that more than 80 percent of consumers who say they "like" or "strongly like" Mujirushi products also say they are either "interested" or "somewhat interested" in environmental issues (fig. CS-1a).

In contrast, the percentage of consumers who say they are either "not very interested" or "not interested" in environmental issues runs in the 30th and 40th percentiles respectively among those who say they either do not like Mujirushi products "very much" or "strongly dislike" them. Similarly, when asked if they like Japan and Japanese culture, 85 percent of consumers who reply that they "strongly like" or "like" Mujirushi also say they "strongly like" or "like" Japan (fig. CS-1b).

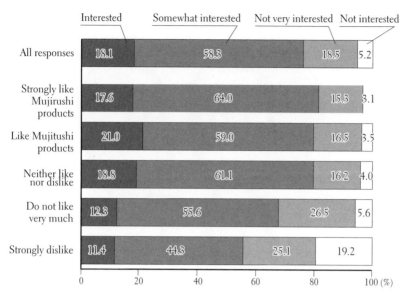

FIGURE CS-1a Interest in Environmental Issues and Affinity for Mujirushi Products

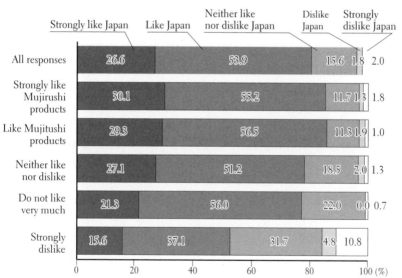

FIGURE CS-1b Attitudes Toward Japan and Affinity for Mujirushi Products

Based on Culturestudies, "Gendai saishin josei chōsa" (Newest Survey of Modern Women), 2010, a survey of women aged 20–39 in greater metropolitan Tokyo by NetMile, Inc.

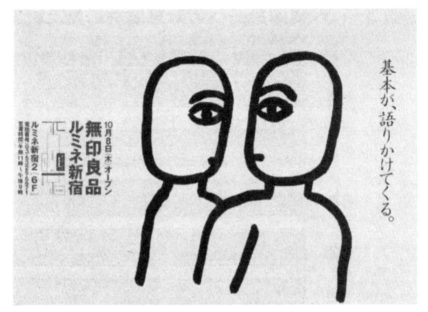

A Mujirushi poster (Advertising Museum Tokyo (ADMT) collection)

It seems that Mujirushi has established an image with consumers of being ecological, simple, and distinctly Japanese.

Thus positioned, Mujirushi in 2003 launched a new endeavor that it called "Found Muji." The concept for "Found Muji" stores was that Mujirushi would not develop the products sold there, but would instead go out and "find" ethnic products from around Japan and the world that one would feel on sight to be classically "Mujirushi." For example, it has not only found eating implements and tableware from all across Japan, but has gone on to acquire metalware from India, Blanc de Chine ceramics, wooden benches and textiles from China, hemp sacks used by the French post office, and other goods from around the world.

It seems that some people have taken to calling Mujirushi the *mingei* (folk crafts) of modern Japan. Its products have been praised for possessing their own *mingei*-like beauty of function (*yō no bi*) in the context of modern life, in short, a beauty that comes directly from their utilitarianism. Now, with its Found Muji stores, Mujirushi is hunting out the "functional beauty" of different regions around the world.

If one of the defining characteristics of fourth-stage consumer society is the value it places on unique local cultures, then it seems extremely natural, perhaps even inevitable, that a fourth-stage brand like Mujirushi would go in this direction.

However, when I visited Mujirushi's Found Muji Aoyama store in Tokyo's high-end Aoyama district, I had a surprising reaction. I could not help but feel that I was in one of those refined antique and collectibles stores you find in well-heeled parts of Tokyo like Nishi-ogikubo and Mejiro.

I suspect that once consumers acquire the capacity to search out and discover "Muji-like" items on their own, Mujirushi Ryōhin the brand may become superfluous. Of course, not that many people will actually develop such a sophisticated taste, and even the few who do may still buy Mujirushi goods to fill in gaps in what they own. Yet the work of Found Muji seems in some sense to refute the *raison d'être* of Mujirushi itself.

Of course, Mujirushi Ryōhin probably knows this better than anyone. I have a feeling that Mujirushi's long-term goal will be the promotion of a philosophy far transcending the "things" it sells.

APPENDIX II. INTERVIEWS

YAMAZAKI RYŌ
Community Designer

Young People Waking Up to the Charms of Local Japan

Yamazaki Ryō is a renowned community designer who leads current local revitalization projects across Japan. Yamazaki uses a unique and practical approach with the various communities in need of his help, emphasizing meeting with local residents face to face. He and his team are constantly called upon to manage projects for the many communities across the country in need of revitalization. Yamazaki also advises on the critical importance of reviving Japan's regional and local communities in today's fourth-generation consumer society, which over time will play an increasingly influential role in Japan's economy.

MIURA: Today, I'd like to talk with you about what is happening in Japan's local communities, and what more should be done for them. Given that you are engaged in the still new profession of community design, when did you realize yourself that going forward it would actually have nothing to do with the design of physical objects?

YAMAZAKI: I'd say the 1995 earthquake in Kobe gave me my first inkling of that.

MIURA: Meaning that, seeing all the damage to the city, you questioned what the point was of knocking buildings down just to build them up again?

YAMAZAKI: That's right. And especially so because I had studied architecture and urban planning at university. Back then I thought that a sort of postmodern architecture, slightly broken down in appearance but still structurally sound, would draw people's attention.

MIURA: That was back during third-stage consumerism, the age of *mono*, of physical things.

YAMAZAKI: That was when I was still trying to work out how to impress the shape of things on people's consciousness, whether it was a building constructed as though the concrete had cracked, or layered like it was falling over, that sort of thing.

MIURA: Design that looked like ruins?

YAMAZAKI: Yes. But then, I saw everything destroyed for real in the Kobe earthquake. That left me thinking that faking damage was actually senseless, you see.

At the time I was with an urban planning research office, and the City Planning Institute of Japan sent me to go over the disaster site, looking at the structures there. I was trying to determine the degree of damage, whether it was partial, severe, or total, and as far as the eye could see in Kobe's Sumiyoshi district, where I was doing my survey, the damage was absolute. There weren't even roads where there should have been roads. The thought that there might be people still trapped in the rubble below shook me up, too. I was on the verge of serious depression, but at least the river was still a river. People were going down to the riverbed to do their laundry and cook their food. Seeing the evacuees gathering there, giving encouragement to one another, was a shock to my system. Old women whose sons had died were offering support to a couple who'd lost their parents, saying things like, "I was sleeping on the second floor, so I ended up crushing my own son who was on the first floor. And you, too . . ." And I thought, "These people are amazing." I was heartened by the thought that it was these sorts of little ties between people that are all that really remain in the end.

I had been educated to think that good design existed to make people happy, that an abundant new age could come just from making things. Now I found myself thinking that the very word "design" had to encompass more than manufacturing things in greater and greater quantities.

MIURA: Was it very long after that that you realized that what really matters aren't things after all, but people?

YAMAZAKI: That came a little later. I started at a design firm that did both architecture and landscape design, and also ran workshops. They said I should take over the workshops because I was a good speaker, and so I did.

MIURA: Was running workshops interesting work?

YAMAZAKI: I wasn't so into it initially. Words like "community" or "workshop" seem kind of highfalutin, you know? [*laughs*].

MIURA: True!

YAMAZAKI: I had figured that workshops were all about putting pink tags on construction paper and well-mannered people saying things like, "I believe everyone is in agreement on the matter concerned." Which all struck me as just a big lie. When I actually started conducting workshops, however, I gradually came to see that it wasn't all lies after all. And that got me to wondering why it was that people who create spaces make the spaces which they themselves want, without getting opinions from anyone who will actually be using those spaces. I mean, if you're going to make something physical, you get various people together around the core element of making such-and-such a product, you build a team of people who bond, and they themselves handle various parts of the process. I came to believe that the right way to create spaces is to focus on forging those kinds of bonds.

MIURA: Spaces as a means to an end.

YAMAZAKI: And because they are means to an end, people really can assemble to create spaces, as they can also assemble to draft comprehensive plans. You can get people together to prepare for events. The real objective is to turn people into a team, to bring together people who are actually doing things in the community. This is what I came to believe.

MIURA: Did your firm start out dealing with local Japan?

YAMAZAKI: I personally didn't have much interest in local communities to start with. I was born in Aichi Prefecture and lived there until I was two, but after that I was always a transfer student, always the new kid in school, every time my parents were relocated for work, whether it was to Hirakata, Nishinomiya, or Nagoya. And whichever city it was, we always lived in some "new town" housing development on the outskirts of the city. My father's corporate housing was always in places like that. Wherever we went, I lived like some military brat, so it's hard for me to imagine life in one of those emotionally rich, down-home *shitamachi* neighborhoods where people all know one another. Notions of city centers or mountain valleys or remote islands didn't evoke any response in me, either. And of course, I had no idea whatsoever what sorts of rules there might be in different communities. Even now, I feel most strongly attached to "new town" housing developments.

MIURA: Hah! That's a surprise [*laughs*].

YAMAZAKI: Someone with a background like that isn't going to want to just suddenly go to the countryside. And I'd also heard about the backbiting and petty gossip there, too.

MIURA: Then how did you actually get into local Japan?

YAMAZAKI: It all began with a staffer at our firm. When she was still in university, I was her advisor on her graduation project. I had her pick a site to do her work by throwing a dart at a map.

MIURA: And the dart hit the island of Ieshima?

YAMAZAKI: That's right. I told her to throw it at Osaka, but she ended up hitting this little island off the Himeji coast instead.

MIURA: So if it had hit Osaka, you wouldn't have done Ieshima?

YAMAZAKI: You got it. I said, "Eh? You hit an island? Okay then, go there." But it was kind of strange to have a student just show up on the island and go around asking people what problems they were having [*laughs*]. Rumors started spreading in the community and the local government offices about the weird girl, so in my ostensible capacity as her academic advisor I went there myself to smooth things out. And that's how it started.

MIURA: And you've been working in local communities ever since?

YAMAZAKI: After that, we were fortunate enough to get inquiries from all over Japan.

MIURA: You got that much recognition from your initial work on Ieshima?

YAMAZAKI: No, I think the real acclaim came for the Amachō project.[*] The mayor of Amachō, Yamauchi Michio, is a fascinating and intriguing character, so there was interest right from the outset.

MIURA: You had a noteworthy mayor.

YAMAZAKI: Right. He had a policy of welcoming persons who had done an "I-turn" with open arms.[**] We were called in to assist with a comprehensive plan involving resident participation at a time when he

---

[*] Amachō is a small town on one of the islands of the Oki Islands archipelago in the Japan Sea.

[**] As opposed to a "U-turn," where a person from the countryside returns home to his or her community of birth after living in the big city, a decision by an urbanite to move to the countryside has come to be called an "I-turn."

was already beginning to get attention as it was. But it was because of Ieshima that we got the call in the first place.

We were carrying out this project with local people in Ieshima-chō and Professor Seki Mitsuhiro of Hitotsubashi University was impressed with how we were going about it. He said we seemed to do things differently from how the usual so-called "community revitalization consultants" would have done it. As I understand it, he personally arranged the introduction to the mayor of Amachō, telling him that it would be worthwhile for him to talk to me.

MIURA: How are you different from conventional consultants?

YAMAZAKI: None of us have any idea, actually. We've just been learning from others' examples, simply doing what we can with our designer training.

MIURA: Maybe your focus of interest is different?

YAMAZAKI: I think our approach has always been to create situations where people who want to do something interesting in their towns will find it easier to do so.

Typically, community revitalization starts with getting persons in leadership positions, such as the head of a community association, the boss of a shopping district cooperative, or the leader of the chamber of commerce, to carry out plans at the local government level. These people are the top leaders in their regions, however, so at some level they don't actually want to change the status quo that much. My sense is that getting these kinds of persons together for community revitalization is not going to produce real action.

With us, we go and talk directly with people in the community. We ask, "Is there anyone doing something interesting in this town? Are there any young people doing interesting things around here?" Now, since these are public works projects, naturally we also solicit public involvement, but we do it in such a way so as to connect on an individual level, saying, "We're holding such-and-such a workshop, and we hope you'll attend." About half the people we invite to our workshops

Yamazaki Ryō (second from left), *doing things differently from how the usual so-called "community revitalization consultants" work. Photo courtesy of studio-L.*

are those whom we personally find of interest. And the other half or so are bureaucrats and those who are attending in response to our announcements to the general public and are strongly interested in community revitalization. That way, we get a good mix.

If all you have are people with a strong interest in community revitalization, then what you get is talk like "what community revitalization is really all about is. . . ." But if you then get some former juvenile delinquents—some people who really hate what the bureaucracy's doing—involved, then pretty soon you've got a fight on your hands. Now you're cooking! [*laughs*]. It's at those moments when the people we personally invited step up to make their town more interesting, turn it into something unlike what it was before.

MIURA: Sounds like a pub meeting!

YAMAZAKI: Right, right! And that might just make for a different kind of community revitalization than what's gone before.

MIURA: And even on that little island there were people who wanted to make something happen?

243

YAMAZAKI: Yes, there were.

MIURA: Do you think there's a lack of awareness in our broader society on this point?

YAMAZAKI: There sure is. I think there are a lot of people who figure, right from the outset, that there are no people like that in the local community.

MIURA: And isn't it the same with the so-called "shutter streets" of empty storefronts, where people figure there's no one left who wants to have anything to do with them, to try to do anything there?
YAMAZAKI: That's the sense I get. But in fact, there are plenty of people with all kinds of notions, all kinds of ideas.

MIURA: What did the juvenile delinquents want?

The Ieshima Project
(Ieshima-chō, Himeji City, Hyōgo Prefecture)

A project carried out with the three primary aims of creating regional specialties based on the island's flourishing fisheries industry, designing packaging which communicated aspects of the island's way of life, and creating and implementing plans for guesthouses and tours of farms and fishing ports. The project's stated goal was "10,000 people visiting 100 times, rather than one million people visiting once."

The Ama Town Fourth Comprehensive Plan: Community Revitalization Assistance (Amachō, Oki-gun, Shimane Prefecture)

A project implemented on Amachō island with the aim of revitalizing the community from within, involving the creation of four teams focusing on people, lifestyle, industry, and the environment. The teams met in a series of workshops and study groups, resulting in the residents themselves drafting their own plan, titled "Twenty-four Proposals for Amachō's Future."

YAMAZAKI: The juvenile delinquents started out with no ideas whatsoever for what to do, as you might expect [*laughs*]. They had this really strong sense that things couldn't go on as they were, but they couldn't figure out what to do about it. In one workshop, we practically forced this one guy onto the team that was focusing on developing human resources, and a bunch of his followers joined as well. I latched on to him when he insisted that he wouldn't have any part of it, and told him to just sit down and participate. I told him that we needed the opinions of people like him if we were to keep this from all being a waste of time. Initially, however, he just seemed to be sleeping right through it. When the talk got serious, though, he'd interrupt and say he didn't get what we were talking about. And when he did that, the earnest participants would have to explain things again in a way that everyone really could get it.

MIURA: Was it your long experience conducting workshops that led to your intuition that you needed to involve people who appeared to have no particular interest in community revitalization?

YAMAZAKI: In the course of doing a number of these workshops, I came to realize that a lot of workshops are just pro forma affairs.

MIURA: With guys coming around wearing string ties?

YAMAZAKI: Yeah [*laughs*]. The old-guard intellectuals. But the ideas that emerged from those meetings were all things I'd already heard somewhere before.

MIURA: You've been involved in a great number of community revitalization projects all across Japan. Having seen the situation from northernmost Hokkaido to southernmost Okinawa, what do you think Japan's local communities should do? I would imagine that the way young people view them has changed. When I was younger, the prevailing attitude—spurred on by third-stage consumerism—was that buying things in Shibuya was the way to go. It seems to me that things are completely different now from how they were then.

YAMAZAKI: The young people who have started thinking of moving out of the big cities are in their twenties, which means they're the "eco-natives."

MIURA: You mean, the generation that's been educated about ecology their whole lives?

YAMAZAKI: This is purely my own feeling, you understand, but it's second nature for these young people to use both sides of a sheet of paper when making photocopies. They say it just doesn't feel right when they don't, whereas to people of my generation it feels like something we have to make a big deal about whenever we do it [*laughs*]. To them, ideas like "grow local, buy local," or that sourcing energy from far away leads to large energy losses, or concepts like "food mileage," "virtual water," "ecologically sound lifestyles," "slow food," and all that are just a natural part of basic education.

MIURA: Like reading, writing, and arithmetic.

YAMAZAKI: But these green things which are as natural, as basic, as reading, writing, and arithmetic require very large outlays of money to do if you're living in Tokyo. It seems to me that there are far more people than

A workshop in Kan'onji City. Yamazaki's community revitalization begins with walking about town and talking to the people he meets. Photo by Miura Atsushi.

you might imagine who are uncomfortable with the old way of doing things. I get the feeling that their vision for their own lifestyle is taking a quite different path from the one we've been on thus far. And so, given the opportunity, they'll pack up and head for the hinterlands. It seems to me that this is happening more and more with these generations.

One thing I've noticed is the number of cafés and the like springing up out in the countryside, in places that make one wonder whether they can actually make a go of it.

MIURA: How far out in the country?

YAMAZAKI: Really far out. There's a café in the Reihoku region of Kōchi Prefecture, just this one, standing by itself in a place where you would see only mountains if you drove for twenty minutes or more in any direction. The owner opened this café right next to an erosion

The Pocchiri-dō (Little Bit), a café in the Kōchi mountains enjoyed by locals who drive there. Snacks made with local ingredients are doing a brisk business online. (Photos courtesy of Pocchiri-dō.)

control dam. He does illustrations and bakes cookies out there. And it's doing so well that he's employed two young housewives who live in the area.

MIURA: The pictures look just like a café you'd find in Tokyo, in Kōenji.

YAMAZAKI: In a complete change from the way we used to envision rural villages struggling with depopulation, places everywhere are now using regional information and communications technology (ICT) for Internet access, so fiber-optic cables are reaching the furthest edges of all these rural communities. When you log onto these connections it's practically like having your own dedicated line. The old women in these rural communities aren't going online, so once the fiber-optic comes to your door you have practically full 100 mbps access.

MIURA: Beats a city high-rise by far.

YAMAZAKI: Luxury apartments in Tokyo are running at about 10-20 mbps, so it's much nicer to suddenly be able to connect at 100 mbps. And then people start making things they can market online. This café owner puts the cookies he makes in tins that he also makes, and sells them online packaged together with different teas. And he explains in detail on his website how his cookies use safe and healthy local ingredients and are baked by people he knows and trusts.

And do people come? Yes, they do. Word of mouth has gotten out to municipalities all around Reihoku that now we have a Kōenji-style café in our own neighborhood. And since it's the only place like it in any of the nearby municipalities, people hop into their cars to go there.

After all, in the countryside most people still live with their parents and their in-laws. So even having friends drop by to chat can get uncomfortable. People even feel nervous about laughing too loud. So they congregate at this place instead.

MIURA: People need an alternative, "third space" to go to, even out in the country.

YAMAZAKI: Right. In a very real sense, this is their alternative place.

Then a student who I taught at the university graduated from my seminar, and now works in Amachō. Even though she's an eco-native, she thought she should probably look for work in Tokyo or Kyoto or Osaka. But I told her: "The Town Hall in Amachō which I'm working with is hiring non-permanent personnel. They're only paying 120,000 yen a month, but maybe you could try it out." She did. And it turns out that she's now saving 100,000 yen a month out of her 120,000 yen salary! She says it's perfectly doable to save 1.2 million yen annually.

The reason is, there are lots of old ladies in the region where she lives. And when they want new clothing, gloves, or books, there aren't any for sale in Amachō. So she goes online to buy these things for them, and in return they give her loads of *daikon* radishes and persimmons [*laughter*]. She gets more food than she can possibly eat. And it's Amachō so there's also plenty of fish. She hardly has to spend anything on food. Seasonings and condiments, maybe, and that's it.

MIURA: It's a kind of barter system.

YAMAZAKI: Right. And her rent is 3,000 yen a month, if memory serves. So she doesn't spend more than 20,000 yen a month.

We have a firmly embedded image of the countryside as a place where wages are low and farming isn't viable anymore. It's similar to the way we've become conditioned to think that there are no motivated people in the "shutter-street" shopping districts, or that there's no one with any ideas about doing things on the outer islands.

MIURA: Like we figure no one in the countryside is reading [simple-life magazine] *ku:nel*.

YAMAZAKI: But they are. They love it out there [*laughs*]. They know that kind of information better than we do. That's one more way in which country living today is completely different from the old preconceptions.

MIURA: The *ku:nel* lifestyle is actually easier there.

YAMAZAKI: A fresh coat of white paint and a few stylish knickknacks, and you're set. And the rent is 3000 yen. People who find that out are likely to head for the countryside, especially those in the eco-native movement.

Now I know this is not a particularly novel conclusion, but I think the Internet has really made a big difference. Whereas the political hierarchy used to run up from struggling, so-called *genkai-shūraku* rural communities to core rural communities to localities to regional cities to medium-sized cities to major cities, nowadays it's possible to sell things directly to the big cities from the end of the line.

MIURA: The hierarchy has gone away.

YAMAZAKI: Yet that old hierarchy is still fixed in our minds. It's possible to link a house in the mountains with a 27-inch display in Tokyo via Skype and converse directly twenty-four hours a day. It would be possible for me to relocate my entire personal library out into the country and say, "Show me page 30 or thereabouts of that book. Yeah, that's it. Send me a scan." And yet, even though it's completely feasible to have my personal library in some other place, I somehow don't feel like I could actually do it.

MIURA: I know what you mean.

YAMAZAKI: But it actually is possible. While it may sound a little cynical to say this, I personally think the Ministry of Agriculture, Forestry, and Fisheries and the Forestry Agency are trumpeting things like "Japanese agriculture is in trouble" or "Japan's forestry won't survive" in what's really little more than an effort to safeguard their budgets. That may in fact be part of the story, or it may not be, but these organizations have issued nothing but data to the effect that "Japan's agricultural sector is in agony" whenever they've gotten into a tug of war with the Ministry of Land, Infrastructure, Transport, and Tourism over their budget.

And the more they send out that message, the fewer young people there are who want to work in agriculture. They say that an annual income of two million yen is terribly low, even when everyone is really living quite well. But there's never much talk about how much you can actually save out of a yearly income of two million yen out in the country.

The real surprise is that people living outside the big cities are actually quite happy. Frustratingly so. It's like, "You mean this person eats fresh raw oysters on his yacht every day?!" In the city we only see things like that on TV. And yet there are elementary school kids out in the countryside who are eating that way every day.

By now even the local people themselves have gotten used to warning city people, "Don't even think about living out here." My own company is moving its office to the country. We're relocating a large part of our office functions to a place called Shimagahara, deep in the mountains in Mie Prefecture, on the site of what used to be a lumber mill covering about 3,300 square meters. We're still keeping our office in Osaka but, like I said earlier, we have connections via Skype twenty-four hours a day, and we're attempting to move all of our books, workshop materials, and the like to Shimagahara. But the villagers themselves are giving us the usual line: "Why are you people coming to this place?!" [laughs].

The consensus seems to be: "A design firm in a shuttered lumber mill? Why do such a thing?" Even the people in the countryside have internalized the notion that there's no work and nothing to do where they live.

MIURA: I feel that the major reason young people want to move to regional Japan but don't think they can actually do so is employment. But even without employment being available . . . ?

YAMAZAKI: The first thing is to just go and try it. They'll at least have no trouble feeding themselves if they just help out the local people with the problems they're facing.

MIURA: And get plenty of *daikon*, too!

251

Yamazaki Ryō, *Community Designer*
Born in Aichi Prefecture in 1973, Yamazaki is the manager of studio-L and a professor at the Kyoto University of Art and Design. He participates in community design, helping people living in regional Japan solve community problems themselves. He is involved in many projects, including community revitalization workshops and developing compre-hensive plans involving resident participation. He and studio-L have received Good Design Awards for the Ama Town Fourth Com-prehensive Plan in Shimane Prefecture, the Maruya Gardens department store project in Kagoshima City, and the "quake + design" social design education project as well as the Ministry of Agriculture, Forestry, and Fisheries' Eighth All Right! Japan Prize Selection Committee Chairman's Prize for the Ieshima project. Yamazaki's many publications include Komyunitii dezain *(Community Design) from Gakugei Shuppansha, 2011. Studio-L's Iga office in Mie Prefecture is now dedicated to the Hozumi Lumber Mill Project.*

ASADA WATARU
"Editor of the Everyday"

Creating the "Public"
by Opening up the "Private"

Asada Wataru, musician, writer, and event producer, describes himself as an "editor of the everyday." With the publication of his 2012 book Sumibiraki: Ie kara hajimeru komyunitii *(Open Living: Community that Begins From the Home), Asada brought together the stories of scores of individuals across Japan who have turned their private residences into public spaces, a process of "opening the home" that he hopes will ultimately rewrite conventional concepts of "uchi" and "soto" — inside and outside — and of ownership and community in tomorrow's Japan.*

I'm thirty-two years old, which makes me part of the so-called "Lost Generation,"[*] and I would say there are more and more people of my generation and the generation just a little behind us living in shared housing today. Back around 2000 and on up to 2005 or so, people were mostly doing this because it was cheaper and you could get more living space. Nowadays, though, I think a bigger reason is the networks — both for work and shared interests — that come out of living with other people Once you are living that way, the question then comes up of what interesting, concrete ways there might be to use the common space that

---

[*] The generation of the "lost decade(s)" after the bursting of the real estate bubble in Japan in the early 1990s.

it effectively generates. And that in turn brings in all kinds of other people in addition to the residents themselves. Once that happens, you've reached that state that I've been advocating, what I call *sumibiraki* ("open living"). . . . In other words, everyone is sharing each other's knowledge, experience, and human networks.

[In time] a whole community could be like a *sumibiraki* house. It would be like, "Hey, so-and-so's house over there is practically everyone's kitchen now, so let's go there!"

What Umeyama Kōsuke, creator of the Ni-jō Daigaku (Two-mat University), which I introduce in *Sumibiraki*, is doing in his own local Karahori Shopping Street in Osaka is something he calls "Karahori Dining." He gets together young people who are thinking they might like to try refurbishing some of the old *nagaya* tenement houses there, and takes them around Karahori to shop at the local greengrocer and fishmonger and other stores on the shopping street, stopping to talk with the owners along the way. And then he takes them to the home of someone who actually lives in Karahori and they all talk about the town while they use the makings they bought to cook and eat dinner together. And then, for a clincher, Umeyama will have shopkeepers they were talking with just a little while earlier drop by and join them for dinner [*laughs*]. In the end, by opening up just one house to the community, the border between home and community begins to dissolve.

As IT technology advances you can just see the growing nomadization of work. I'm totally a nomad worker myself. Now, I don't think the *raison d'être* of the home has been "re-edited" as much [as the workplace has been]. But even so, after the March 11, 2011, earthquake and tsunami a lot of my friends in music and the arts just up and evacuated from Kantō to Osaka with their whole families. They didn't use bureaucratic assistance to do it. They just used their own professional networks that they'd been building from before the disaster to look for places where they could live temporarily. And then, while they've been staying in Osaka, they've been going out and meeting local folk who'd been wanting to have a chance to talk with them. I feel that in a way it has liberated the whole notion of living the nomadic life. I don't want anyone to misunderstand me [about how terrible the disaster was], but at the same time I do feel some new possibilities emerging after it. . . .

The basic idea of *sumibiraki* is to once again think about opening up the home to the outside, only to do it on a modernized base. When I'm interviewed by the press there are always reporters who, when they write it up, extol *sumibiraki* as "reviving traditional community" or the like. But in fact I think it's something completely different.

For one thing, we only have the option of opening our homes to the outside today because of this new age that we're living in. And for

A sumibiraki *party at Minamimori-cho led to the birth of this idea.*

another, what's especially important to *sumibiraki* is the interesting new ways that individuals are finding to express this option for themselves.

Which leads me to one more thing. If you ask whether those local communities of old were really so open or not, I think the answer is that—while they may have been open to the people of the local community—there were many ways in which they were completely closed to people from the outside, to *yosomono*, to strangers.

What's happening now, though, is that people are using modern urban communication to come together, not around *chien*, the old ties of land or place, but around shared interests and knowledge bases. It's not the traditional *kyōdōtai* community, but what you have termed *kyōitai*, Miura-san. A community of different individuals.

People want to be connected, but not in rigid, restrictive relationships. And I think the sense that somewhere you do have an out is what, ultimately, has given birth to these new modes of sharing. If things get too rigid again, then I think the circle of sharing will close.

Further, ever since the experiences of March 11 there has clearly been a spreading sense of, "Well, we'll just take care of things ourselves." As just one example, when I was doing research for *Sumibiraki* I interviewed people living the share-house life [in Tokyo] who tweeted on the very day of the disaster things like, "Our doors are open all day long, so anyone out there, just drop on in." And they actually did give people who couldn't get home because the transportation network was down a place to stay. I believe the *sumibiraki*-style activities that are already happening all over Japan are functioning very effectively as a living lesson on the importance of *tsunagari* (human connections) in an emergency.

This interview is an edited and in some places expanded version of a conversation between Asada Wataru and the author in Sumibiraki, *pp. 150–159.*

Asada Wataru, *"Editor of the Everyday"*
Born in Osaka in 1979. Graduated from Osaka City University Faculty of Law. Asada's activities range from music performance and recording to designing and producing multidisciplinary cultural projects and related writing and speaking engagements. He has extended his own range of self-expression from "sound" to "places" and to "happenings" as he uses abandoned facilities, old temples, private homes, ryokan inns, and vacant shops to create spaces and communities all over Japan. Asada is also a member of the interactive music group SjQ++, which received an Award of Distinction in Digital Music and Sound Art at the 2013 Ars Electronica Festival in Linz, Austria.

NARUSE YURI

Assistant professor, University of Tokyo

A Café Rises in the Disaster Zone: Creating a New Public Commons

Naruse Yuri of Naruse Inokuma Architects had been searching for a new kind of architecture that could help give structure to communities. Then the devastating March 11, 2011, earthquake and tsunami in northeastern Japan brought her face to face with exactly that challenge on the ground, as she joined the effort to build a new community café for the shattered coastal town of Rikuzen-Takata.

In the coming years the population in Japan will be aging, there will be more and more unmarried people, and the number of single households will increase. When I was thinking as an architect about what kind of houses, what kind of residences would be best for this future Japan, I became interested in "share houses," and eventually tried my hand at designing some myself. More recently I have been doing research on space sharing at the university.

My parents are in their sixties, the generation that always kept buying up to bigger and bigger cars and televisions. They bought their house with a thirty-year loan. When I tell them that I'm conducting research on sharing, the expression on their faces says clearly, "Why on earth would anyone do that?" You can hardly blame them [*laughs*]. They're the "private ownership" generation.

But after the March 11 earthquake and tsunami, I think it has become a little easier for people to understand the value of sharing. After the disaster, our design office, Naruse Inokuma Architects, was asked by *Kāsa Burūtasu* (Casa Brutus) magazine to come up with a concrete proposal informed by the disaster, and we developed a concept for wooden, share-style, post-disaster temporary housing. By adopting sharing, we were able to reduce the amount of exclusive floor space per individual, while sharing the amenities also holds down construction costs, making it easier for people to come together and live there securely. We thought the disaster zone might also need a housing option like this, considering how many elderly people are living alone there.

Another project we started at about the same time was the Rikuzen-Takata Living Project. There we worked on the project together with local Tōhoku residents and with a team led by Dr. Koizumi Hideki of Tokyo University. As one part of that effort, in January 2012 we opened the Riku Café, a temporary community space in Rikuzen-Takata in Iwate Prefecture.

Dr. Koizumi had friends in the community before the disaster, and I understand that they contacted him for help in community revitalization, his area of specialty. Based on his experience with the relief efforts after the Kobe earthquake of 1995, he felt that it was very important that temporary rebuilding take place even before formal reconstruction plans could be implemented. If there were no shops left at all, no places where the town's residents could rest and relax for even a little, then people would simply disappear from the community. Once that happened, there could be no reconstruction in the true sense of the word.

We located Riku Café in the same location where in April 2011, immediately after the disaster, local clinics and dentists had begun operating out of temporary facilities, as that had become a center for the local citizenry. There had already been a number of people in the disaster zone opening up their own privately-owned spaces to others, as Gotō Chikako of Tokyo University's Urban Design Center Kashiwa (UDCK), which is participating in operational support for the project, found in her research. In Rikuzen-Takata as well, an old acquaintance of Dr. Koizumi had opened his own house to be used as a distribution center for relief supplies and as a space where people could simply stop

The Riku Café, a temporary community space in Rikuzen-Takata in Iwate Prefecture. Photograph courtesy of Naruse Inokuma Architects.

by and have some tea. When he was still doing that there had been a number of calls for the creation of a place where everyone could gather more easily and comfortably, and that led in turn to the building of a community café.

A local landlord offered land for the project, while Dr. Koizumi and I worked on the cafe design. We took no architectural design fee, and the Tokyo University team explained to potential financial backers that this was a new public commons project conceived by local citizens—their support would be directly helping people in the disaster zone in a way that everyone could see. Sumitomo Forestry Company, Ltd. and numerous other companies agreed to cooperate.

We did not want this simply to be a payout for our corporate backers, so we allowed them to use the project in their advertising. Pamphlets are available at Riku Café explaining the materials that were used in its construction, so in a sense it also functions as a showroom.

In fact, we have had people who came to visit the café say they would like to have a house of their own like it, or who have been impressed by the quality of the insulation and have said they want to use the same materials themselves. You might call it another kind of space sharing. Right now volunteers run the café, but we are thinking of converting the project into an NPO to make it self-sustaining.

Not just in Tōhoku but all over Japan, populations will be declining in the years ahead. If we don't consciously act to create places where people can come together, the towns are going to be really lonely places, and they are not going to be generating any new businesses, either. Sharing creates density. I believe sharing has the power to gather people together.

What is most important in making sharing work is how to cooperate together, how to share things together, and how to sustain those mechanisms over the long term. When you say "sharing," the image most people have is of everyone jointly owning and using a single item. What it really means, however, is to pool our personal resources and to create mechanisms for governing that process. The challenge before us now, I think, is how to bring this about in a creative fashion, to design new methods for encouraging and drawing out this kind of sharing among us all.

Just the other day I was back in Rikuzen-Takata for our regular meeting with the local operating team. I was just delighted to see how they keep finding new ways to use the café. Since it was never really the custom in that part of Japan to go sit in a café, it seems they still haven't reached a point where just anyone in the community can feel comfortable popping in. However, they do have regulars now who come in every morning to have some tea, chat, and eat a *bentō* box lunch. I'm looking forward to seeing what develops next.

I have been thinking about how I can commit myself more to people's lives through my daily design work. The Tōhoku disaster gave me new impetus — it was an incredibly precious opportunity for me to be able to participate in this project, and to work together with the people of Rikuzen-Takata directly in actually creating a new center for community life.

Again, I think that my encounter with the idea of "sharing" has expanded my world outside of architecture. I hope that by thinking more about what I and the people around me really want, by thinking of how to make tomorrow's society better, I will be able to help give shape to a new architecture. In the future I want to work on architecture as a mechanism for benefitting society.

Naruse Yuri, *Assistant professor, University of Tokyo Born in Aichi Prefecture, Japan, in 1979. Completed her master's degree from the University of Tokyo School of Engineering, Department of Architecture, in 2004. Since 2007, joint owner of the architectural design studio, Naruse Inokuma Architects. Assistant professor at the University of Tokyo since 2009.*

NISHIMURA HIROSHI
Architect

From Vacant Lots to Green Lawns: Revitalizing the Downtown

Nishimura Hiroshi's award-winning architectural career has taken him far from his hometown of Saga City in northern Kyushu, but the decline of Saga's struggling downtown shopping district prompted him to return with a radically different approach to curing the plague of "shutter streets" and parking lot "vacuums" that is sucking the life out of Japan's regional cities: "Plant it, and they will come."

NISHIMURA: I believe that Saga City can become one of Japan's "top runners." That's because the time will inevitably come when the community revitalization models of regional Japan are exported to Tokyo. In recent years Tokyo has loosened its regulations to encourage investment, and this has resulted in new towns and clumps of skyscrapers and apartment towers. But this cannot continue forever.

When you look at the population statistics, they're already declining for regional cities, but in Tokyo they are still going to go up for another ten to twenty years. Right now Japan's hinterlands are already working desperately to address the crisis that's almost upon them. But two decades from now—when Tokyo's population begins to slide— then it will be Tokyo that's frantically trying to learn from regional Japan. So this is Saga's chance to turn the tables.

MIURA: There are all kinds of different narratives in regional Japan. Yet until now everyone's tried to follow the Tokyo model.

NISHIMURA: For years the Tokyo model was regional Japan's utopia. So even after the times changed, it wasn't easy for them to change their way of thinking.

MIURA: Please tell me the specifics of what you're doing here in Saga City.*

NISHIMURA: The central shopping district of Saga City covers an area with a radius of about three hundred meters. But when you walk through the district it has already become, not just a "shutter town" of empty storefronts, but what you could call a "parking lot vacuum," with parking lots everywhere where there used to be buildings. We call our plan for reviving this town center the Yonkaku Kōsō, or Four Point Plan. The four "points" are the S-platz building, a third-sector community development project that went bankrupt in 2003 but has now been revived; the old classic local department store Saga Tamaya; the Saga Jinja shrine; and the site of the old abandoned Mado-no-ume supermarket, now home to the new headquarters of the public Saga Health Insurance Organization.

Instead of redeveloping these four points in the old twentieth century way, our goal is to first re-establish foot traffic between them while making careful use of resources that are already there.

Saga City is built on a plain, so bypasses right out of some urban planning textbook have been flung up, development has spread further and further into the suburbs, and big box stores are popping up everywhere while the city core withers. Even if you wanted to compress this sprawl it would be impossible. So the real question is how to take the current, hollowed-out city core and create a new environment there.

When you ask the people at city hall what they're doing about the city center, it turns out they're actually holding events there all year

---

* Saga City is the capital of Saga Prefecture on the island of Kyushu in southern Japan. Its population in 2009 was 238,934.

The central shopping district of Saga City, full of parking lots where there used to be buildings. Illustration courtesy of Workvisions.

long. But no matter how many events you stage, once they're over the foot traffic returns to what it was before. That approach does nothing to create lasting change.

Based on that premise, we created our Downtown Revitalization Project in March 2011. What is key here is how to manage vacant lots. In the past, you would buy up all the vacant lots, redevelop them, put up new buildings, bring in tenants to fill them, and then presumedly the people would pour in and the place would come alive. That was the twentieth-century model, but if you try doing that now, even if it went well at first, before long you would have more and more empty shops again. So the point of our plan is to see what we can do—while leaving these empty spaces empty—to create an environment where people will come and walk around the downtown again.

Our idea was that if we tore out all those empty parking lots and created attractive open spaces it would transform the city. If they were turned into open spaces, first of all the living environment would improve. There would be more people who wanted to live downtown. It would create an environment where more young couples would feel they could raise children. In which case, we would probably see a movement to convert many of the empty stores into residences.

So, in order to just try it and see what would happen, we implemented what we call the "Waiwai Container Project." The Saga city government rented land owned by a bank, and we created a plaza with a lawn and modified shipping containers and essentially ran a social experiment to see what kind of activities would lead people to gather at the site.

Inside the containers we placed some three hundred different magazines, children's picture books, and *manga* comic books. Visitors can go and read them for free.

MIURA: Did the cost of the publications come out of the Saga City Business Promotion Section's budget?

NISHIMURA: Yes, in addition to donations and other sources. In order to get a selection of titles that would draw a broad range of age groups to the site, we checked what was currently popular at the city library and studied popularity rankings on the Internet. We also threw in foreign magazines and picture books. You normally can't even buy foreign magazines, not in Saga! [*laughs*]. And as a result, we get children, adults, elderly gentlemen, a cross-section of generations. Sometimes there are so many children playing on the grass it makes you wonder where on earth they've all been hiding until now. Even the nursery schools bring their pupils around on their daily walks.

MIURA: Do you have food and drinks there?

NISHIMURA: You can bring your own, or you can have food delivered here by shops we've established tie-ups with. We sell sweets on consignment. During the summer, after it cools down in the evening all kinds of people gather here. We even get folk playing recorders [*laughs*].

MIURA: It sounds like Inokashira Park in Kichijōji, near where I live!

NISHIMURA: Until now Saga's citizens used to say that even if they did come downtown there wasn't anything to do, there weren't any people around, it just didn't make sense to go there. The city would tell the local merchants to try harder to get people to come, and the merchants would answer right back, "People just won't come. We can't try any harder than we are already" [*laughs*]. It went around and around in circles. Sometimes they would hold events and appeal to people to come. But you can't sustain that turnout once the event's over.

The goal of the Waiwai Container Project is not to siphon all the district's activity into these two sites. Instead, by having the shopping district merchants advertise here, deliver food to our visitors, introduce their products on-site, we want people to fan out from the containers into the town. After they spend some time here, go have something to eat, or do some shopping on their way home. That's the kind of activity we want this to encourage.

And another thing. We had the local residents themselves plant the grass lawns. When you have the children plant the lawns, no one tosses their trash there anymore. People take care of things they have a hand in creating. Even the wooden decks are like that. Our staff worked

Once a lawn was planted in the vacant lot, the children poured in. Photo courtesy of Workvisions

together with city hall staff and college students to go to home centers to buy the materials, work them, and ultimately install them themselves.

Inside the containers the children hunt for picture books they want to read and listen to book readings. Foreign residents drop in to teach English classes. Other local people have held art exhibitions. We even had a visiting dancer from the United States who performed in front of the containers, in the rain. It's all been things like that.

Next, if you ask what the local shopping district is doing in response to all this, one day a downtown *gyōza* pot sticker shop suddenly put photos on its website of *gyōza* placed on the

Stocking containers with books and magazines created a place where people wanted to be. Photograph courtesy of Workvisions.

lawn under the slogan, "*Shibafu ni gyōza*" (*Gyōza* on the Grass) And in the next day's newspaper, there was an advertisement titled: "There are lawns downtown. And there's a *gyōza* shop downtown, too!" Complete with coupons [*laughs*]. You don't need permission to take or use photographs of the site. The important thing is for the citizens themselves to use their imagination to come up with ideas on how to use the lots.

When it came to maintaining the lots, we also decided not to rely solely on government. Instead, we arranged to have a local landscape gardener use the lot for his own PR and offer for-pay lectures to citizens with an interest in gardening. The revenues cover his expenses for maintaining and managing the lawn. It's good advertising for the gardener and boosts his income. And as a result, we have an automatic process in place for maintaining the property, while Saga citizens get an opportunity to learn gardening. We want to try doing more things like this from fiscal 2012 on.

We are also planning to invite the famous Saga-born architect Baba Masataka to join us in thinking about how to promote the reutilization of vacant stores via media like a Saga version of Tokyo R Fudōsan (Real Tokyo Estate). Yet another idea is community activism, which is why we have invited in community designer Yamazaki Ryō. Our goal is to produce the conditions for Saga's citizens to use vacant lots for their own activities on an everyday basis.

Nishimura Hiroshi, *architect*
Born in Saga Prefecture, Japan, in 1967. Completed his master's degree from the University of Tokyo School of Engineering in 1993. Founded the architectural firm Workvisions in Tokyo in 1999. Nishimura's genre-transcending work encompasses architecture, civil engineering, community revitalization, and other disciplines as he focuses on creating new things while keeping the issues of "town/city/community" always in mind. Major projects include the Saga City Downtown Revitalization Plan, the Iwamizawa Compound Station Building (recipient, Japan Industrial Design Promotion Organization 2009 Good Design Awards Good Design Grand Award and 2010 Architectural Institute of Japan Architectural Design Division Prize). The Waiwai Container Project received a Good Design Award in 2013.

TSUJII TAKASHI

Poet, novelist, founder of the Saison Group

Toward the Muji "Non-brand" Era

Tsujii Takashi (the nom de plume *of Tsutsumi Seiji) was a living witness to the history of Japan's economy and society from before World War II up until his death on November 25, 2013, at the age of eighty-six. In the postwar years he was commander in chief of the Saison Group, not only a retail and distribution business but an integrated lifestyle industry in its own right, as well as a celebrated poet and novelist. In the following interview I asked Tsujii about Japan's past, present, and future from the perspective of the history of postwar consumer society.*

THE FIRST LIBERATION OF THE JAPANESE CONSUMER: THE 1960s

MIURA: I personally consider your greatest business achievement to be the creation of Mujirushi Ryōhin (known abroad as Muji Store), so I would like to begin by asking you, from the perspective of the history of postwar consumer society, why you decided to create the brand?

TSUJII: Japanese consumers used to be quite unsophisticated. The overwhelming majority of consumers were amateurs. From the Meiji period [starting in 1868] through to Japan's defeat in World War II, they had never been given time to mature. Just when it seemed they were starting to grow up, they would be snatched away to be soldiers.

It was the same with specialty stores. Just about the time a craftsman or a shopkeeper was beginning to think to himself, "I've finally
got a handle on bags and purses now. Let's turn this into a specialty
store," he'd get his *akagami* draft notice. It was impossible for anyone to
become a real specialist.

That's why, when you walk along the Ginza today, you can practically count the number of Japanese brand stores on one hand. Even
the ones that do exist don't have the wherewithal to compete with a
Hermes or the like.

Even after the war ended, from 1945 to 1960—up until the era of
rapid economic growth, in fact—there were no structures in place for
developing specialty brands, and I think Japan's consumers, too, were
essentially still in the old *sakoku*, "closed country," mentality.

In Europe, you understand, craftsmen didn't have to go to war.
They were considered to have specializations of their own.

MIURA: They protected their craftsmen?

TSUJII: They did. The Europeans were conscious that a product's value
came from the craftsman who made it. But Japan's government from
the Meiji period on did not share that attitude. For them it was all,
"*Zeitaku wa teki da*" (Luxury is our enemy).* In the Imperial Rescript
of 1908, issued in the forty-first year of Meiji when people were still
exuberant over Japan's victory in the Russo-Japanese War, it was all
about simplicity and fortitude being Japan's national policy. Later, after
the Great Kantō Earthquake of 1923, Yamamoto Gonnohyōe** used the
Taishō Emperor's name to declare that *keichō fuhaku* (Frivolity and
Western ways) were what had led Japan astray. And now, leaping ahead
across eras, we have "Lord" Ishihara Shintarō calling the 2011 Tōhoku

---

* A widely used government slogan during the war years, codified in a July 7, 1940, min-
isterial ordinance restricting production of luxury goods and imposing other austerities,
known popularly as the Shichi-shichi Kinrei (7.7 Prohibition Ordinance).
** Admiral Yamamoto Gonnohyōe (Gonbei), appointed Japan's eighth prime minister in
1913 and named prime minister again shortly after the Great Kantō Earthquake of 1923
to lead a reconstruction cabinet.

earthquake and tsunami *"tenbatsu,"* or divine punishment.* It's always been this way. When I heard "Lord" Ishihara's *tenbatsu* comment I was profoundly disappointed. I thought, "Meiji still lives!" [*laughs*].

After that stage, however, the "closed country" mentality began to lift, and we entered a period when people began to think that maybe foreign products weren't half bad, that maybe it was fine to go ahead and buy them all you want. We opened up to foreign countries.

That's how it was that the Takashimaya Department Store tried holding an "Italian Fair" in 1956. Everything sold like crazy! Up until then, Japanese consumers had thought that European goods were "untouchable," something forever beyond their reach. So essentially, from the 1868 Meiji Revolution up to 1945, and then again from 1945 until 1960, Japan's consumers were trapped in *sakoku*.

Come 1959 I decided that we should do our own France Exhibition, and I went to Paris to select the merchandise. As a simple department store owner, I couldn't let the other guys outdo us, right? And indeed, it sold very well. Everything went, down to the ashtrays and wastebaskets. We sold absolutely everything we had. There wasn't a single thing left. And I thought to myself, *sakoku* really has lasted a long, long time in Japan. We've censored ourselves with all those old slogans: "*Hoshigarimasen, katsu made!*" (We won't want anything, not until victory!), "*Konna zeitaku na mono o, wareware ga mi ni tsukete wa mōshiwake arimasen.*" (We'd be ashamed to wear such luxurious things"). But as we entered the 1960s that self-restraint loosened at last.

Given that state of affairs, up until about 1980 I devoted myself exclusively to introducing foreign brands. If I count them all up now it comes to around fifty different brands.

And the Europeans were quite willing to oblige. Just looking at the numbers, Japan's economy seemed to be getting a lot stronger, so if some Japanese department store showed up saying that they wanted to represent them in Japan, it was a perfect way to get in some test marketing.

---

* Ishihara Shintarō: Outspoken novelist, conservative politician, and the governor of Tokyo from 1999 to 2012. On March 14, 2011, three days after the Tōhoku earthquake and tsunami, Ishihara told reporters that he considered the disaster to be "divine punishment" for modern Japan's rampant greed and self-interest.

THE SECOND LIBERATION OF THE JAPANESE CONSUMER:
THE LATTER HALF OF THE 1970S

TSUJII: For me there was a by-product in all this. Namely, when I wasn't working I would go out and visit the museums of Paris. Everywhere I went it was, "This is amazing! I've never seen anything like this before!" It made me realize that I had been in a kind of *sakoku* myself when it came to the arts and art history. My own awareness of painting stopped, at the very most, at the late Impressionists.

MIURA: Or it did until 1959?

TSUJII: Exactly. Once in Paris I saw work the likes of which I had never seen before. [Vassily] Kandinsky, [Paul] Klee. I might be thinking to myself, "What the heck is that?" but it was all still fascinating. I thought to myself, "I've been locked away too." Then when I got back to the apartment all tired out and turned on the radio, this time it would be all this perplexing music pouring out. Again, I'd think to myself, "What the devil is this?" But when I listened more closely it would turn out to be a piece by [Karlheinz] Stockhausen taped by the WDR Köln Rundfunkorchester Broadcasting Station. I realized that I'd been in a "closed country" state about music, too. So that was the by-product of my trip to France.

There was another kind of by-product when I moved to Los Angeles in 1961 to spend a year there. I never want to live in such a boring place again for the rest of my life! [*laughs*]. There was nothing there to see except Disneyland and the luxury restaurants of Hollywood, and all those idiots, flush with money but no different inside from average people you might see anywhere. I couldn't bring myself to even feel like talking to them.

What I wound up looking forward to were my occasional trips to New York for our corporate bond issues and other business. When I first visited New York it was the beginning of the Pop Art movement. In Paris I'd been irradiated with contemporary art. Now in New York I crashed into Pop Art.

MIURA: There wasn't any Pop Art in Los Angeles yet?

Tsutsumi Seiji, then representative director and store manager of the Seibu Ikebukuro head store, in 1961.

TSUJII: Nothing at all. But you can say that as a by-product of these travels, from 1959 to 1961 I experienced an internal revolution. How shall I put it? My own liberation from *sakoku* moved ahead.

So in that sense, on the consumption side Japan's first liberation from *sakoku* began around 1960, but I cannot help feeling that there was also a second revolution readied for me personally in terms of arts and culture and the way I lived.

Our Mujirushi business then occurs as a *Merkmal*, a characteristic, of the second lifting of *sakoku*. When I try to pull it all together, that seems to be its place in the broader current. If I were to divide Japan's postwar consumer society into two stages, I would say there was a strong element of social reformation up through the end of the 1960s. As an effect of the first liberation from *sakoku*, you understand.

However, once we enter the 1970s, that sense of liberation largely disappears. So within that larger current, I think I can say that Mujirushi was for me my own second liberation from *sakoku*.

Marx himself wrote that consumption is not part of the reproduction of labor-power. There's some element of that, of course. But the product of consumption is the individual himself, the "restoration of man to himself." Viewed that way, we had already achieved our first liberation, but I could not help but feel that we were not doing quite so well on achieving the second stage, in other words the restoration of man to himself.

At the same time, I had become quite fed up with all the talk about "brand" this and "brand" that.

MIURA: About when was it that you got so fed up?

TSUJII: By the second half of the 1970s I was already feeling that it was something I really had to give some thought to. Slap a label on something, and it would sell for 20 percent more than before. I had a growing sense inside me that this was akin to fraud [*laughs*].

So it struck me that an integrated lifestyle industry had to free itself from first-stage *sakoku*, not just about things like textiles or cosmetics but about every aspect of living. Our housing, every part of our lives needed to be liberated from that "closed country" mentality.

MIURA: I see. In other words, by creating Mujirushi [literally, "no-brand"], something that was neither a brand nor worshipping things Western, you were trying to reach that second stage of liberation?

TSUJII: But even so, when we opened our Mujirushi store in Aoyama in 1983 it took three months of debate inside the company. Please remember that at the time Mujirushi was a division of Seiyū. Seiyū had a policy of not opening any stores unconnected to its main [department store] business, so was it really okay to create this new place at all? What makes you think you have any business opening a store in an upscale location like Aoyama? That kind of thing. Seiyū had already launched several private brands before Mujirushi, brands like Kokyō Meihin (Hometown Best) and Shufu no Me Shōhin (The Housewife's Eye), but they never really caught on.

MIURA: I seem to remember buying a "Housewife's Eye" chopping board [*laughs*].

TSUJII: You did, did you? Thank you very much!

MIURA: It was a very simple, no-frills product.

TSUJII: As an object, I think it wasn't bad.

MIURA: A Mujirushi forerunner.

TSUJII: It was. And when I was trying to figure out what the problem was, I realized that partly it was about price.

MIURA: "Housewife's Eye" wasn't very cheap?

TSUJII: It wasn't cheap. After all, in a way it was all small-lot production. Things like that can't be mass-produced. So I got to thinking. The products were good, but the prices were no good. And that led to the idea that if we were going to be in a weak position competing on single items, then we had to focus on presentation, on presenting a complete line of products.

That's why when we first started up Mujirushi I hardly brought in anyone from Seiyū or our department stores at all. I just had all these secret conversations with people [on the creative side] like Tanaka Ikkō, Koike Kazuko, and Sugimoto Kishi. Itoi Shigesato was in it, too. We'd get together in a bar in Yoyogi and hash things out.

For my part, during the daytime I spent all my time visiting different Seiyū stores to see which products were expensive, and weren't selling because of their price. Asking myself things like, why can't we sell shiitake mushrooms that aren't perfect in appearance, even in pieces? Or, can we lower our production costs if we stop lining up all the crab legs in our canned crabs. I went and visited sheep farms to buy the wool for our sweaters. I think Uniqlo is doing the same thing nowadays.

Both Uniqlo and we began by going right to the start of the production chain when we created our goods. This is something department stores can't do. That's because they want to be able to send unsold goods back to the wholesaler.

MIURA: You've said that Mujirushi doesn't worship foreign brands, that its products are anti-establishment products. The activities you've been describing just now don't sound corporation-centric at all. They sound like anti-establishment consumer rights actions.

TSUJII: I don't think anything else I ever said whle I was still on the job fell as flat as "anti-establishment products" [*laughs*]. "Establishment" itself was still a new word to a lot of people. "Anti-establishment" all the more so.

MIURA: Was Tanaka Ikkō the first person you called in from outside the company?

TSUJII: That's right.

MIURA: And the name Mujirushi Ryōhin [literally, "No-brand good merchandise"]. That was Tanaka?

TSUJII: He coined it.

MIURA: But the concept was yours?

TSUJII: I think at first I was saying "Nonburando Shōhin" ("Non-brand merchandise"). It was Tanaka who hit on "Mujirushi."

MIURA: Nowadays a lot more companies are going back to Japanese for their product naming.

TSUJII: It's finally begun to increase.

MIURA: Thirty years ago it really took some courage.

TSUJII: Back then using Japanese felt so old-fashioned, so out of it. But when I visit Muji branches overseas today they're playing Buddhist *shōmyō* chants as background music.

MIURA: Right in the stores?

TSUJII. That's right. And they light *o-kō* incense, too.

MIURA: The staff overseas think that's more "Japanese"? That it's a good idea to do that?

TSUJII: I think so . . . . And also because in fact it's proven quite effective.

MIURA: It's so Zen?

TSUJII: Well, maybe just more exotic. As for myself, I've been telling them that exoticism is fine for now, but that it's only going to work for them for, at the most, seven or eight years. If they don't use that time to build up their ties with local production centers, eventually they're going to run out of steam. That's been my advice.

MIURA: When you launched Mujirushi did you have any notion of making Muji a kind of standard that could spread around the world?

TSUJII: In the beginning we were only concerned about securing our position in Japan itself [*laughs*]. To be perfectly honest.

MIURA: I see. But, it's actually quite rare for products like these to travel outside of Japan and catch on overseas.

TSUJII: I do think it's rare.

MIURA: Not machinery, not instant cup noodles. . . .

TSUJII: I think it's extremely rare to see a whole line of products make it abroad the way Muji has.

READING THE ZEITGEIST

MIURA: Of course this isn't true just of you, Tsujii-san, but managers have to stay on top of the changing times. In your case, you were in the retail industry, and you were an exceptionally astute reader of the times. I imagine there must have been a few failures along the way, too, but tell me, how do you stay in touch with the zeitgeist?

TSUJII: If you'll pardon me starting with a joke, my trick is to go to the ō-gosho, the very inner sanctum of the business and financial community, the *zaikai*. And if I then do the exact opposite of the consensus opinion of the *zaikai* ō-gosho, I'm pretty much guaranteed to stay on top of the times [*laughs*]. That's because those people don't even want to read the times.

MIURA: They don't?

TSUJII: Their authority all rests upon the eras that came before.

MIURA: You have a point there.

TSUJII: This may also sound like I'm joking, but I've found that another thing to do is to do the opposite of the mass media consensus. Miura-san, Japan's mass media are truly terrible. The so-called Big Six newspapers? Dismal. If you flip the consensus of Japan's *zaikai* and the mass media on its head, you can get a pretty good reading of the times and see where we're headed.

MIURA: It's pretty alarming if even the mass media can't read the times, or are deliberately not even trying to.

TSUJII: It is. And then the third thing—and this is really the key—is to just walk the streets. It really doesn't matter where. It can be a Matsumoto Kiyoshi drugstore, or Uniqlo. Strolling through places like that and eavesdropping on people's conversations are what will give you the best hints of all. This is absolutely true. Listening to what people are talking about on the train is good, too.

With mass consumption, you can't get a grasp of what changes are happening just by doing a little research here and there. An earthquake sends a tsunami washing ashore, and cars are sent tumbling over and over like toys. You see that, and suddenly you stop wanting to own a car after all. Just from [those TV scenes of the disaster] alone, I think there is a feeling spreading among a lot of people that we can get by without owning all those things we used to think we couldn't live without.

That's why now, when the Cabinet Office or the Ministry of Internal Affairs and Communications or I don't know who runs around shouting things like "Japan is strong!" or "*Ganbare* (Fight on), Japan!" I personally find them the most execrable catchphrases possible. Their mentality is locked in place as if the sixty years since World War II never happened.

If you ask me, I think that in the future regional Japan is going to be the new center, and we will find ourselves trying to create new communities unlike any we have ever seen before. Once that happens, society is going to be transformed, in all senses of the word. I think the challenges we are going to face in the future cannot be overcome by the center [in Tokyo].

MIURA: It has also been my feeling that the [2011] disaster may be the most difficult problem Japan has faced in its history. Kobe is a modern city without much of a past. So when it gets destroyed [in the 1995 Kobe earthquake], you can basically just rebuild. But the Tōhoku region is different. I often hear people saying that if [former prime minister] Tanaka Kakuei was still around he would have had a reconstruction plan in place by now, but I don't think that's true.

TSUJII: This time is different.

MIURA: The area is so vast, there are so many different local characteristics, and the cities are not modern. There may be factories, but there are also rice paddies and fields and fishing villages. You don't know where to begin. Most important of all, people's consciousness has changed. If Tōhoku had been devastated thirty years ago, the thinking would have been, we'll build some expressways, put up buildings. It would have been seen as a chance to modernize the region. But right now nobody thinks modernization is a good thing. They want to preserve Tōhoku's own unique qualities. That's why we can't do a Tanaka Kakuei-style reconstruction.

TSUJII: Speaking of Tōhoku, actually the disaster has given me some hope that Japan is not a lost cause after all. That's because it has shown us a different image of Japan than what has come to be considered "Japanese" for so many years.

MIURA: What might that be?

TSUJII: For example, it's that Tōhoku came right out and opposed the center. That has never happened before. The instant "Lord" Ishihara Shintarō called the disaster "divine punishment" the region's local governments, the prefectural governors, the mayors, village heads, all came out and said, "What is he saying? How dare he call this *tenbatsu* when everyone's suffering like this." Even that arrogant Ishihara Shintarō had to bow his head the next day.

SMALL COMMUNITIES AS THE NEW CORE

TSUJII: I think that local government leaders—governors, mayors, village and town heads—discovered that even without the help of the center, they could do it themselves. This is a huge discovery.

MIURA: It's truly "Muji-Nippon."

TSUJII: Exactly right. This is something we should make special note of about this disaster. Until now, people thought that they could not do anything without the center. But actually, governors and the mayors in Japan are given considerable authority. I think it was a discovery for the entire Japanese people to find out that there were such capable people among Tōhoku's town and village leaders.

MIURA: Even though our national legislators are no good.

TSUJII: Compared to the foot-dragging of the central government ministers and officials, it's hard to believe they're the same Japanese. I have a feeling that we're entering a new stage.

Or another way of putting it might be to say that Japan's old, premodern village societies still exist in Tōhoku. But if you were to ask who destroyed Japan's village societies in the first place, it was without a doubt national mobilization, it was government by the military faction during World War II, it was the Tōjō Hideki cabinet. They destroyed Japan's village communities.

And then there were those virtues of Japanese-style management, the lifetime employment system and seniority-based pay hikes. Tōjō Hideki broke these as well. During World War II the national system was totalitarianism. The declarations of the government back then were to an astonishing degree identical in content to the declarations of the Soviet Communist Party's Central Committee. So perhaps the Tōhoku region was not as contaminated by the demagoguery of history as the center was. It may sound paradoxical, but it may be that it was in Tōhoku that the good qualities of the old Japan still survived.

MIURA: There was a way in which the [2011] disaster washed away the dirt and grime of our old conventional wisdom.

TSUJII: It was also truly a surprise to me to find that there were so many people with such strong independent decision-making skills, such leadership, among Tōhoku's town and village heads.

MIURA: That's why this idea that the center has to take care of regional Japan because regional Japan can't take care of itself may actually be a fantasy created by the center itself.

TSUJII: It's the same kind of fantasy as the fantasy of nuclear power. And now it's collapsed.

MIURA: Now that this has happened, I expect we will see a mood building that it would be better for the taxes collected locally to all be used locally.

TSUJII: It became a huge issue when I said something just like that while I was still serving on the Tax Commission. What's wrong with having the localities collect the taxes and take out what they need at the local level, I asked, and then send the central government whatever's left? Germany does it. Japan's the only one that forces everyone to line up with the center. But when I said that in the committee, I was told I'd made an unthinkably dangerous statement.

MIURA: This time it's the people of Tōhoku themselves who are saying, given how bad things are, just lift the central government regulations and let us do things our way.

TSUJII: That they are.

MIURA: From the central government's perspective, however, they must feel that once they permit that to happen there's no telling where it might lead. They just can't let them do that, not even in a crisis situation.

TSUJII: The central government ministries and agencies do seem to feel this is a crisis. If they manage to rope everything back together again under "*Ganbare*, Japan!" we're in trouble.

And another thing. When you look at Tōhoku, you can see how there has never really been any such thing as city planning anywhere in Japan.

MIURA: I think that's right.

TSUJII: The general feeling is, "It's my money and it's my land. What's the big problem with me building on it?" So people just throw up anything, anywhere. Then, after some time goes by, they begin to think, "Oh, I guess we do need a park, and a kindergarten" and add them on after the fact. Our cities today are the result of that kind of thinking.

But I think one of the lessons of this disaster will be that, while we don't refute the system of private ownership, and while it is all right for people to be able to have what they want, at the same time there is a limit. I think people's attitudes are shifting in that direction, that, if it's for reasons affecting the public good, it may be necessary for individual rights to be curtailed to some degree.

MIURA: I think that's true. And at the same time, I think it is essential that Japan's politicians and business and financial leaders have some kind of sense of how our cities should be changed. The distribution industry nowadays just runs computerized population analyses and puts up stores wherever it looks like they can get a lot of traffic. There's no urban theory or even Tokyo theory behind it at all.

It's my feeling from personal experience that, just to take one example, the center of Tokyo is becoming more and more boring. Everyone is putting up new buildings, or stations, or shopping malls that are like fortresses, driven by a philosophy that says, get everyone into one place and don't let them spend a single yen anywhere else. Even if you do want to walk around the streets to feel the zeitgeist, the "street" itself is disappearing.

TSUJII: It's just as you say. I remember someone saying to me some-time back that the streets feel really deserted, and I think it may finally be beginning to happen now. They really have become deserted. But when you ask what can be done to revive them, I think that there are actually a number of new, little communities—communities that merge where we live with where we work, with stores and shops attached to them—being built already. It may take thirty years, it may take forty years, but after our big metropolises decline we will see the formation of new blocs with these new mini-communities at their core, and the creation of new modes of public administration. There will be trees planted between all these neighboring blocs, and someday they will grow into forests.

Well. It may take a hundred years for that to happen, a dizzyingly long time. But it is inconceivable that Tokyo can continue to grow the way it is now. If we don't inject an element of community into our thinking, it will be impossible to find our way to reviving our cities and towns.

MIURA: That's very true. Some time back I did a reconnaissance of Tokyo's suburbs and the *shitamachi* low town for a dialogue with Dr. Jinnai Hidenobu of Hōsei University to run in the sixtieth anniversary special edition of *Toshi Keikaku* (City Planning), the magazine of the City Planning Institute of Japan. And it really was just as you say. There are fresh little shoots of small-scale community-building cropping up all over. One housewife around forty years old had asked the owners of some nearby uncultivated agricultural land to let her use it to set up a community garden. Local residents work the garden, and those who come to tend it on any given day take home whatever is ready for picking that day. They make their own fertilizer from the raw garbage created by the surrounding residential districts. It's just one little example, but these kinds of movements are happening. Meanwhile the housewife who started the garden has been motivated by the project to study urban planning, and is learning about the Building Standards Act.

TSUJII: This is another thing I just happened to have heard, but when someone ran a survey of where you could find a good town to live in the environs of Tokyo itself, at the top of the list was the Ningyō-chō district. I think second place was Kagurazaka? Those are both places in the city where there is still a sense of community.

MIURA: That's because the people doing business there still live there themselves.

TSUJII: Build communities that use for their yardstick whether or not the people living there can really enjoy a decent human life.

MIURA: Maybe your "Muji" way of thinking—unbound by the old, establishment value systems of brands and their ilk—can begin to spread, not just as *mono*, as "things" like Mujirushi Ryōhin products, but as *koto*, as the things we do, and as people. Maybe someday we'll see the creation of "Muji-style" towns.

TSUJII: Yes. And if you do try building a "Muji" town, before you know it, it might outgrow even this thing we call "Muji" and start generating new concepts of its own.

MIURA: Certainly not just a town that only uses Mujirushi Ryōhin, Mujirushi's "good products."

TSUJII: Yes. Yes.

MIURA: Mujirushi *"ryōji"* (Mujirushi good things) and Mujirushi *"ryōnin"* (Mujirushi good people)!

TSUJII: I think you've got it [*laughs*].

Tsujii Takashi

Nom de plume *of Tsutsumi Seiji, poet and novelist and founder of the Saison Group. Born in Tokyo in 1927. Died November 2013 at the age of 86. Recipient of the 1994 Tanizaki Jun'ichirō Prize for Literature for his novel* Niji no misaki *(Rainbow Cove) (Tokyo: Chūō Kōronsha, 1994). Recipient in 2006 of the 62nd Japan Art Academy Onshi Prize. Appointed a member of the Japan Art Academy, member of the board of the Japan P.E.N. Club, and vice-chairman of the Japan Art Academy. His later works included the poetry collection,* Tsujii Takashi Zenshishū *(Complete Poems of Tsujii Takashi) (Tokyo: Shichōsha, 2009), the novel* Akaneiro no sora *(A Madder Red Sky) (Tokyo: Bungei Shunjūsha, 2010), and the essay collection,* Ryūri no jidai *(The Age of Wandering) (Tokyo: Genki Shobō, 2012).*

A Timeline of Consumer Society:
1851 to 2012

Principal Periods of Modern Japan

Edo (Tokugawa)	1600–1867
Meiji	1868–1912 *(to July 29)*
Taishō	1912–1926 *(to December 24)*
Shōwa	1926–1989 *(to January 6)*
Heisei	1989–

Nengō	JAPAN	Year
		1851
Tokugawa Period Kaei		1852
6	• Commodore Matthew Perry leads a flotilla into Edo Bay, today's Tokyo Bay, effectively ending more than two centuries of Japan's *sakoku* seclusion policy.	1853
Ansei		
1	• The Treaty of Kanagawa signed, opening the ports of Shimoda and Hakodate to U.S. vessels.	1854
5	• Japan-U.S. Friendship and Trade Treaty signed.	1858
Keiō		
2	• Fukuzawa Yukichi publishes Seiyô jijô (Conditions in the West) after returning from an international study mission.	1866
3	• Japan participates in the 1867 Exposition Universelle d'Art et d'Industrie in Paris, its first international exposition. • Nakagawa Kahei opens Japan's first butcher shop handling beef in Tokyo's Takanawa, later opens Nakagawaya restaurant serving *gyūnabe*, forerunner of sukiyaki.	1867
Meiji Period		
1	• Meiji Revolution launches the modern Japanese state. Edo renamed Tokyo.	1868
2	• Public telegraph service begins between Tokyo and Yokohama. • First public horse-drawn coach service begins between Tokyo and Yokohama.	1869
4	• *Yokohama Mainichi Shimbun* (Yokohama Daily News) published. First daily newspaper in Japanese and the first to use domestically produced lead type. • Modern postal service begins between Tokyo, Kyoto, and Osaka.	1871
5	• Rail service links Tokyo's Shimbashi and Yokohama. • Gas streetlights installed in Yokohama.	1872
7	• Kimuraya opens its first store on the Ginza, sells sweet *anpan* buns.	1874
		1875
10	• The First National Industrial Exposition held in Tokyo's Ueno Park.	1877
11	• American educator George Adams Leland teaches athletics in Japan at the invitation of the Japanese government.	1878
		1879
14	• The Second National Industrial Exposition held in Ueno Park with nearly four times as many products and nearly double the attendance.	1881
15	• The first electric arc light is installed in Tokyo's Ginza. • Tokyo's first permanent museum and zoo open in Ueno Park. • Kimuraya's *anpan* the rage on the Ginza.	1882

Themes	WORLD
	• The Great Exhibition of the Works of Industry of All Nations, the first world's fair, opens in London.
	• Le Bon Marché, the world's first department store, opens in Paris.

Pax Britannica

The Crystal Palace in Hyde Park, an iron-framed glass building designed by Joseph Paxton and erected for the Great Exhibition of 1851. From a painting by P. Le Bihan. Photo courtesy of Aflo.

• First U.S. transcontinental rail line completed.

• The first incarnation of Bloomingdale's department store opens in New York.

• Liberty department store opens in London.

• England's first official tennis tournament is held at Wimbledon.

Westernization

• Werner von Siemens presents the world's first electric locomotive at the Berlin Industrial Exhibition.

Nengō	JAPAN	Year
Meiji 16	• The governmental Rokumeikan (House of the Cry of the Stag) lodging, social club, and ballroom opens in Tokyo's Kojimachi-ku (now Uchisaiwai-cho), next to the site of today's Imperial Hotel.	1883
		1884
		1885
21	• Kahisakan, Japan's first full-fledged café, opens in Tokyo's Shitaya just north of today's Ueno Station.	1888
22	• Public telephone service begins between Tokyo and Atami.	1889
23	• The **Asakusa Ryōunkaku tower**, popularly known as the Asakusa Twelve Storys, becomes a Tokyo landmark boasting Japan's first elevator.	1890
25	• Watchmaker Hattori Kintarō establishes Seikōsha, today's Seikō.	1892
		1893

The Third National Industrial Exposition of 1890 (Ad Museum Tokyo Collection). | 1894 |
30	• Inabata Katsutarō holds the first showing of cinematographic films in Osaka's Namba.	1897
31	• Japan's first bicycle races held in Ueno Park.	1898
32	• Nippon Beer K.K., forerunner of Sapporo Breweries, opens Ebisu Beer Hall, Japan's first full-scale beer hall, in Tokyo's Shimbashi (now Ginza).	1899
		1900
		1901
35	• Singer Sewing Machine Co. (today's Singer Corporation) opens a Japan branch on the Ginza.	1902

*Letchworth, the first "garden city" (1903).
(Photo by author).*

Themes	WORLD

<!-- Left margin vertical labels: "Asakusa Era" and "Rise of the United States" -->

- *Ladies' Home Journal* published in the U.S.

- The London Underground Inner Circle line completed.
- The forerunner of the Marks & Spencer, Ltd. department store chain founded in Leeds' Kirkgate Market.
- Germany's Karl Benz sells the three-wheel Benz Patent Motorwagen, the world's first commercial car.
- The Tiffany glasswork studio opens in New York.

- England's John Boyd Dunlop invents the inflatable rubber bicycle tire.

- **Eiffel Tower** erected in Paris as the entrance arch to the 1889 Exposition Universelle world's fair on the centenary of the French Revolution.
- British businessman Thomas Lipton begins buying tea estates in Ceylon (today's Sri Lanka).

- The Coca-Cola Co. founded in the U.S.
- The Parker Co. fountain pen maker founded in the U.S.
- *Vogue* magazine launched.

- The Chicago World's Columbian Exposition marks the 400th anniversary of Christopher Columbus' voyage to the Americas. The ornate Japan Pavilion influences many American architects and designers.

- ***Billboard Magazine*** published.

Fashion leader Vogue, *April 1924.*
Photo courtesy of Vogue Magazine.

- Campbell Soup Co. devises condensed canned soup.

- England's Sir Ebenezer Howard founds Garden Cities Association, the future Town and Country Planning Association.

- 47 million attendees throng the 1900 Paris Exposition Universelle.
- Paris's first subway line enters service.
- Kodak starts selling a one-dollar camera.

- Luxury department store Bergdorf Goodman opens in New York.
- England's Gramophone & Typewriter Co. invents the standard play record.

- Pepsi-Cola Co. founded.
- Cadillac builds its first car.

Paris Exposition Universelle 1900.
Photo courtesy of Yomiuri Shashinkan.

Nengō	JAPAN	Year
Meiji 36		1903

Meiji 36 — 1903
- Socialist philosopher Sakai Toshihiko launches *Katei Zasshi* (Home Journal) promoting reformations in Japanese home life.
- Pioneering woman journalist Hani Motoko publishes *Katei no Tomo* (Friend of the Home) magazine, predecessor of *Fujin no Tomo* (Woman's Friend).
- The Fifth National Industrial Exposition in Osaka's Tennôji, with light illuminations, an observation tower with an elevator, and a merry-go-round.
- Tokyo's central Hibiya Park completed.
- Tokyo Densha Tetsudō, Japan's first trolley company, starts service between Shimbashi and Shinagawa.
- Japan's first movie house, Denkikan (Electricity Hall), opens in Asakusa.
- A refrigerator goes on show at the National Industrial Exposition.

37 — 1904
- Mitsukoshi Gofukuten, Japan's first department store, opens in Tokyo.

38 — 1905
- *Fujin Gahō* (Ladies' Illustrated) published.

39 — 1906
- *Fujin Sekai* (Ladies' World) published.

40 — 1907
- Permanent ice-skating rink opens at Lake Suwa in Nagano Prefecture.

41 — 1908

Mitsukoshi Gofukuten department store sales floor. (National Diet Library).

42 — 1909

The Imperial Theater. (National Diet Library).

43 — 1910

44 — 1911
- The Imperial Theater opens in Tokyo. Mitsukoshi department store uses the advertising slogan, "Today the Imperial, tomorrow Mitsukoshi."
- Birth of the Tokyo Shiden, the city's municipal trolley system.

Taishō Period

1 — 1912
- Both phonograph production and record sales top 50,000 a month.
- Tokyo Taxicab Co., Japan's first, opens in Tokyo's Sukiyabashi.
- The Luna Park amusement park opens on the site of the Fifth National Industrial Exposition in Osaka's Tennôji, dominated by the Tsūtenkaku observation tower.

2 — 1913
- Hashimoto Masujirō's Kwaishinsha Co. produces the Dat Car, leading to Nissan Motor Co.'s Datsun cars.
- Morinaga Seika starts selling caramel candy.
- Ginza Senbikiya opens its first "Fruits Parlor."
- Singer's Japan subsidiary, Singer Mishin, markets home sewing machines in Japan.
- The Takarazuka Shōkatai chorus group established, forerunner of today's Takarazuka Music School and the all-female Takarazuka revue.
- Tokyo Denki, forerunner of Toshiba Corp., mass-produces the "Matsuda Lamp" tungsten light bulb.

Themes	WORLD

U.S. Mass Production

- The Boston Americans defeat the Pittsburgh Pirates in the first World Series.
- **Letchworth**, the first "garden city," built in the London suburbs.
- Harley-Davidson Motor Co. sells its first motorcycles.
- Ford Motor Co. founded.
- The Wright Brothers achieve powered flight, staying airborne for 42 seconds.
- Germany's Siemens AG electric locomotive sets a 210 kph speed record.
- France's Lumière brothers patent the Autochrome color photography process.

- England's Rolls-Royce, Ltd. founded.

- The first Grand Prix auto race held in Le Mans, France.
- The De Forest Radio Telephone & Telegraph Co. makes the first successful radio studio broadcast.

- Thomas Edison and major U.S. production companies collectively patent the movie camera.
- General Motors Co. founded.
- The **Model T Ford** goes on sale.
- Hoover Co. markets an electric vacuum cleaner.
- Olivetti & Co., SPA, founded in Italy.

- General Electric sells the first electric toaster.

- Thomas Edison develops the "talkie."

- Hotpoint Electric Heating Co. starts selling electric irons in the U.S.
- Founding of CTR (Computing Tabulating Recording Co.), today's IBM.

Taishō Modernism

First-stage consumer society 1912–41

- Coco **Chanel** opens her first store in France's Deauville.
- Home electric refrigerators go on sale in the U.S.
- Thomas Edison presents the first talkie.
- Camel, the world's first pre-packaged mixed tobacco cigarette, goes on sale in the U.S.

Nengō	JAPAN	Year
Taishō		
3		1914
4	• Hayakawa Tokuji markets the "screw pencil" mechanical pencil, later renamed the "sharp pencil"; goes on to found Sharp Co. • First Household Exposition opens in Ueno.	1915
5	• *Fujin Kōron* (Women's Review) magazine published.	1916
6	• Publication of *Shufu no Tomo* (Housewife's Friend). In just three years it has the highest circulation of all women's magazines.	1917
8	• Long-selling Calpis fermented soft drink goes on sale.	1919
9	• Hankyu railway company builds a five-story building in front of Osaka's Umeda Station, with Shirokiya as a tenant.	1920
10	• Morinaga Seika releases powdered milk (still manufactured and sold today by Morinaga Milk Industry Co).	1921
11	• Ezaki Shōten (today's Glico Group) introduces Glico candy. • The Bunka Sewing School (today's Bunka Gakuen University) founded. Remains a women's college until 2012. • Peace Memorial Tokyo Exposition held at Ueno Park. Western-influenced houses in the Bunkamura ("culture towns") display catch on as **bunka jūtaku** ("culture homes"). • *Shūkan Asahi* (Weekly Asahi) and *Sandē Mainichi* (Sunday Mainichi) news and entertainment weeklies published.	1922
12	• **"Maru-biru"** (Marunouchi Building) completed in front of Tokyo Station. The nine-story office building housed 350 companies and 10,000 workers, as well as the beauty parlor of New York-trained beautician Yamano Chieko who popularized the perm in Japan. • First subdivision of garden city **Den'en Chōfu** opens. • *Bungei Shunjū* opinion journal and the illustrated *Asahi Gurafu* (Asahi Graphic) published. • Kujaku Curry (Peacock Curry), forerunner of S&B Curry, goes on sale. • Cemedine Co. starts selling popular Cemedine glue. • Kikuchi Seisakusho (today's Tiger Corp.) begins selling tiger-mark vacuum bottles. • Cosmetics pioneer Shiseidō launches its chain-store system. • Opening of new **Imperial Hotel building designed by Frank Lloyd Wright**. • The **Great Kantō Earthquake** of September 1, 1923, devastates Tokyo.	1923
13	• Takarazuka Grand Theater opens.	1924
14	• **Tokyo Broadcasting Station launches Japan's first radio broadcasting**.	1925
Shōwa Period		
1	• Japan Broadcasting Corporation (NHK) established.	1926
2	• Japan's first subway line opens in Tokyo between Asakusa and Ueno.	1927

Themes	WORLD

First-stage consumer society 1912–41

Culture

Suburbs

Urban Mass Consumption

- Warner-Lambert markets Listerine mouthwash.

- Citröen releases the 10HP Type A, Europe's first mass-produced automobile.
- American Telephone and Telegraph Co. (AT&T) introduces dial telephones.
- Lipton's enters the teabag market.

- Cluett, Peabody & Co., maker of Arrow brand shirts, releases the Arrow Trump, a men's shirt with a fixed collar.
- Johnson & Johnson sells Band-Aids in the U.S.

- France's Chanel releases its signature fragrance Chanel No. 5.
- England's British Broadcasting Corporation (BBC) begins radio broadcasts.
- Radio commercials debut.
- *Reader's Digest* published in the U.S.
- Hollywood produces its first color feature movie, *The Toll of the Sea*, using the Technicolor 2 Process.

- Britain's Cutty Shark scotch whiskey released.
- Yankee Stadium opens in New York.
- Germany's Bauhaus school of design and architecture has its first show, the Bauhaus Exhibition in Weimar, and "Bauhaus Week" on the theme of the "unity of art, technology and science."
- Germany's Mercedes-Benz manufactures the first diesel trucks.
- *Time* magazine goes on sale in the U.S.

Frank Lloyd Wright's Imperial Hotel.
http://architectstudio3d.org/AS3d/about_imperial.html

- Germany's Leica Camera AG releases the legendary Leica A.
- *New Yorker* magazine starts publishing.
- Scotland's John Logie Baird achieves the first transmission and reception of television images.

- **Weissenhof Settlement Estate** housing exhibition in Stuttgart, Germany; helps create the "International Style" of architecture.

Nengō	JAPAN	Year
		1928
Shōwa		
3	• Shirokiya opens a department store in front of Tokyo's Gotanda Station. • Mitsukoshi Gofukuten renamed Mitsukoshi.	
4	• The full-fledged train terminal department store **Hankyū Hyakkaten** opens in Osaka's Umeda. • **Shinjuku Mitsukoshi** opens. • Kotobukiya Ltd. (today's Suntory Group) sells Japan's first domestic whiskey.	1929
5	• **Ginza Mitsukoshi** opens.	1930
6	• **Matsuya Asakusa** Department Store opens.	1931
7	• NHK radio reception licenses top one million. • The **Mitsukoshi-mae subway station** opens in Tokyo. • **Tokyo 35-ward system** established.	1932

"Take the subway to Mitsukoshi." (Ad Museum of Tokyo collection).

8	• **Shinjuku Isetan** Department Store opens. • **Nihonbashi Takashimaya** Department Store opens.	1933

A poster for the opening of the Shinjuku Isetan Department Store. It conveys what a special event it was to visit Tokyo's giant downtown department stores. Poster by illustrator Kazama Shirō. (Ad Museum of Tokyo collection).

9	• **Shibuya Tōkyū Tōyoko** Department Store opens.	1934
10	• *Kissaten* coffee shops all the rage in Japan's cities. Some 2,500 open in Tokyo alone. • Expansion of the Nihonbashi Mitsukoshi complete. Seven stories high with two basement levels, the building's grand Central Hall has its own pipe organ.	1935
11	• The Nichigeki Dance Team chorus line gives its first performance at the Nichigeki theater in Yurakuchō.	1936
12	• Second Sino-Japanese War begins.	1937
13		1938

Themes	WORLD

Rail Terminals

- Walt Disney screens *Steamboat Willie*, the first Mickey Mouse cartoon.
- First regular TV broadcasts begin in the U.S.: three times a week for 90 minutes each.
- Daven Television Receiver and Tri Standard released in the U.S., the first commercially available TV sets. Owners assemble them themselves.
- Stock market crash and start of the **Great Depression**.
- New York's Museum of Modern Art (MoMA) founded.
- Clarence Birdseye markets his quick frozen food technology in the U.S.
- First tape recorders using magnetized plastic tape appear in Germany, making possible high quality sound reproduction and editing.

The Ginza Age

- **Chrysler Building** completed in New York.
- French architect Le Corbusier's final design for the landmark Savoye House.
- First Christmas tree erected on construction site of New York's Rockefeller Center. 1933 brings the first official tree lighting.
- AT&T inaugurates Teletypewriter eXchange Service (TWX) service, forerunner of the telex.
- Radio City Music Hall opens in New York. World's largest movie theater seats 6,000.
- Annual U.S. radio set sales top 4 million, with one in more than half of all households. Annual U.K. radio set sales reach 1.5 million.
- The first dishwashing machine goes on sale.
- RCA Corporation of America (today's RCA Corporation) holds first public demonstration of a cathode ray tube television set.

Rise of Shinjuku and Shibuya

- Founding of aircraft maker Lockheed Corporation (today's Lockheed Martin).
- Chicago World's Fair opens with the theme "A Century of Progress."
- Weekly news magazine *Newsweek* goes to print.
- England's ICI [Imperial Chemical Industries] develops polyethylene.
- Zippo lighter product registration (patented in 1937).
- Invention of the Hammond organ.
- Penguin Book paperbacks published in England.
- Boeing Airplane Co. (today's Boeing Co.) develops the B-17, a four-engine bomber and the first with a low mono wing and all-metal construction. To become famous as the Flying Fortress in World War II.
- Landmark photojournalism weekly *Life* published.
- Disney releases the first full-length, all-color sound animation movie, *Snow White and the Seven Dwarfs*.

Fascism

- Eastman Kodak Co. releases the Super Kodak Six-20, the world's first camera with automatic exposure.
- Benny Goodman gives the first jazz concert at New York's Carnegie Hall.
- Orson Wells broadcasts a radio dramatization of H. G. Wells's *War of the Worlds* in the U.S., panicking some listeners who believe it is real.
- Dr. Ferdinand Porsche reveals the final prototype of the Volkswagen "Beetle."
- DuPont begins nylon production in the U.S. Its first commercial products are nylon bristles for toothbrushes.

Department Stores

Radio

First-stage consumer society 1912–41

Nengō	JAPAN	Year
Shōwa 14		1939
15	• Musashino Department Store, forerunner of the Seibu Department Store, opens in Tokyo's Ikebukuro.	1940
16	• **Japan attacks Pearl Harbor.**	1941
		1942
		1944
		1945
22	• Lotte Co. starts producing chewing gum.	1946
		1947

Dior's elegant fashions became popular around the world. New Look by Christian Dior, 1947 (Photo credit: dovima_is_devine_II @) Flickr Creative Commons).

A poster for the 1939 New York World's Fair, designed by Herbert Matter, appointed designer for the Swiss National Pavilloin.

Nengō	JAPAN	Year
23	• Nichiban Yakuhin Kōgyō (today's Nichiban Co.) sells Cellotape, the brand name becoming synonymous with adhesive tape in Japan. • Tokyo's Kabukichō district created.	1948
24	• Dressmaker Jogakuin sewing school (today's Sugino Gakuen) publishes *Doresumēkingu* (Dress-making) magazine. • First Bireley's orange juice enters Japan from the U.S. • *Asahi Shimbun* newspaper serializes the "**Blondie**" comic strip in Japanese.	1949
25	• Kotobukiya (today's Suntory) releases its top-of-the-line whiskey Suntory Old. Torys Bars serving cheaper Torys Whiskey pop up across Japan in 1955. • Men's style magazine *Danshi senka* (Men's Quality Magazine) published by Sutairu-sha. • Odakyū Electric Railway starts running its iconic Romance Car express between Shinjuku Station and the Hakone Yumoto hot springs resort. • Tokyo Tsūshin Kōgyō, today's Sony Corp., releases its first tape recorder.	1950

Themes	WORLD

First-stage

Fascism

- New York World's Fair opens in April 1939.
- Rockefeller Center completed in New York.
- Germany invades Poland on September 1, launching World War II.

- Raymond Loewy, godfather of industrial design, redesigns the Lucky Strike cigarette pack.
- DuPont starts selling nylon stockings, creating an instant sensation.

- Kodacolor goes on sale in the U.S.

- Society of Industrial Designers founded, forerunner of American Society of Industrial Design.

- World War II ends.

- Tupperware Corp. starts selling kitchen containers, switches over to sales through home demonstration parties the following year.
- Italy's Corradino D'Ascanio, inventor of the helicopter, designs Piaggio & Co.'s Vespa scooter.

Second-stage consumer society 1945–74

Americanization

- William Levitt builds the first **Levittown** on New York's Long Island, with 17,400 manufactured houses, helping define the American suburbs.
- Invention of the microwave oven.
- France's Christian Dior presents his revolutionary "New Look," the polar opposite of wartime fashions, with long skirts asserting an extreme femininity.
- Le Corbusier designs the radical Unité de Habitation apartment building in Marseille. The "vertical garden city" offering communal spaces and services to foster community is completed in 1952.

- The U.S. Polaroid Corp. markets the first instant camera.

- Columbia Broadcasting System Records (today's Columbia Records) releases the first LP records.

- "Peanuts" comic strip serialized in the U.S.
- Diners Club, the first independent credit card company, founded in the U.S.
- World's first color TV broadcasts begin.

Nengō	JAPAN	Year
Shōwa		1951
26	• Nakauchi Isao founds Sakae Yakuhin Kōgyō, a cash-basis medicinal wholesaler, in Osaka, forerunner of giant Daiei, Inc. retail chain.	
	• Asahi Bakushu (today's Asahi Breweries) starts selling Bireley's orange drink.	
	• International Terminal completed at Tokyo's Haneda International Airport.	
	• The quality of public housing improves with the Kōei Jūtaku Hō (Public Housing Act), including south-facing kitchens and dining rooms. The DK (combined dining room & kitchen) floor plan is adopted for the first time.	
	• Fujiya introduces Milky candy featuring mascot character Peko-chan.	
27	• Japan Tobacco adopts the famous dove logo for its Peace cigarettes; Raymond Loewy's design commission is 1.5 million yen.	1952
	• Meidi-Ya grocery chain starts producing concentrated orange juice. In April, Sapporo Breweries starts selling its Ribbon Juice, later renamed Ribbon Orange.	
28	• NHK broadcasts the first Kōhaku Uta-gassen ("Red and White Song Battle") from Tokyo's Nichigeki with a live audience, launching an enduring New Year's Eve ritual.	1953
	• Kinokuniya, the first supermarket in Japan, opens in Tokyo's Aoyama.	
29	• Electric refrigerators, washing machines, and televisions are dubbed the **"Three Sacred Treasures."**	1954
30	• The Jiyūtō and Nihon Minshutō political parties merge into the Jiyūminshutō (Liberal Democratic Party) that holds power nearly continuously to the present day. Dubbed the 1955 Taisei (**1955 Establishment**).	1955
	• Toyota Motor Co. introduces the upscale Toyopet Crown. In 1958 the Toyopet becomes the first Toyota sold in the United States.	
	• **Japan Housing Corporation** (JHC) established, predecessor of the Urban Renaissance Agency (UR). JHC's ad copy, "Sutenresu kagayaku kicchin setto" (Gleaming stainless steel kitchen set) is a hit, and the stainless steel kitchen becomes a symbol of the modern lifestyle.	
	• Ministry of International Trade and Industry (today's MEITI) announces the **"People's Car Concept."**	
	• Fashion designer Mori Hanae opens a salon on the Ginza.	
31	• Sun Wave Corp. (now part of the LIXIL Group) develops a stainless steel sink, which quickly becomes another symbol of modern living.	1956
	• Takashimaya Department Store holds an Italian Fair.	
	• **Japan Highway Public Corporation** (JH) established (today's privatized NEXCO companies).	
	• Shūkan Shinchō (New Tide Weekly) magazine published, launching a weekly magazine boom.	

Themes	WORLD
Second-stage consumer society 1945–74 — Modernization	• U.S. household automobile ownership hits 60 percent. • Video recording technology developed. • CBS inaugurates the world's first regular color television broadcasts. • Deutsche Grammophon releases 33-rpm LPs.
Home Electrification	• *TV Guide* published in the U.S. • *Playboy* published in the U.S.
	• A shopping center housing 100 stores opens in Detroit. The next year there are 1,800 shopping centers across the U.S. • Burger King founded. • RCA Victor Record Co. releases first prerecorded music tapes, using reel-to-reel tape. • The first Newport Jazz Festival. • Elvis Presley makes his professional recording debut.
Pax Americana	• U.S. housing starts peak at 1.65 million units. • **Disneyland** opens in southern California's Anaheim. • Ray Croc starts franchising **McDonald**'s throughout the U.S. • James Dean dies in a car crash, age 24. • RCA demonstrates the music synthesizer. • Allen Ginsburg reads his experimental poem "Howl" at San Francisco's Six Gallery. It comes to symbolize the American Beat Generation and is praised as an elegy to the passing of the American dream. • Architect and industrial designer Eero Saarinen creates his elegant Tulip chair from aluminum and plastic (1955–56).
	• Nikita Khrushchev denounces Joseph Stalin's legacy at the 20th Congress of the Communist Party and calls for a new start for the Soviet Union. • The U.S. interstate highway plan underway. • Bell Telephone Labs develops the Picture-Phone, the first video telephone. • Ampex Corp. introduces the VRX-1000 videotape recorder in Chicago, raising the curtain on the video age.

Nengō	JAPAN	Year
Shōwa 32	• JHC's Hikari-ga-oka *danchi* complex completed in Kashiwa north of Tokyo. Popularizes the term "new town" for giant housing complexes. • Japan's first women's weekly magazine, *Shūkan Josei* (Woman's Weekly), published by Kawade Shobō. Relaunched in August the same year by Shufu-to-seikatsu Co. • Tokyo Tsūshin Kōgyō releases the world's smallest transistor radio, the Pocketable Radio TR-63, using the brand name Sony. Sold in the U.S. as the Transistor Six. • Daihatsu Motor Co. releases the Midget three-wheel mini-truck. • Toyota releases the first Corona. • The **Good Design Award** (**G-Mark**) inaugurated by the Japan Institute of Design Promotion. • Avant-garde artist and lingerie designer Kamoi Yōko holds a show in Osaka, challenging Japan's conservative notions of lingerie. • *I Love Lucy* and *Lassie* air on Japanese TV. • Nippon Inryō Kōgyō (today's Coca-Cola (Japan) Co.) markets Fanta Orange and Fanta Grape.	1957
33	• Isetan Department Store sells Valentine's Day chocolates for the first time. • Takeda Shokuhin Kōgyō uses rice sales routes to market the Plussy vitamin C drink (now sold by House Wellness Foods Corp.). • *Josei Jishin* (Women, Ourselves) magazine published. • The first of fifty-six Nichigeki Western Carnivals launches Japan's Rockabilly Boom. • JVC (Victor Company of Japan) sells the Victron, the first domestically built electric organ, and Japan's first stereo system. In August it markets Japan's first stereo records. • Fuji Heavy Industries releases the **Subaru 360 Ladybird**. • Nisshin Food Products markets **Chicken Ramen**, the world's first instant noodle product. • Kao Sekken (today's Kao Group) releases Wonderful-K kitchen detergent. • An article in *Shūkan Asahi* coins the phrase, ***danchi-zoku***, the "*danchi*-tribe." • The hula hoop craze reaches Japan. • **Tokyo Tower** completed. At 333 meters (1,092.5 feet), it is the tallest tower in the world. • The engagement of the Crown Prince to commoner Shōda Michiko is announced, triggering the **Micchi Boom**. • Shufu-no-mise Daiei (Housewives' Store Daiei) as Daiei's first chain store opens in Kobe's Sannomiya. • *Father Knows Best* on Japanese TV. • Honda sells the **Super Cub C100** motorcycle.	1958

Themes	**WORLD**

Second-stage consumer society 1945–74

Pax Americana

American TV Shows

High Growth Takes Off

Cars

Supermarkets

Instant Foods

- *West Side Story* debuts on Broadway.
- The Soviet Union launches Sputnik 1 into orbit, shaking American confidence.
- The Frisbee goes on sale in the U.S.
- First stereo recordings sold in the U.S.

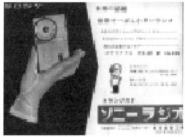

Sony TR-63 ad. (Courtesy of Kawasaki AA676).

- Texas Instruments invents the IC integrated circuit.
- American Express Card launched.
- The U.S.S.R. displays a Sputnik at the Brussels World's Fair Soviet Pavilion.
- The Seagram Building completed in New York.

Empress Michiko ignited the "Micchi Boom." The cover of the December 14, 1959 Asahi Gurafu read: "Warera no purinsesu!" (Our Princess!).

Daihatsu Midget ad from Asahi Gurafu, May 3, 1959. (Miura collection).

Josei Jishin from May 21, 1962. (Miura Collection).

Nengō	**JAPAN**	Year

Shōwa 1959
34 • *Shūkan Shōnen Magajin* (Weekly Boy's Magazine, Kōdansha) and *Shūkan Shōnen Sandē* (Weekly Boys' Sunday, Shōgakukan) are published on the same day, triggering the weekly boy's *manga* boom.
• *Shūkan Gendai, Shūkan Bunshun,* and other news and entertainment magazines launch as the weekly magazine boom gains strength.
• Nissan Motor Co. releases the Bluebird, known as the Datsun 510 in the U.S. and Canada and as the Datsun 1600 in other foreign markets.
• Olympus Optical Co. (today's Olympus Corp.) sells the Olympus Pen, the first half-size compact camera.
• Seibu Department Store holds a France Exhibition.
• Nippon Gakki Seizō, today's Yamaha Corp., introduces the Electone electric organ.
• Daiwa House Industry Co. develops Japan's first prefabricated structure, the Midget House prefab classroom, forerunner of Daiwa's prefab dwellings.
• Sony announces the world's first portable transistor television.
• *The Donna Reed Show, Leave It to Beaver, Perry Mason,* and *Rawhide* start on Japanese TV.

35 • Inoue Kōgyō releases the Kurinappu (Cleanup) stainless steel sink. 1960
• Morinaga & Co. markets the first Japanese instant coffee, introducing *insutanto* (instant) into the vocabulary.
• Leading journalist and commentator Ōya Sōichi coins the word *rejā,* derived from the English "leisure."
• Van, Jun, and other fashion brands launch the "Ivy Look" for men.
• *77 Sunset Strip* airs in Japan.
• Mitsubishi 500, Mazda R360 coupe go on sale.
• Prime Minister Ikeda Hayato's **Income-doubling Plan**.

36 • Atsugi Nylon Industrial Co. (today's Atsugi Co.) begins full-scale marketing 1961
of seamless nylon stockings and tights.
• Morinaga Seika introduces Marble Choco candy, sales explode in 1963.
• Morinaga Milk Industry Co. sells Creap powdered creamer. The TV commercial catchphrase, "Goodness, drink coffee without Creap?!" (*Kurīpu o irenai kōhii nante*) is a hit.
• Toyota Motor Corp. sells the people's car Publica UP10, its name contracted from "Public Car."
• Long-running women's magazine *Misesu* (Mrs.) published by Bunka Publishing Bureau.
• *The Mickey Mouse Club* begins on Japanese TV.

37 • Taishō Pharmaceutical Co. markets nutrition drink Lipovitan-D. 1962
• Coca-Cola adopts the Japanese catchphrase, "*Sukatto sawayaka, Koka-Kōra*" (Coca Cola! It's refreshing!).
• Lion Dentrifrice Co. (today's Lion Corp.) introduces Vitalis hair styling tonic for men.
• The Mazda Carol, Mitsubishi Minica, and Suzuki Suzulite Fronte "light van" minicars released.

Themes	WORLD

The Manga Age / Instant Foods

- The American National Exposition opens in Moscow. Scene of the "Kitchen Debate" between Premier Nikita Khrushchev and VP Richard Nixon.
- Austin Motor Co. releases the Mini-Cooper.
- The first Barbie doll goes on sale.
- Amway Corp. founded in the U.S.
- America's Xerox Corp. markets its copy machine.

Prefabs

The Leisure Age

Advertisement for Seibu's "La Foire de France" exhibition from Asahi Shimbun, *October 4, 1959.*

- The Southland Corp. founded in the U.S., includes the 7-Eleven chain in its holdings.
- Hit movie version of Leonard Bernstein's *West Side Story* wins ten Academy Awards.
- The U.S.S.R.'s Yuri Gagarin rides Vostok 1 into space. The first human to orbit the Earth.

Income Doubling

Men's Fashion

- Benny Goodman, the King of Swing since the 1930s, performs in Moscow with Premier Khrushchev in attendance.
- Bob Dylan releases *Blowin' in the Wind.*
- The Beatles sign with EMI, release their first single, "Love Me Do."
- England and France agree to develop the Concorde, the world's first supersonic airliner.
- Rachel Carson's **Silent Spring** published, warning of the threat to the ecosystem from DDT and other chemical products.

Second-stage consumer society 1945–74

Nengō	JAPAN	Year
Shōwa		1963
38	• Dai Nippon Bungu Co. (today's Pentel Co.) markets its felt-tip Sign Pen with water-based ink. The next year brings the "sign pen" boom after reports that U.S. President Lyndon Johnson signs his papers with a Pentel. • Shiseidō markets **MG5** hair and skin care line, launching the men's cosmetics wars.	
39	• Calbee Food & Confectionary Co. (today's Calbee, Inc.) introduces long-selling Kappa Ebisen shrimp crackers. • Jun Co. (Ltd.) opens its Jun men's fashion store on the Ginza. • *Heibon Panchi* (Heibon Punch) magazine published. • **The Tokyo Olympics.** • **Tokaidō Shinkansen** bullet train service begins. • Ōzeki Sake Brewing Co. (today's Ōzeki Corp.) markets the first single-serving size *sake*, Wan-kappu (One-cup Ōzeki). • Tōyō Kōgyō Co. (today's Mazda Motor Corp.) launches the bestselling **Familia 800 sedan.** • Joint-venture Jūjō Kimberley K.K. markets Kleenex Tissue in Japan.	1964
40	• Otsuka Pharmaceutical Co. releases Oranaomin C, a carbonated energy drink. • The Economic Planning Agency conducts its first survey of spending patterns of single workers. With an average monthly income of 23,200 yen and average savings of 138,000 yen, the "privileged single" takes the limelight. • The Meishin Expressway, Japan's first superhighway, completed between Nagoya and Kobe.	1965
41	• Hayakawa Electric Industry Co., forerunner of Sharp Corp., sells the R-600, the world's first microwave oven for the home. • Weekly *manga* magazines *Shōnen Magazine* and *Shōnen Sunday* circulations both top one million. • Nissan Sunny and **Toyota Corolla** released. 1966 is later dubbed Mai-kā Gannen (Year One of "My Car"). • The "3 C Era." The color TV, the air conditioner (cooler) and the car are Japan's new **Three Sacred Treasures.** • *Bewitched*, *Flipper*, and *The Andy Williams Show* air in Japan.	1966
42	• Japanese domestic color television set ownership hits one million. • **Toyota's monthly vehicle production reaches 80,000.** The Corona alone accounts for 30,000. • The Rika-chan doll goes on sale. • Fashion model Twiggy visits Japan and the miniskirt craze begins. • JHC introduces the 3LDK (living-dining-kitchen and three bedrooms) floor plan. Living rooms become the rage.	1967
43	• **Environmental Pollution Prevention Act** takes effect. • Otsuka Foods Co. launches Bon Karē (Bon Curry) curry sauce, the world's first food product in a plastic retort bag. • Meiji Seika (today's Meiji Co.) markets Karl cheese curls, the first Japanese savory snack. • Chifuren (National Federation of Regional Women's Organizations) launches a "100 Yen Cosmetics" campaign for affordable and safe cosmetics. Sells own beauty care products under the brand name Chifure.	1968

Themes	WORLD

Second-stage consumer society 1945–74

Income Doubling

- Estée Lauder announces Aramis fragrance for men.
- The Rolling Stones release their first single, "Come On."
- Cosmonaut Valentina Tershkova, the first woman in space, orbits the earth forty-eight times on Vostok 6.

- British designer Mary Quant introduces the **miniskirt**.
- The New York World's Fair opens.
- IBM develops the word processor.
- The world's first disco, Whiskey a Go-Go, opens on the Los Angeles Sunset Strip.
- Hysterical fans mob the Beatles' first New York performance.
- Austin Mini production tops one million.
- Ford Motor Co. debuts the Mustang, creating the "specialty car" category.

Priviliged Singles

男性の時代・MG5の時代

The age of the fashionable man begins.
An ad for MG5.
(Courtesy Shiseidō).

- The April 18, 1966, *Jiefangjun Bao* (Liberation Army Daily) publishes an editorial titled "Hold High the Great Red Banner of Mao Zedong's Thinking; Actively Participate in the Great Socialist Cultural Revolution." The Chinese Communist Party announces the start of the Great Proletarian Cultural Revolution on May 16.

3 Cs & My Car

The Familia.
(Courtesy Mazda).

- Canada hosts Expo '67, the Montreal World's Fair.

Shōwa Genroku Prosperity

Twiggy fever sweeps the world.
(Photo courtesy Asahi Shimbun Co.).

Snacks & Candy

- Students riot and workers strike in France's "May Uprising."
- The *Whole Earth Catalog* published in the U.S.
- The first Isle of Wight Festival held in England, drawing 250,000 attendees.

Nengō	**JAPAN**	Year
	Shōwa 43 (*continued from page 310*) • Famed composer Yamamoto Naozumi appears in a TV commercial for Morinaga Yell chocolate, marketed with the slogan "**Bigger is better**. More delicious is more delicious." • The Shibuya Seibu Department Store opens.	1968
44	• **Tokyo University's student-occupied Yasuda Auditorium falls to riot police.** • Construction begins on JHC's Takashimadaira *danchi* in Tokyo's Itabashi Ward. • Tamagawa Takashimaya SC opens, Japan's **first suburban shopping center**. • Model and actress Rosa Ogawa's *"Oh! Mōretsu"* (**Oh! Burning!**) commercial for Maruzen Oil Co. (today's Cosmo Oil Co.) becomes the catchphrase of the day.	1969
45	• The **Japan World's Fair Expo '70** opens in Osaka on the theme "Progress and Harmony of Mankind." • **Kentucky Fried Chicken** debuts in Japan at Expo '70, opens first store in Nagoya. • Family restaurant chain **Skylark** opens first outlet (the Kunitachi branch) in Tokyo's Fuchū. • Fashion magazine *an-an* published. • Dunkin' Donuts chain opens first branch on the Ginza. • Fuji-Xerox Co. airs the commercial *"Mōetsu kara byūtifuru e"* (From Driven to Beautiful). • Japan National Railways "**Discover Japan**" **campaign** launches, runs through 1977. • **Toyota Celica** goes on sale. Japan's first specialty car.	1970
46	• Sekisui Chemical Co. markets Sekisui Heim modular homes. • **McDonald's** opens its first Japan branch on the Ginza. • Shūeisha, Inc. publishes fashion magazine *non-no*. • Nissin Food Products sells its first Cup Noodle, noodles that can be eaten just by pouring hot water into the container. • Meiji Dairies Co. (today's Meiji Holdings Co.) links up with Borden of the U.S. to sell Lady Borden high-end ice cream in Japan. • Residents begin moving into **Tama New Town**. • Lotteria Co. opens its first fast-food branch in Ueno's Matsuzakaya Department Store. • Doit Co. opens Japan's first do-it-yourself (DIY) store in Saitama's Yono City. • NHK viewer contracts for color TV service reach 11.8 million, passing black-and-white contracts. • **Environment Agency** established.	1971
47	• The Red Army Faction hostage siege at Asama Mountain Lodge grips Japan. • **Daiei** sales pass Mitsukoshi's, making it Japan's largest retailer. • Suntory commercial, *"Kinyōbi ni wa wain o kaimashō"* (**Let's buy wine on Friday**) (print ad photo p. 315). • Nissan Skyline's Ken and Mary commercials air.	1972
48	• Shibuya Parco opens. The ad copy for the opening is, "The people you're passing are all so beautiful. Shibuya Park Drive." • **First Oil Crisis.**	1973

Themes			WORLD

Shōnen Magazine *when its circulation passed one million.*
(September 14, 1969 edition; Miura collection).

- America's Apollo 11 lands on the moon.
- Woodstock Festival held in upstate New York.
- The French-British Concorde breaks the sound barrier in test flights (enters service in 1976).

First issue of an-an.
(Miura collection).

First issue of non-no.
(Miura collection).

- Robert Moog patents the electronic synthesizer.

Japan National Railways "Discover Japan" campaign.
Ad Museum of Tokyo collection.

- The Club of Rome releases **The Limits to Growth**, warning that if population growth and environmental pollution continued, growth on Planet Earth would reach its limit within one hundred years.
- U.S. supermarkets start using barcodes.

- British economist E. F. Schumacher's **Small is Beautiful** becomes a best-seller. Proposes ways to save the Earth from man's destruction.

Vertical labels (left to right):

Second-stage consumer society 1945–74

The Shinjuku Era — The An-Non Tribe — New Family

Snacks & Candy — Industrial Development — Eating Out — Ecology

Nengō	**JAPAN**	Year

Shōwa 48 (*continued from page 312*) — 1973
- Inoue Yōsui's hit song, "*Kasa ga nai*" (I can't find my umbrella).
- Brilliant art director **Sugiyama Toshi** commits suicide. Creator of "Let's just let it all hang out" (*kiraku ni ikō yo*) ad for Mobile Oil ad and commercials for Shiseidō, Calpis, Toyota, and other clients since the 1960s.

49 — 1974
- Kirin-Seagram Co. (today's Kirin Distillery Co.) releases Robert Brown, its first domestic whiskey.
- Asahi Culture Center opens in Shinjuku.
- B-R 31 Ice Cream Co., a joint venture between Fujiya and U.S. Baskin-Robbins, opens its first branch in Tokyo's Meguro Ward.
- **7-Eleven opens** a branch in the Toyosu district of Tokyo's Kōtō Ward, the first convenience store in Japan.
- The catalog magazine *Saison de non-no* published.

50 — 1975
- Sony releases the world's first home VTR, the Betamax SL-6300.
- Japan Recruit Center (today's Recruit Group) publishes the job-hunting magazine *Shūshoku Jōhō*.
- The **Seibu Museum of Art** (today's Sezon Museum of Art) opens in Tokyo's Ikebukuro.
- Kōbunsha Co. publishes Japan-oriented fashion magazine *JJ*.
- Yamazaki-Nabisco Co. sells Chip Star, Japan's first fabricated potato chip, made from potato dough instead of slices.
- Yamato Transport Co. starts its Kuroneko parcel delivery service.
- The first store in the Hokka-Hokka Tei franchise selling freshly made *bentō* lunches opens in Sōka City, north of Tokyo.
- Nihon Keizai Shimbunsha publishes *Shōhisha wa kawatta* (The Consumer Has Changed).
- Parco runs ads, "Don't look at nudes. BE nude" and "It takes more than a [pretty] face to be a model."
- *Made in U.S.A. Catalog, An-An Expanded Edition: The Catalog Collection,* and *Weekly Sankei Special Expanded Edition Do Catalog* published.
- Kadokawa Shoten Publishing Co. runs Ishioka Eiko ad, "Women, turn off your televisions!"

51 — 1976
- Pioneering "fashion building" Aoyama Bell Commons opens.
- Heibon Shuppan (today's Magazine House) publishes **Popeye magazine**.
- Honda Motor Co. sells the women's 50 cc mini-bike Road Pal.
- The first Tokyū Hands DIY store opens in Fujisawa City, Kanagawa Prefecture.
- JICC Shuppankyoku (today's Takarajima Co.) publishes *Whole City Catalog*, first of the Takarajima "mooks" (magazine-books).
- Yamaha Motor Co. releases the women's motorbike Passol.

52 — 1977
- Long-selling Mild Seven cigarettes launched.
- ASCII Corp. (today's ASCII Media Works) founded to create Japanese video games and publications on gaming and computing.
- Proctor & Gamble Sunhome Co. (today's Proctor & Gamble Japan Co.) releases Pampers disposable diapers in Japan.
- *Kurowasan* (Croissant), *More, Watashi wa Onna* (I Am Woman) released as the women's magazine boom continues.

Themes	WORLD

Second-stage consumer society

New Family

Individualization

Conservation, Low Growth

Advertising began stressing a couple's private life: "Friday is the day to buy wine" ad. (Courtesy Suntory).

Third-stage consumer society 1975–2004

Catalog Culture

"It takes more than a [pretty] face to be a model." Parco's ads promoted the independent woman. (Courtesy Parco).

Seeking New Women's Lifestyles

Going Mild

The inaugural issue of Popeye. *(Miura collection).*

Takarajima's *Whole City Catalog. (Miura collection).*

Nengō	**JAPAN**	Year
Shōwa		1978
53	• Boutique Takenoko opens in Tokyo's Harajuku. Helps launch the 1980s Takenoko-zoku (Takenoko Tribe), first of a wave of Harajuku youth trends.	
	• High-end fashion house Hanae Mori Building and youth fashion mecca LaForet Building both open in Harajuku.	
	• Tokyū Hands opens in Shibuya.	
	• "Space Invaders" triggers the video game boom.	
	• Start of the karaoke craze.	
54	• Interior décor magazine *Futari no heya* (A Room for Two), today's *Plus1 Living*, published by Shufunotomo Co.	1979
	• Kibun Foods Inc. markets the first soymilk.	
	• NEC Corp. releases its PC8001 personal computer, igniting Japan's PC boom.	
	• The Sony **Walkman** goes on sale.	
	• Tokyū's 109 Building opens in Shibuya.	
	• Amano Yūkichi publishes *Kōkoku hihyō* (Advertising Critique), a magazine that will critique Japan's advertising scene for the next thirty years.	
	• **Seiko ad: "Why don't you change your watch along with your clothes?"**	
55	• Otsuka launches the sports drink Pocari Sweat.	1980
	• Magazine House publishes men's magazine *Brutus*.	
	• Toto Ltd. sells the first Washlet electric toilet seat.	
	• Tanaka Yasuo's urban youth novel **Nantonaku, kurisutaru (Somehow, Crystal)** receives the Bungei Prize.	
	• Women's magazines *Torabāyu* and *Cosmopolitan* go to press.	
	• Reikōdō, Japan's first record rental shop, opens in Tokyo's Mitaka. Record rental stores pop up all over Japan.	
	• Style and gossip magazine *25 Ans* published.	
	• **Japan becomes the world's top car manufacturer.**	
	• Seibu Department Store's **"Yourself, re-discovered"** campaign.	
	• **Mujirushi Ryōhin** products go on sale.	
56	• Aerobics introduced in Japan.	1981
	• Honda releases its fuel-efficient City model with a 1200 cc engine.	
	• With Shōgakukan launching *CanCam* magazine and radio stations featuring girl disk jockeys, the coed boom is in full fling.	
	• Funabashi LaLaport shopping center opens, the first in Mitsui Fudōsan Retail Management Co.'s LaLaport chain.	
	• Roppongi AXIS Building opens with design and craft shops and three art galleries.	
	• **Myōjō Foods markets Chūka Zanmai "luxury" instant ramen.**	
	• **Toyota announces the hit *haiso-kā* ("high-society car"), the Soarer, named Japan Car of the Year.**	

Themes	WORLD

Third-stage consumer society 1975–2004

Women's Lifestyle / **Going Mild**

Do-it-yourself / **Video Games**

• France's Pierre Bourdieu publishes *La Distinction*, pointing out class differences in taste and consumption. Japanese edition published in 1990.

Interiors / **The Shibuya Age**

The inaugural issue of More. *(Miura collection).*

• Harvard's Ezra Vogel writes ***Japan as Number One***.
• Founding of CNN.

Japan As Number 1 / **Luxurification**

The first Walkman. The product went on to be a hit around the world. (Courtesy Sony).

• The IBM 5150 Personal Computer (IBM PC) goes on sale.

Keihakutanshō / **Coeds**

The Soarer "high-society" car. (Ad Museum of Tokyo collection).

Nengō	**JAPAN**	Year
Shōwa		1982

57
- Japan the first country to commercialize **CD players**.
- *Nikkei Business* publishes special feature "Industrial Structure: The 'Lighter, Thinner, Shorter, Smaller' Shockwave."
- NEC releases 16-bit PC-9801 for business applications.
- Honda rolls out the second-generation Prelude. With a reclining passenger seat controlled from the driver's side, it spawns the term "date car."
- Tama Plaza Tokyu shopping center opens in the Yokohama suburbs; other station shopping buildings open in outlying Ōmiya and Fuchū.
- Seibu Department Store's **"Delicious Life" campaign** (1982–83).

58   **1983**
- Nintendō Co. releases the Family Computer System videogame console, triggering the Famicon boom.
- PC market penetration tops one million units.
- Fuji Television Network launches *All Night Fuji*, a popular, sometimes naughty, late night variety show, as lifestyles diversify.
- **Tokyo Disneyland** opens.
- Seiyū opens the first dedicated Mujirushi Ryōhin store (Muji store) in Tokyo's Aoyama.
- Asada Akira publishes *Structure and Power: Beyond Semiotics*. Surprise hit sells 150,000 copies.

59   **1984**
- Dutch quality ice cream brand Haagen-Dazs opens first Japan branch in trendy Aoyama; long lines form outside the new landmark.
- Monthly *Classy* magazine published, riding a wave of interest in *ojōsama*, the extravagant daughters of Japan's elite.
- Yamazaki Masakazu publishes *The Birth of Soft Individualism*.
- Fujioka Wakao publishes *Farewell to the Masses*, coins the phrase *shōshū* ("micro-masses").
- Watanabe Kazuhiro publishes **Picture Scrolls of Wealth and Soul**.
- Yūrakuchō Seibu opens as a "Life Information Building."
- 3.5 million Family Computer consoles sold to date.

60   **1985**
- 8 mm video camera introduced.
- Video game "Super Mario Brothers" released.
- Mild Seven Light cigarettes go on sale.
- Wave of books on the growing stratification of consumption in Japan, including Hakuhodo Institute of Life and Living (HILL)'s **"Bunshū" no tanjō** (The Birth of the "Micro-masses" and **Shin "Kaisō shōhi" no jidai** (The New Era of "Stratified Consumption") by Ozawa Masako of the Long-Term Credit Bank of Japan research department.
- Japan's equal opportunity employment act takes effect.

61   **1986**
- Toyota releases hit, second-generation **Soarer**, selling 300,000 over the next five years.
- Shogakukan publishes consumer magazine *Dime*.
- ENIX launches "Dragon Quest" series, the first console-based role-playing game.

Themes		WORLD

Third-stage consumer society 1975–2004

Keihakutanshō — Suburban Shopping Centers

- Walt Disney Productions releases *Tron*, the world's first full-length computer graphics (CG) movie.
- England's Reebok's 1982 Freestyle women's athletic shoe wins over dancers as aerobics shoe, fueling the company's popularity.

Digitalization — "Neaka" Optimism

- China establishes "economic and technological development zones" in fourteen coastal cities, including Shanghai. The ETDZs let foreign investors hire Chinese workers and ease tariffs and regulations.
- The postmodern AT&T Building opens. Designed by architects Philip Johnson and John Burgee.
- Apple Computer releases breakthrough personal computer, the box-shaped Macintosh 128K.
- Michael Jackson's album *Thriller* nets more than $75 million.
- AT&T Bell Laboratories sends 20 billion bits of data per second over a single optical fiber, equivalent to 300,000 telephone calls.

Tokyo Disneyland became a fixture in Japan. (Photo: Asahi Shimbunsha).

Masses vs. Micro-masses

- CNN launches CNN International.
- Scientists announce discovery of the "ozone hole," a widening gap in Earth's protective ozone layer. Fosters awareness of the impact of human activity on the planet.
- Mikhail Gorbachev implements his *glasnost* ("openness") policy toward the mass media and the arts, especially literature. A flood of previously banned Western works become available to Soviet citizens.
- America's Cray 2 supercomputer the most powerful in the world at the time with a performance of 1.72 gigaflops (billions of calculations per second); runs virtual wind-tunnel simulations for NASA.

Nengō	**JAPAN**	Year
Shōwa		1987
62	• Matsushita Electric Industrial Co. (today's Panasonic) automatic bread maker a runaway hit. • **Shibuya Loft** opens. • *Nikkei Trendy* magazine published. • Ueno Chizuko publishes *The "Find-myself" Game.*	
63	• Tokyo Dome completed. • Nissan releases the Cima luxury sedan. Sells 36,400 in a year. • Nissan releases the fifth-generation Silvia sports coupe. Sells more than any previous version. • Magazine House publishes **Hanako** women's lifestyle magazine. • Seibu Department Store's **"I want something to want"** campaign.	1988
Heisei Period		
1	• Nintendo releases the Game Boy hand-held video-game player. • Stocks in Tokyo hit record highs (the peak of the Bubble).	1989
2	• Popular *Chibi Maruko-chan* cartoon character gets her own evening television show. Ratings hit 39.9 percent.	1990
3	• **Juliana's Tokyo discotheque** opens.	1991
4	• Land prices start falling from their peak, leading to Japan's "lost decade(s)."	1992
5	• J. League founded. The first professional soccer league in Japan. • JR East railway's "*Sō da. Kyoto, ikō*" (I know! Let's go to Kyoto) campaign. • Akita Aeon Mall, the largest shopping center in Tōhoku, opens in Akita City. • *Ko-gyaru* (*ko*-gals) is the new slang for girl high-school students (*kōkōsei*) as the "loose socks" look spreads among students.	1993
6	• The Komuro Tatsuya boom begins as the music producer invents contemporary Japanese dance music and introduces a string of hit pop acts. • Youth flock to vintage clothing shops in Tokyo's Kōenji.	1994
7	• **Great Hanshin Awaji Earthquake** devastates the city of Kobe. • Popularity of Nike and other sports brands soars. • **Working population (age 15–64) peaks** and begins to decline.	1995
8	• The first Starbucks in Japan opens on the Ginza.	1996
9	• Sales of first Nintendō "Pocket Monster" game software top 8 million. • Toyota releases the first Prius hybrid automobile. • Sony introduces the Vaio notebook computer. • "Ura-Harajuku," fashion from hip boutiques on the backstreets of Harajuku, comes into vogue. • *Chiruchinbito* natural living magazine goes on sale. • **Yamaichi Securities bankruptcy.** • **Hokkaido Takushoku Bank bankruptcy.**	1997

Themes	WORLD

Third-stage consumer society 1975–2004

Soaring Stock & Land Prices

- Gorbachev uses the 1988 CPSU Party Congress to implement reforms weakening the party's role and bringing in free elections, the effective end of seven decades of party control. Gorbachev is elected first and last President of the Soviet Union in 1990.

Hanako Tribe

- Solar Mobile 1989, a solar-powered automobile show, held in West Germany.
- Fall of the Berlin Wall.

First issue of Hanako. *The magazine's ad copy declared "Shigoto to kekkon dake ja iya!" (I want more than just work and marriage!).*

End of Cold War Structure

- The British Antarctic Survey announces two-thirds of the ozone layer above the South Pole has already been destroyed.
- France's Centre d'Étude Polymorphisme Humain (CEPH) and Genethon lab lead the race to decode the human genome. Genethon releases a first-generation map of 90 percent of the genome.

College Gals

- China's population tops 1.2 billion.

- Microsoft introduces **Windows 95** with a graphical interface; it becomes the most popular OS of its day.

Eco Cars

Vintage Clothes

Apple Macintosh ad. Courtesy Ad Museum of Tokyo.

Surf's up.

321

Nengō	JAPAN	Year
Heisei		1998
10	• **Long-Term Credit Bank of Japan fails.** Three senior executives arrested the following year. Later reorganized into the foreign-owned Shinsei Bank. • **Uniqlo** opens its first downtown store in Tokyo's Harajuku. • The J-Pop girl group Morning Musume debuts. • Flea markets flourish in Inokashira Park, other parts of Tokyo. • Tachibanaki Toshiaki publishes *Confronting Income Inequality in Japan*.	
11	• Docomo launches the i-Mode mobile data service for cellphones. • Sony releases Aibo, the robot dog. • *Sotokoto* goes on sale. The world's first environmental fashion magazine. • Novelty song "Dangō 3 Kyōdai" (The Three Dango Brothers) tops Oricon singles list; sells 2.91 million copies. • *Ko*-gals flock to Egoist store in Shibuya 109 building, stroll streets in dyed brown hair, miniskirts, and thick-soled shoes based on the store's trendy "charisma" staffers.	1999
12	• Tatsumi Nagisa publishes "*Suteru!*" *Gijutsu* (The Art of Throwing Things Away) on how to shed unnecessary possessions. • Satō Toshiki publishes *Japan, Land of Inequality*. • Honda presents the ASIMO humanoid robot. • South Korea's PC Bang Internet cafes arrive in Japan. • Beginning of the **café boom.**	2000
13	• Miyazaki Hayao's *Spirited Away* becomes biggest box office hit in Japanese history; goes on to win "best animated feature" at the 75th Academy Awards. • ***Tokyo Renovation: 93 Stories of Reconstruction*** published.	2001
14	• "Jimotees," from the Japanese word *jimoto* for "local," cause a buzz; people are choosing to stay in outlying centers like Machida, Ōmiya, or Kashiwa instead of going to downtown Tokyo to play. • J-Phone (today's Softbank Mobile Corp.) leaps into second place in cellphone contracts on the popularity of its Sha-Mail photo mail feature. • Shipments of Sony PlayStation 2 consoles break 40 million.	2002
15	• Doors open at Tokyo's Roppongi Hills skyscraper. • Seibu Department Stores and Sogō Co. merge into the Millenium Retailing Group. • *Fuyu no Sonata* (Winter Sonata) triggers a South Korean TV drama boom in Japan. • Magazine House publishes the LOHAS magazine *ku:nel*. • Chikyūmaru Co. publishes the LOHAS magazine *Tennen Seikatsu* (Natural Life). • The net-based **Tokyo R Fudōsan** realty company opens for business.	2003
16	• Ebi-chan OL fashion takes off as "office ladies" (OL) adopt the cardigan and skirt look of top *CanCam* cover model Ebihara Yuri. • Nakano Hitori publishes a book version of *Densha Otoko* (Train Man), the tale of a shy *otaku* finding true love; said to have started as a thread on the Japanese Internet bulletin board 2-Channel.	2004

Themes	**WORLD**

Third-stage consumer society: 1975–2004

Eco Cars / Flea Markets / Cellphones / The Lost Decade / Cafés / Renovation / LOHAS

- Apple releases the iMac.

The 1999 Gal's up! Karisuma Style *(*Gal's up! Charisma Style*) from publishing company Bunkasha put the staff of the Shibuya 109 Building Egoist store on its cover. (Miura collection).*

Shoes with soles 10 centimeters thick or more were all the rage. (Photo: Ōi Natsuyo).

- The iPod goes on sale.

- Apple's online iTunes Music Store opens.

The back cover of ku:nel's *first issue was a Prius ad.*

- **Facebook** opens.
- China's Lenovo Group buys IBM's personal computer division.

Nengō	**JAPAN**	Year
Heisei		2005
17	• Seven & i Holding Group brings Millennium Retailing (today's Sogo & Seibu Co. Ltd.) under its umbrella. • Energy-conserving "Cool Biz" introduced. Office workers are allowed to dress lighter in summer in exchange for less air conditioning. • Miura Atsushi's *The Underclass Society* becomes a bestseller. • The Lexus luxury car goes on sale in Japan, after Toyota releases it first in the U.S.	
18	• The hit girl singing group AKB48 releases its debut single. • Online music downloads pass CD singles in market scale. • Nintendo sells the DS Lite handheld dual-screen console, while Sony releases the PlayStation 3.	2006
19	• **Japan's population peaks** and begins to decline.	2007
20	• Popular Wii Fit exercise software released for Nintendo's Wii game system. • Swedish clothing giant H & M opens its first Japan store on the Ginza. • **Aeon Lake Town** opens in Saitama Prefecture's Koshigaya City. With 710 stores, 245,223 square meters of retail floor space, and 14,000 parking spaces, it is Japan's largest mall. • Rush to open outlet malls: Mitsui Outlet Park Iruma (April), Nasu Garden Outlet (July), Mitsui Outlet Park Sendai Port (September), Sendai-Izumi Premium Outlets (October).	2008
21	• May figures show the Toyota Prius to be the best-selling car in Japan on a monthly basis for the first time.	2009
22	• Hituji Real Estate publishes *Tōkyō Shea Seikatsu* (Tokyo Share Life). Popularity of "share-houses" grows.	2010
23	• **March 11 Tohoku earthquake and tsunami** and ensuing Fukushima nuclear plant crisis. • Mitsukoshi and Isetan merge. • Lumine takes over Yūrakuchō Seibu. • The K-Pop boom reaches Japan.	2011
24	• Panasonic, Sony, Sharp and other top corporations report sharp losses.	2012

Themes	WORLD

Fourth-stage consumer society 2005–2034

Stratification & Inequality

Shopping Malls

- The iPod nano released.

- Twitter launched.

CanCam magazine, the popular girl's bible.
(May 2006 issue; Miura Collection).

Fast-fashion

Yoga

- The first **iPhone** goes on sale.
- Subprime loan crisis triggers a global **financial crisis** and recession.
- India's Tata Motor Co. releases the Nano, the **"world's cheapest car."**

Sharing

- Apple introduces the iPad.

The March 2011 Earthquake.
The city streets of Kesen'numa after the tsunami.
Photo courtesy of Asahi Shimbun.

- China's Tianhe-2 supercomputer fastest in the world at 33.86 petaflops (quadrillions of calculations per second).

NOTES

Preface to the English Edition

1. Miura Atsushi, *Ōinaru meisō: Dankai sedai samayoi no rekishi to genzai* (The Great Run-around: The Wandering History and Present Day of the Japanese Baby Boomers) (Tokyo: Parco, 1989).
2. Miura Atsushi, *Dankai sedai o sōkatsu suru* (Summing Up the Baby-boom Generation) (Tokyo: Makino Shuppan, 2005).
3. Miura Atsushi, *Dankai sedai no sengoshi* (A Postwar History of the Baby-boom Generation) (Tokyo: Bungeishunju, 2007).
4. Miura Atsushi, *Dankai kakusa* (*Dankai* Divided: The Stratification of the Baby Boomers) (Tokyo: Bungeishunju, 2007).
5. Miura Atsushi, *"Kazoku" to "kōfuku" no sengoshi* (Family and Happiness: A Postwar History of Suburbanization in Japan) (Tokyo: Kodansha, 1999).
6. Miura Atsushi, *Kōgai wa kore kara dō naru? Tokyo jūtakuchi kaihatsu hiwa* (What Will Become of the Suburbs Now?: The Secret History of Housing Site Development in Tokyo) (Tokyo: Chuokoron-Shinsha, 2011).
7. Miura Atsushi, *Tokyo wa kōgai kara kiete iku!* (The Vanishing Suburbs: The Coming Decline of Metropolitan Tokyo) (Tokyo: Kobunsha, 2012).

PART ONE:
THE FOUR STAGES OF CONSUMER SOCIETY

Epigraph. Shimomura Osamu, *Nihon keizai seichōron* (A Theory of Japanese Economic Growth) (Tokyo: Chuokoron-Shinsha, 2009), p. 13.

Chapter One: An Overview of Consumer Society in Japan

1. "Sangyō kōzō—kei-haku-tanshōka no shōgeki," *Nikkei Business*, (February 8, 1982).
2. See Yamada Masahiro, *Parasaito shakai no yukue* (The Future of a Parasite Society) (Chikumashobo, 2004), pp. 24–30.

PART TWO:
THE TRANSITION FROM SECOND-STAGE TO THIRD-STAGE
CONSUMER SOCIETY

Epigraph. Fujioka Wakao, *Sayonara taishū* (Farewell to the Masses) (Tokyo: PHP Kenkyūjo, 1984), pp. 178–79.

Chapter Two: Differences Between Second- and Third-stage Consumer Society

1. For more, see the author's *"Kazoku" to "kōfuku" no sengoshi* (Family and Happiness: A Postwar History) (Tokyo: Kodansha, 1999).

2. Economist Yoshikawa Hiroshi writes authoritatively on this in *Kōdo seichō* (High Economic Growth) (Tokyo: Yomiuri Shimbunsha, 1997). Or you might review the author's *Kore kara no jūnen: Dankai junia 1,400 mannin*.

3. See Iwama Natsuki's *Sengo wakamono bunka no kōbō* (The Dynamism of Postwar Youth Culture) (Tokyo: Nihon Keizai Shimbunsha, 1995), pp. 81–83.

4. They were perhaps equally shocked to learn that the university's famously intellectual students also had a fan club for pop idol singer and actress Yamaguchi Momoe.

Chapter Three: Individualization and Sophistication of Demand

1. A Japanese coinage with the "D" from "designer" and the "C" from "character." In this case "designer" brands referred to the fashions of independent fashion houses like Kawakubo Rei and Issey Miyake, while "character" referred to brands with a distinct flavor or "character" launched by larger clothing manufacturers.

2. *The Tale of the Heike*, translated by Helen Craig McCullough (Stanford, Calif.: Stanford University Press, 1988), p. 23.

3. For more on *"Daiyon Yamanote,"* see the author's 2011 *Kōgai wa kore kara dō naru?* (What Will Become of the Suburbs Now?) (Tokyo: Chuokoron-Shinsha, 2011).

4. "Nigenka suru kachikijun to 'sōhi'-māketto no kōzō" (Bifurcating Value Standards and the Structure of the "Sōhi" Market").

5. *Nakashoku* refers to takeout and other ready-to-eat foods purchased outside but eaten at home or the workplace; this is also known as the home meal replacement (HMR) sector.

6. Since *nakashoku* is essentially food that people do eat around town rather than at a sit-down restaurant, I have taken to calling it *gaishoku* 街食, or "town food," in a play of words on the usual term for eating out, *gaishoku* written 外食.

7. For a more detailed discussion of Tokyū/Tokyu Hands, see chapter six.

Chapter Four: Evolving Consumer Psychology

1. *Mōretsu* (intense, fierce) is used in a positive sense in the phrase *mōretsu shain* to refer to a hard-working employee utterly devoted to his job and company.

2. Fujioka Wakao, *Fujioka Wakao zenshigoto/purodyūsu* (2) *Mōretsu kara byūtifuru e* (Fujioka Wakao Complete Works/Productions (2): From Driven to Beautiful) (Tokyo: PHP Kenkyūjo, 1988), pp. 13–14.

3. Fujioka Wakao, *Fujioka Wakao zenshigoto/purodyūsu* (1) *Disukabā Japan* (Fujioka Wakao Complete Works/Productions (1): Discover Japan) (Tokyo: PHP Kenkyūjo, 1987), p. 23.

4. Ibid., pp. 27–28.

5. Hasegawa Machiko's immensely popular four-panel comic and television cartoon series about life in an everyday Japanese family that virtually all Japanese have read or watched at least once in their life.

6. Okamoto Tarō, "Bankokuhaku ni kaketa mono" (My Challenges in the World Exposition) in Taro Okamoto Museum of Art (ed.), *"Okamoto Tarō, Expo '70, Taiyō no Tō kara no messēji" ten* ("Okamoto Tarō, Expo '70, A Message from the Tower of the Sun" exhibition) (Kawasaki: Taro Okamoto Museum of Art, 2000), pp. 6–9. First published in Tange Kenzō and Okamoto Tarō (eds.), *Nippon Bankokuhaku: Kenchiku, zōkei* (The Japan World Exposition: Architecture and Design) (Tokyo: Kōbunsha, 1971).

7. "Shakai ishiki ni kansuru yoron chōsa."

8. NHK Hōsō Yoron Chōsajo, ed., *Zusetsu sengo yoronshi* (A Visual History of Postwar Public Opinion) (Tokyo: Nihon Hōsō Shuppan Kyōkai, 1975), p. 196.

9. Komatsu Sakyō, *Mirai no shisō* (A Philosophy of the Future) (Tokyo: Chūō Kōronsha, 1967), pp. 90–91.

10. Ibid., pp. 206–8.

Chapter Five: Splintering of the Masses and Harbingers of a Divided Society

1. Fujioka Wakao, *Sayonara taishū: Kansei jidai o dō yomuka* (Farewell to the Masses: How Do You Read the Era of Sensibility?), PHP Kenkyūjo, 1984), p. 13.

2. Ibid., p. 18.

3. Ibid., p. 19.

4. Ibid., p. 20.

5. Ibid., p. 57; italics added.

6. *Oishii Seikatsu*. This famous catchphrase was created by leading Japanese copywriter and social critic Itoi Shigesato.

7. *Kinkonkan—Gendai ninki shokugyō sanjūichi no kanemochi bin-bōnin no hyōsō to chikara to kōzō* ("Kinkonkan"—Thirty-one Popular Contemporary Professions: The Appearance, Power, and Structure of the Rich and the Poor) (Tokyo: Shufu no Tomo Sha, 1984).

8. Ibid., pp. 2–3.

9. Ibid., p. 3.

10. Translated into English by Richard Nice in 1984 as *Distinction: A Social Critique of the Judgment of Taste* (Cambridge: Harvard University Press, 1984).

11. Hakuhōdō Seikatsu Sōgō Kenkyūjo (Hakuhodo Institute of Life and Living) ed., *"Bunshū" no tanjō: Nyūpīpuru o tsukamu shijō senryaku to wa* (The Birth of the "Divided Masses": What Market Strategy Can Capture the "New People"?) (Hakuhodo Institute of Life and Living, 1985).

12. Ozawa Masako, *Shin "Kaisō shōhi" no jidai: Shotoku kakusa no kakudai to sono eikyō* (The New Era of "Stratified Consumption": The Widening of Income Inequality and Its Impact) (Nihon Keizai Shimbunsha, 1985).

13. *"Bunshū" no tanjō*, p. 1.

14. Ibid., p. 14.

15. For a case study on Mujirushi see the Appendices. It now also operates the Muji Stores outside of Japan.

16. Tsujii Takashi (the penname of Tsutsumi Seiji, president of the Saison Foundation and founder of Mujirushi when he was chairman of the Saison group) confirms this strategy in an interview at the back of this book.

17. "Maku akeru 'kaisō shōhi' jidai: 'Chūryū gensō' no hōkai to taishū shōhi jidai no shūen" (The Curtain Opens on the "Age of Stratified Consumption": The Collapse of the "Middle-class Illusion" and the End of Mass Consumption)," *Nippon Chōki Shin'yō Ginkō Chōsa Geppō* (Long Term Credit Bank of Japan Research Reports), July, 1985.

18. Tachibanaki Toshiaki, *Nippon no keizai kakusa: Shotoku to shisan kara kangaeru* (Confronting Income Inequality in Japan: A Comparative Analysis of Causes, Consequences, and Reform) (Iwanami Shoten, 1988).

19. Satō Toshiki, *Fubyōdō shakai Nihon: Sayonara sōchūryū* (Japan, Land of Inequality: Farewell to the Middle-Class Nation) (Tokyo: Chuokoron-Shinsha, 2000).

20. Yamada Masahiro, *Kibō kakusa shakai: "Makegumi" no zetsubōkan ga Nihon o hikisaku* (Society of Unequal Hope: The Despair of the "Defeated" Will Tear Japan Apart) (Chikumashobo, 2004).

21. Miura Atsushi, *Karyū shakai: Arata na kaisō shūdan no shutsugen* (The Underclass Society: The Emergence of a New Social Stratum) (Kobunsha, 2005).

Chapter Six: An Age of Amorphous Desire

1. Mizuno Seiichi, *Loft Graffiti: "Hoshii mono sagashi" no jidai* (Loft Graffiti: The Age of Searching for Something to Want) (President Sha, 1990).

2. Ibid., p. 26.

3. In his 1970 book *Motivation and Personality*, American psychologist Abraham Maslow proposed a five-stage hierarchy of human needs, ranging from the most pressing needs to the least, which he depicted graphically in a pyramid. The levels of the pyramid climb from the most pressing ("Physiological needs") at the base to the least pressing ("Self-actualization needs") at the fifth, top level of the pyramid.

4. *Loft Graffiti*, p. 28.

5. Ibid., p. 30.

6. Not to mention that Juliana's Tokyo, home to the most famous of the dance podiums, only opened in 1991 and did not even exist at the peak of the Bubble.

7. Tōkyō Marketing Kenkyūkai (Tokyo Marketing Research Society), *"Hanzu genshō": Tōkyū Hanzu kara mono=koto shakai o yomu* (The Tokyu Hands Phenomenon: Reading the *"Mono* Equals *Koto"* Society in Tokyu Hands) (MIA, 1986).

8. Ibid., pp. 38–39.

9. Ibid., p. 48.

Chapter Seven: Consumer Society at Saturation Point

1. Ueno Chizuko, *"Watakushi"-sagashi gēmu: Yokubō "shimin"-shakai-ron* (The "Find-myself" Game: A Theory of the "Private Citizen" Society of Desire) (Tokyo: Chikumashobo, 1987). Paperback edition: Chikuma Gakugei Bunko, 1992.

2. Ueno Chizuko and Miura Atsushi, *Shōhi shakai kara kakusa shakai e: Chūryū dankai to karyū junia no mirai* (From Consumer Society to Divided Society: The Changes Since the 1980s) (Tokyo: Chikumashobo,

2007). Paperback edition: Chikuma Bunko, 2010, subtitle changed to *Hachijū nendai kara no henyō* (The Changes Since the 1980s).

3. *"Watakushi"-sagashi gēmu*, p. 57.

4. Ibid., p. 67.

5. Ibid., p. 71.

6. Ibid., p. 73.

7. Ibid., p. 80.

8. Inoue Shun, *Akumu no sentaku: Bunmei no shakaigaku* (The Nightmare Choice: The Sociology of Civilization) (Tokyo: Chikumashobo, 1992).

9. "Hachijū-nendai no bohimei" (Epitaph for the 1980s). *Across*, December 1989–January 1990.

10. Miura Atsushi, *"Yutaka na Shakai" no yukue: Amerikan uei Japaniizu uei* (The Endpoint of the "Affluent Society": American Way, Japanese Way) (Tokyo: JMA Management Center, 1992).

11. *Tokyo Shimbun*, January 13, 2003.

12. "Takotsubo-ka" (Octopus Pot-ification). *Across*, February 1981.

13. Miyadai appropriated Immanuel Kant's "island universe" theory that the universe was composed of islands (galaxies) separated from one another by great distances rather than being a single field of stars, and used it as a metaphor for the widening gulf between individuals in contemporary Japanese society.

PART THREE:
THE TRANSITION FROM THIRD-STAGE TO FOURTH-STAGE CONSUMER SOCIETY

Epigraph. Hara Kenya, *Dezain no dezain* (The Design of Design) (Tokyo: Iwanami Shoten, 2003), p. 110.

Chapter Eight: Fourth-stage Consumer Society: An Age of Sharing

1. Cabinet Office, *Shakai ishiki ni kansuru yoron chōsa* (Public Opinion Survey on Social Consciousness).

2. In Japan it was and in many cases still is customary to receive a large lump-sum payment upon retirement in lieu of a company pension.

3. "Do we really have to be first? Is there something wrong with being second?" (*Ichiban ja nai to dame desu ka? Niban ja dame nan desu ka?*). This phrase took its cue from a moment that symbolized the controversial cost-cutting "budget screenings" of government ministries and programs

implemented by the Government Revitalization Unit, established in 2010 during the short-lived administration of the Democratic Party of Japan (DPJ). In deciding to cut funding for Japan's next-generation supercomputer project during a screening of the Ministry of Education, Science and Culture budget, Japanese politician Murata Lien-Fang was quoted as saying "*Sekai-ichi ni naru riyū wa nani ga aru'n deshō ka? Ni-i ja dame nan deshō ka?*" (What reason is there for us to be the best in the world? Is there something wrong with being second?). Critics said her comment was symbolic of Japan's economic malaise and declining stature in the world.

4. *Danshari* 断捨離 is a slogan derived by combining Japanese characters used in a popular Japanese-language description of the philosophy behind yoga: 断行 (*dangyō*) cut out, 捨行 (*shagyō*) throw away, 離行 (*rigyō*) step away. *Danshari* was pitched as a way to simplify one's physical and spiritual life by purging one's home and life of unnecessary items and clutter.

5. For more on this movement, see the author's interview with Yamazaki Ryō in the Appendices.

6. In recent years charities and relief organizations have received an increasing number of anonymous donations of items like school knapsacks, often made in the name of fictional characters like the masked hero of the famous pro wrestling manga *Taigā Masuku* (Tiger Mask).

Chapter Nine: The Sharing Lifestyle

1. I discuss the "share house" phenomenon in depth in my 2011 book, *Kore kara no Nihon no tame ni "shea" no hanashi o shiyō* (Let Us Talk About Sharing for the Good of Future Japan) (Tokyo: NHK Publishing, 2011).

2. "One-room mansions" are apartment buildings containing only studio apartments that are marketed to singles and young couples. They are called *manshon* (mansion) both to evoke the luxury of larger and fancier *manshon* apartment buildings and to differentiate themselves from Japan's traditional *apāto* (apartments), often older, wooden structures with limited amenities.

3. For one example, see my 2002 joint research project with Hakuhōdō's Research and Development Division, "*Kyōhi shakai no sōzō*" (Creating a Shared-consumption Society).

4. Miura Atsushi, "*Kazoku*" to "*kōfuku*" no sengo-shi (A Postwar History of Family and Happiness) (Tokyo: Kōdansha, 1999).

5. Ibid., p. 214.

6. Ibid., pp. 214–15.

7. For more about these experiences, see Miura Atsushi, *Maihōmu-resu chairudo* (A "My-Home"-less Child) (Tokyo: Club House, 2001); reissued by Bunshun Bunko in 2006.

8. Miura Atsushi, *"Kazoku to kōgai" no shakaigaku* (The Sociology of Family and Suburb) (Tokyo: PHP Institute, 1995).

9. Matsushita announced his "tap water philosophy" (*suidō tetsugaku*) to his employees on May 5, 1932, after pondering the shared goals of religion and business management during a visit to a Shinto shrine.

10. Iwasawa Miho, "Shokon-rikon no dōkō to shusseiritsu e no eikyō" (Recent Trends in First Marriage and Divorce and Their Effects on Fertility Rates in Japan). *Jinkō mondai kenkyū* (Journal of Population Problems), 64–4 (2008.12).

Chapter Ten: Simplicity, Localism, and the Japanese Way

1. Miura Atsushi, *Shinpuru-zoku no hanran* (Revolt of the Simplicity Tribe) (Tokyo: KK Bestsellers, 2009).

2. The demographic acronym LOHAS, for "Lifestyles of Health and Sustainability," was coined in 1999 by Conscious Media, publisher in the United States of the *LOHAS Journal*, and was based on the work of American sociologist Paul Ray on what he termed "cultural creatives." LOHAS was quickly picked up in Japan, where it is written as ロハス , pronounced "rohasu."

3. Miura Atsushi, *Aikoku shōhi: Hoshii no wa Nihon bunka to Nihon e no hokori* (Consumption as Nationalism: The Pull of Japanese Culture and Pride in Japan) (Tokyo: Tokuma Shoten, 2010).

4. NHK Hōsō Bunka Kenkyūjo (NHK Broadcasting Culture Research Institute), "Nihonjin no ishiki" (Survey of Japanese Value Orientations).

5. Hiroi Yoshinori, *Sōzōteki fukushi shakai: "Seichō"-go no shakai kōzō to ningen, chi'iki, kachi* (The Creative Welfare Society: Post-Growth Social Structure and People, Regions, and Values) (Tokyo: Chikumashobō, 2011), pp. 47–48.

6. "Ke (ケ)." The Japanese ethnologist Yanagita Kunio pointed to two different perceptions of the world and the times in traditional Japan, *hare* and *ke*, where *hare* (as in the *hare* in *haregi*, one's best clothing) were special events and occasions when one might dress up and make other special preparations, and *ke* indicated the normal and the day-to-day.

7. *Genkai shūraku*, or "terminal villages," are rural communities that have suffered extreme depopulation as young people have moved to the cities. Kōchi University professor Ōno Akira defined *genkai shūraku* as rural

communities where more than half of the residents are sixty-five years or older.

8. Kanze Noh. The Kanze school of Noh, founded in the fourteenth century in Nara, one of the four oldest schools of Noh and the school of Zeami Motokiyo, who created the basic form of the art as it is known today.

9. Okuni Kabuki. Kabuki is said to have its origins in dance performances on a dry riverbed in Kyoto by Izumo no Okuni and her troupe in 1603.

10. Motoori Norinaga (1730–1801). Doctor and scholar, and one of the foremost proponents of Kokugaku, or National Learning, which emphasized the study of Japanese instead of Chinese classics.

11. Yamagata Bantō (1748–1821). Osaka rice merchant, scholar, and early atheist who proposed that the solar system was heliocentric.

12. *Yomiuri Shimbun* (Yomiuri Newspaper), March 21, 2010, morning edition, page 1. "*Chikyū o yomu*" (Reading the World) column.

13. Hara Kenya, *Nihon no dezain* (Japanese Design) (Tokyo: Iwanami Shoten, 2011), p. i.

14. Industrial designer Yanagi Sōri (Munemichi) (1915–2011) won world attention when he received the golden prize at the eleventh Milan Triennial in 1957 for his "Butterfly Stool." He was known for his aesthetically satisfying yet highly functional designs. His stainless steel kettle is still in production.

15. Hara, *Nihon no dezain*, p. 43.

16. Ibid, p. 105.

17. *Fasuto fūdo* is a play on words based on the English phrase "fast-food," pronounced *fasuto fūdo* in Japanese. I replace the *fūdo* フード of "food," with the Japanese homonym, *fūdo* 風土 meaning the culture and traditions of different localities.

Chapter Eleven: The Ultimate Consumer Society

1. Mita Sōsuke, Kurihara Akira, and Tanaka Yoshihisa, eds., *Shakaigaku Jiten* (Dictionary of Sociology) (Tokyo: Kobundo, 1988), p. 324.

2. Yamazaki Masakazu, *Yawarakai kojinshugi no tanjō: Shōhi shakai no bigaku* (The Birth of Soft Individualism: The Aesthetics of Consumer Society) (Tokyo: Chūō Kōron, 1984). Reissued in Chūō Kōron Bunko edition, 1987.

3. Ibid., p. 136.

4. Ibid., pp. 140–141.

5. Ibid., p. 141.

6. Ibid., pp. 141–142.

7. *Asahi Shimbun*, January 19, 1976.

8. The Kinokuniya bookstore outside the east exit of Shinjuku Station for years has been a symbolic center of contemporary Japanese intellectual and artistic life.

9. Yamazaki, *Yawarakai kojinshugi no tanjō*, p. 144.

10. Ibid., p. 165.

11. Ibid., p. 167.

12. Ibid., p. 144.

13. Ibid., p. 145.

14. Ibid., p. 149.

PART FOUR:
THE FUTURE OF CONSUMER SOCIETY

Epigraph. Yamazaki Masakazu, *Sekai bunmeishi no kokoromi: Shinwa to buyō* (A History of World Civilization: Mythology and Dance) (Tokyo: Chuokoron-Shinsha, 2012), p. 461.

Chapter Twelve: The Search for New Ways of Living

1. Please see the author's *Karyū shakai* (The Underclass Society), *Mai hōmuresu chairudo* (A "My Home"-less Child), and others.

2. Yamamoto Riken, *Chiikishakaiken moderu* (Modelling the Local Community Sphere) (Tokyo: INAX Shuppan, 2010), pp. 3–4.

4. Yamamoto Riken, *Chiikishakaiken-shugi* (Local Community Area Principles) (Tokyo: INAX Shuppan, 2012), pp. 4–6.

4. Ibid., p. 6.

5. Ibid., p. 8.

6. Sakaguchi Kyōhei, *Zero kara hajimeru toshigata shuryōsaishū seikatsu* (Starting from Zero: The Urban Hunting and Gathering Life) (Tokyo: Ohta Publishing, 2010).

7. Asada Wataru, *Sumibiraki: Ie kara hajimeru komyunitii* (Open Living: Community that Begins From the Home) (Tokyo: Chikumashobo, 2012).

8. Sakaguchi Kyōhei, *Zero kara hajimeru toshigata shuryōsaishū seikatsu*, pp. 10–11.

9. Ibid., p. 49.

10. Asada Wataru, *Sumibiraki*. Garden café, p. 94; library, p. 90; university, p. 98; art study, p. 54.

11. Ibid., p. 14.

12. Miura Atsushi, *Kore kara no Nihon no tame ni "shea" no hanashi o shiyō* (Let Us Talk About "Sharing" for the Good of Future Japan) (Tokyo: NHK Publishing, 2011).

13. *Setagaya o "chiiki kyōsei no machi" ni shiyō daisakusen* (Grand Operation to Make Setagaya a "Local Symbiosis Community").

14. For a more detailed discussion, please see my book co-written with architect Fujimura Ryūji, *3.11-go no kenchiku to shakai dezain* (Post-March 11 Architecture and Social Design) (Tokyo: Heibonsha, 2011).

15. "Wissenschaft als Beruf," *Gesammelte Aufsätze zur Wissenschaftslehre* (Tubingen, 1922), pp. 524–55. Originally a speech at Munich University, 1918, published in 1919 by Duncker & Humblodt, Munich; and other writings.

Chapter Thirteen: Creating the Sharing Society

1. See, for example, the author's *Korekara no jūnen: Dankai junia 1400 man-nin ga koa shijō ni naru* (The Next Ten Years: 14 Million *Dankai* Juniors Will Be the Next Core Market) (Tokyo: Chūkei Shuppan, 2002).

2. Judy Corbett and Michael Corbett, *Designing Sustainable Communities: Learning from Village Homes.* (Washington, D.C.: Island Press, 1999).

3. Shirakawa-gō in Gifu Prefecture is home to several villages that are known for their distinctive thatched-roof houses that residents help re-thatch as a community effort. It has been designated a UNESCO World Heritage Site.

4. *Yuimāru* is a word from the Ryukyuan dialect spoken on Okinawa that means to live in a community and to help one another.

5. Ministry of Internal Affairs and Communications Statistics Bureau, "Kakei Chōsa."

6. Yamazaki Ryō, *Komyunitii dezain* (Community Design) (Kyoto: Gakugei Shuppansha, 2011), p. 194.

7. *Tōkō kyohi*, or children refusing to go to school, often in response to school bullying, has become a major issue in Japan.

8. Zygmunt Bauman (1921–). Author of *Community: Seeking Safety in an Insecure World* (Cambridge: Polity, 2010) and other works.

9. Miura Atsushi, *Kakusa shakai no sabaibaru-jutsu: Ikinokori o kakeru hito to kigyō* (Survival Skills for an Unequal Society: People and Companies Who Are Betting on Surviving) (Tokyo: Gakushū Kenkyūsha, 2008).

BIBLIOGRAPHY

Across. "Hachijū-nendai no bohimei" (Epitaph for the 1980s). December 1989–January 1990.

Across. "Nigenka suru kachikijun to 'sōhi'-māketto no kōzō" (Bifurcating Value Standards and the Structure of the "Sōhi" Market"). April, 1983.

Asada Wataru. *Sumibiraki: Ie kara hajimeru komyunitii* (Open Living: Community that Begins From the Home). Tokyo: Chikumashobo, 2012.

Bauman, Zygmunt. *Community: Seeking Safety in an Insecure World.* Cambridge: Polity, 2010.

Bourdieu, Pierre. *La Distinction: Critique sociale du jugement.* Paris: Le Editions de Minuit, 1979.

Baudrillard, Jean. *La Société de Consommation: Ses Mythes, Ses Structures.* Paris: Gallimard, 1970.

Corbett, Judy and Michael Corbett. *Designing Sustainable Communities: Learning from Village Homes.* Washington, D.C.: Island Press, 1999.

Fujimura Ryūji. *3.11-go no kenchiku to shakai dezain* (Post-March 11 Architecture and Social Design). Tokyo: Heibonsha, 2011.

Fujioka Wakao. *Fujioka Wakao zenshigoto/purodyūsu* (1) *Disukabā Japan* (Fujioka Wakao Complete Works/Productions (1): Discover Japan). Tokyo: PHP Kenkyūjo, 1987.

———. *Fujioka Wakao zenshigoto/purodyūsu* (2) *Mōretsu kara byūtifuru e* (Fujioka Wakao Complete Works/Productions (2): From Driven to Beautiful). Tokyo: PHP Kenkyūjo, 1988.

———. *Sayonara taishū: Kansei jidai o dō yomuka* (Farewell to the Masses: How Do you Read the Era of Sensibility?). Tolyo: PHP Kenkyūjo, 1984.

Hakuhōdō Seikatsu Sōgō Kenkyūjo (Hakuhodo Institute of Life and Living), ed. *"Bunshū" no tanjō: Nyūpīpuru o tsukamu shijō senryaku to wa* (The Birth of the "Divided Masses": What Market Strategy Can Capture the "New People"? Hakuhodo Institute of Life and Living, 1985.

Hara Kenya. *Dezain no dezain* (The Design of Design). Tokyo: Iwanami Shoten, 2003.

———. *Nihon no dezain* (Japanese Design). Tokyo: Iwanami Shoten, 2011.

Hiroi Yoshinori. *Sōzōteki fukushi shakai: "Seichō"-go no shakai kōzō to ningen, chi'iki, kachi* (The Creative Welfare Society: Post-Growth Social Structure and People, Regions, and Values). Tokyo: Chikumashobo, 2011.

Inoue Shun. *Akumu no sentaku: Bunmei no shakaigaku* (The Nightmare Choice: The Sociology of Civilization. Tokyo: Chikumashobo, 1992).

Iwama Natsuki. *Sengo wakamono bunka no kōbō* (The Dynamism of Postwar Youth Culture). Tokyo: Nihon Keizai Shimbunsha, 1995.

Iwasawa Miho. "Shokon-rikon no dōkō to shusseiritsu e no eikyō" (Recent Trends in First Marriage and Divorce and Their Effects on Fertility Rates in Japan). *Jinkō mondai kenkyū* (Journal of Population Problems), 64-4 (2008.12).

Komatsu Sakyō. *Mirai no shisō* (A Philosophy of the Future). Tokyo: Chūō Kōronsha, 1967.

Mita Sōsuke, Kurihara Akira, and Tanaka Yoshihisa, eds. *Shakaigaku Jiten* (Dictionary of Sociology). Tokyo: Kobundo, 1988.

Miura Atsushi. *Aikoku shōhi: Hoshii no wa Nihon bunka to Nihon e no hokori* (Consumption as Nationalism: What We Want is Japanese Culture and Pride in Japan). Tokyo: Tokuma Shoten, 2010.

———. *Dankai kakusa* (*Dankai* Divided: The Stratification of the Baby Boomers). Tokyo: Bungeishunju, 2007.

———. *Dankai sedai no sengoshi* (A Postwar History of the Baby-boom Generation). Tokyo: Bungeishunju, 2007.

———. *Dankai sedai o sōkatsu suru* (Summing Up the Baby-boom Generation). Tokyo: Makino Shuppan, 2005.

———. *Kakusa shakai no sabaibaru-jutsu: Ikinokori o kakeru hito to kigyō* (Survival Skills for an Unequal Society: People and Companies Who Are Betting on Surviving). Tokyo: Gakushū Kenkyūsha, 2008.

———. *Karyū shakai: Arata na kaisō shūdan no shutsugen* (The Underclass Society: The Emergence of a New Social Stratum). Kobunsha, 2005.

———. *"Kazoku" to "kōfuku" no sengo-shi* (A Postwar History of Family and Happiness). Tokyo: Kodansha, 1999.

———. *"Kazoku to kōgai" no shakaigaku* (The Sociology of Family and Suburb). Tokyo: PHP Institute, 1995.

———. *Kōgai wa kore kara dō naru? Tokyo jūtakuchi kaihatsu hiwa* (What Will Become of the Suburbs Now?: The Secret History of Housing Site Development in Tokyo). Tokyo: Chuokoron-Shinsha, 2011.

———. *Korekara no jūnen: Dankai junia 1400 mannin ga koa shijō ni naru* (The Next Ten Years: 14 Million *Dankai* Juniors Will be the Next Core Market). Tokyo: Chūkei Shuppan, 2002.

———. *Kore kara no Nihon no tame ni "shea" no hanashi o shiyō* (Let Us Talk About "Sharing" for the Good of Future Japan). Tokyo: NHK Publishing, 2011.

———. *Maihōmu-resu chairudo* (A "My-Home"-less Child). Tokyo: Club House, 2001. Reissued by Bunshun Bunko in 2006.

———. *Ōinaru meisō: Dankai sedai samayoi no rekishi to genzai* (The Great Run-around: The Wandering History and Present Day of the Japanese Baby Boomers). Tokyo: Parco, 1989.

———. *Shinpuru-zoku no hanran* (Revolt of the Simplicity Tribe). Tokyo: KK Bestsellers, 2009.

———. *Tokyo wa kōgai kara kiete iku!* (The Vanishing Suburbs: The Coming Decline of Metropolitan Tokyo). Tokyo: Kobunsha, 2012.

———. *"Yutaka na Shakai" no yukue: Amerikan uei Japaniizu uei* (The Endpoint of the "Affluent Society": American Way, Japanese Way. Tokyo: JMA Management Center, 1992.

Mizuno Seiichi. *Loft Graffiti: "Hoshii mono sagashi" no jidai* (Loft Graffiti: The Age of Searching for Something to Want). Tokyo: President Sha, 1990.

NHK Hōsō Yoron Chōsajo, ed. *Zusetsu sengo yoronshi* (A Visual History of Postwar Public Opinion). Tokyo: Nihon Hōsō Shuppan Kyōkai, 1975.

Nikkei Business. "Sangyō kōzō—kei-haku-tanshōka no shōgeki." February 8, 1982.

Okamoto Tarō. "Bankokuhaku ni kaketa mono" (My Challenges in the World Exposition). In Taro Okamoto Museum of Art, ed., *"Okamoto Tarō, Expo '70, Taiyō no Tō kara no messēji" ten* ("Okamoto Tarō, Expo '70, A Message from the Tower of the Sun" exhibition). Kawasaki: Taro Okamoto Museum of Art, 2000.

——— and Tange Kenzō, eds. *Nippon Bankokuhaku: Kenchiku, zōkei* (The Japan World Exposition: Architecture and Design). Tokyo: Kōbunsha, 1971.

Ōno Akira. *Sanson kankyō shakaigaku josetsu: Gendai sanson no genkai shūraku ka to ryūiki kyōdō kanri* (An Introduction to Mountain Village Sociology: On "Terminal Villages" and Joint-Controlled Watershed Areas in Contemporary Mountain Villages). Tokyo: Nōson Gyoson Bunka Kyōkai, 2005.

Ozawa Masako. "Maku akeru 'kaisō shōhi' jidai: 'Chūryū gensō' no hōkai to taishū shōhi jidai no shūen" (The Curtain Opens on the "Age of Stratified Consumption": The Collapse of the "Middle-class Illusion" and the End of Mass Consumption)." *Nippon Chōki Shin'yō Ginkō Chōsa Geppō* (Long Term Credit Bank of Japan Research Reports), July, 1985.

——. *Shin "Kaisō shōhi" no jidai: Shotoku kakusa no kakudai to sono eikyō* (The New Era of "Stratified Consumption": The Widening of Income Inequality and Its Impact. Nihon Keizai Shimbunsha, 1985.

Sakaguchi Kyōhei. *Zero kara hajimeru toshigata shuryōsaishū seikatsu* (Starting from Zero: The Urban Hunting and Gathering Life). Tokyo: Ohta Publishing, 2010.

Satō Toshiki. *Fubyōdō shakai Nihon: Sayonara sōchūryū* (Japan, Land of Inequality: Farewell to the Middle-Class Nation. Tokyo: Chuokoron-Shinsha, 2000.

Shimomura Osamu. *Nihon keizai seichōron* (A Theory of Japanese Economic Growth). Tokyo: Chuokoron-Shinsha, 2009.

Tachibanaki Toshiaki. *Nippon no keizai kakusa: Shotoku to shisan kara kangaeru* (Confronting Income Inequality in Japan: A Comparative Analysis of Causes, Consequences, and Reform). Iwanami Shoten, 1988.

Tōkyō Marketing Kenkyūkai (Tokyo Marketing Research Society). *"Hanzu genshō": Tōkyū Hanzu kara mono=koto shakai o yomu* (The Tokyu Hands Phenomenon: Reading the *"Mono* Equals *Koto"* Society in Tokyu Hands). Tokyo: MIA, 1986.

Ueno Chizuko. *"Watakushi"-sagashi gēmu: Yokubō "shimin"-shakai-ron* (The "Find-myself" Game: A Theory of the "Private Citizen" Society of Desire). Tokyo: Chikumashobo, 1987. Paperback edition: Chikuma Gakugei Bunko, 1992.

—— and Miura Atsushi. *Shōhi shakai kara kakusa shakai e: Chūryū dankai to karyū junia no mirai* (From Consumer Society to Divided Society: The Changes Since the 1980s). Tokyo: Chikumashobo, 2007. Paperback edition: Chikuma Bunko, 2010, subtitle changed to *Hachijū nendai kara no henyō* (The Changes Since the 1980s).

Watanabe Kazuhiro and Tarako Production. *Kinkonkan—Gendai ninki shokugyō sanjūichi no kanemochi binbōnin no hyōsō to chikara to kōzō* ("Kinkonkan"—Thirty-one Popular Contemporary Professions: The Appearance, Power, and Structure of the Rich and the Poor). Tokyo: Shufu no Tomo Sha, 1984.

Yamada Masahiro. *Kibō kakusa shakai: "Makegumi" no zetsubōkan ga Nihon o hikisaku* (Society of Unequal Hope: The Despair of the "Defeated" Will Tear Japan Apart) (Chikumashobo, 2004).

——. *Parasaito shakai no yukue* (The Future of a Parasite Society. Chikumashobo, 2004.

Yamamoto Riken. *Chiikishakaiken moderu* (Modelling the Local Community Sphere). Tokyo: INAX Shuppan, 2010

——. *Chiikishakaiken-shugi* (Local Community Area Principles). Tokyo: INAX Shuppan, 2012

Yamazaki Masakazu, "*Chikyū o yomu*" (Reading the World) column. *Yomiuri Shimbun* (Yomiuri Newspaper), March 21, 2010, morning edition, page 1.

——. *Sekai bunmeishi no kokoromi: Shinwa to buyō* (A History of World Civilization: Mythology and Dance). Tokyo: Chuokoron-Shinsha, 2012.

——. *Yawarakai kojinshugi no tanjō: Shōhi shakai no bigaku* (The Birth of Soft Individualism: The Aesthetics of Consumer Society). Tokyo: Chūō Kōron, 1984. Reissued in Chūō Kōron Bunko edition, 1987.

Yamazaki Ryō. *Komyunitii dezain: Hito ga tsunagaru shikumi o tsukuru* (Community Design: Creating Human Connections). Kyoto: Gakugei Shuppansha, 2011.

Yoshikawa Hiroshi. *Kōdo seichō* (High Economic Growth). Tokyo: Yomiuri Shimbunsha, 1997.

INDEX

Readers are also directed to the Timeline, which is not indexed here.